The Selected Letters of **Allen Ginsberg** and **Gary Snyder**

The Selected Letters of
ALLEN GINSBERG
and GARY SNYDER

Edited by Bill Morgan

COUNTERPOINT

BERKELEY

Library of Congress Cataloging-in-Publication Data
has been applied for.

ISBN 10: 1-58243-444-1
ISBN 13: 978-1-58243-444-5

Jacket design by David Bullen
Interior design by David Bullen
Printed in the United States of America

COUNTERPOINT
2117 Fourth Street
Suite D
Berkeley, CA 94710

www.counterpointpress.com

Distributed by Publishers Group West

10   9   8   7   6   5   4   3   2   1

Editor's Preface

During the twentieth century, letters were a literary form that nearly everyone practiced. In today's world of cell phones, text messaging and email, it all seems quaint and old-fashioned, but in the days before inexpensive long-distance telephone service became commonplace, the main avenue for communication was the written word.

Gary Snyder and Allen Ginsberg were no exception. After they met in the summer of 1955 they kept in touch by a correspondence that lasted through the next forty years. Both faithfully saved their friends' letters even as they traveled around the world. When the editorial director of Counterpoint books, Jack Shoemaker, discovered that their letters still existed, he asked me to edit them into a book. I knew of Ginsberg's letters from my earlier work on his biography, but I was surprised by the wealth of information that Snyder's side of the correspondence provided. Together they reveal a friendship that helped shape American literature, environmental concern, and spiritual discovery in the second half of the twentieth century. It was through Snyder's studies in Japan and Ginsberg's continual proselytizing that so many people in the West came to discover Eastern spirituality and Buddhism. They were the poet/ magnets to whom other like-minded people were attracted after the pair appeared onstage together as hosts for the first San Francisco Human Be-In of 1967. That event heralded the "Summer of Love" that changed midcentury popular culture forever. Through their example they passed along a knowledge of Eastern meditation practice to countless members of the youthful counterculture during the following decades. Without them would the sixties have unfolded in the same way?

The letters that follow are arranged chronologically. In the few instances where the editor has omitted extraneous passages, an ellipsis [. . .] is inserted in the text. Anything that appears within square brackets [ ] is an editorial note and does not appear in the original letter. There are a few gaps in the sequence where (for whatever reason) the letters from one or the other poet could not be located. Editorial notes have been added in an attempt to provide information that might have been lost with those letters. Footnotes give some background on people, events, and unfamiliar terms. In the case of East Asian names, scholarly practice has been followed, giving the surname entirely in uppercase letters to distinguish which is which. The family name always comes first and the given name second for names from China, Japan, Korea, Taiwan, and Vietnam. In Southeast Asia and India the family name comes second as it does with Western names.

To clean up the text, phone numbers, some addresses, and irrelevant postscripts have been eliminated. Copies of poems, form letters, and other materials that were originally included with letters are generally not reproduced. In the case of poems, those are readily available in collections of Snyder's and Ginsberg's work.

Because so many Asian terms were used within the letters, I have relied heavily on dictionaries for definitions and these can often be found in the footnotes following the first use of the word. In addition to standard dictionaries, I am indebted to the editors of *The Shambhala Dictionary of Buddhism and Zen* (Shambhala, 1991), *The Encyclopedia of Eastern Philosophy and Religion* (Shambhala, 1994), and *Dictionary of Hindu Lore and Legend* (Thames and Hudson, 2002). However, the most important resource used in the preparation of this book was a living one. Gary Snyder was always willing to be of help during the editorial process. In spite of his busy schedule he answered my every question quickly and thoroughly. It was through his knowledge and experience that many of the letters were deciphered and interpreted. Without his help, this book would have lacked the focus it now has.

Behind the scenes, many people have graciously helped during the preparation of this book. In addition to the patient assistance of Gary Snyder, the people at the Allen Ginsberg Trust were always there to lend support. Peter Hale, who is the unheralded master of all things Ginsberg, worked tirelessly on every query I posed him. He, along with co-trustees Bob Rosenthal and Andrew Wylie, supported this project from the beginning. The extraordinary staff at Counterpoint Press, Jack Shoemaker, Laura Mazer, Adam Krefman, Abbye Simkowitz, and Julie Pinkerton, conceived the project and saw it through to the final stage of this handsome production. All of Gary Snyder's letters are preserved with the Allen Ginsberg Papers in the Special Collections Department of Stanford University and Allen Ginsberg's letters are available in the Special Collections Department of the University of California at Davis. The librarians of those two institutions gave their unreserved support to this project.

Acknowledgement is also due to those who gave this editor an extra measure of help along the way: Jack Hagstrom, Joanne Kyger, Peter Orlovsky, John Suiter, and especially to my most steadfast supporter, Judy Matz.

BILL MORGAN

A Note from Gary Snyder

Allen and I came from the far ends of the nation. I was from the German and Scandinavian working farmer/logger/fisherman world of pre-WW II Puget Sound, Allen from the New York City Immigrant Left. We met in a backyard in Berkeley, and again in Kenneth Rexroth's wood-floored apartment in the foggy Avenues zone of San Francisco. The fall of 1955 was the end of graduate school for both of us. We argued a lot and were not easy on each other. I made him walk more, and he made me talk more. It was good for both of us. In that first Bay Area eight months, he and his buddy Jack Kerouac managed to push the already strong but reticent Bay Area poetic culture into public light, with a deliberate intention for some sort of transformation, first literary and then social.

We hitchhiked to the Canadian border and back in the middle of winter giving uninvited readings in Portland and Seattle. I left the coast in May of 1956 for a long stay in Japan (sailing by passenger-freighter), and that was the beginning of our correspondence. Living in different parts of the world as we did for most of the later years, we stayed in touch the old way, with letters. Allen was remarkable for his transgressive sanity. I swung between extremes of Buddhist scholar and hermit nerdiness and tanker-seaman craziness at bars and parties. I sense, reading these letters again, that our mutual respect continued to grow.

A lot of the time we were just working out the details, trail routes, land-management plans—and that's what the "real work" is. His apartment on the lower East Side, my hand-built house at the end of a long dirt road in the far far West, were our hermitages, base camps, and testing grounds. It was all just dust in the wind, but also, the changes were real.

GARY SNYDER
26.IX.08

The Selected Letters of
ALLEN GINSBERG
and GARY SNYDER

EDITOR'S NOTE: *Allen Ginsberg and Gary Snyder were both living in Berkeley, California, during the summer of 1955. Acting as a literary gadfly, poet Kenneth Rexroth suggested that Ginsberg and fellow poet Michael McClure organize a poetry reading that was to feature young, unknown Bay Area writers like themselves. Rexroth had even gone so far as to offer a list of aspiring poets he felt deserved exposure. On that short list was the name of Gary Snyder. In mid-September Ginsberg arranged to have dinner with Snyder. Coincidentally it was on the same day that Ginsberg's close friend Jack Kerouac arrived in town from Mexico. Snyder and Ginsberg hit it off immediately, and the Six Gallery reading, as the October 7, 1955, event became known, was a tremendous success.*

By the time the earliest existing letter from their forty-year-long correspondence was written, Snyder had moved to a tiny unfinished cabin behind Locke McCorkle's house on Montford Avenue in Mill Valley. The letter was a simple note from Gary, suggesting the text to be used for a postcard advertisement of their next reading. That event was the March 18, 1956, Berkeley Town Hall Theater encore of the now famous Six Gallery reading.

1. GARY SNYDER [348 MONTFORD, MILL VALLEY, CA]
   TO ALLEN GINSBERG [1624 MILVIA ST., BERKELEY, CA]

[February 24, 1956]

Good-time poetry / Nobody goes home sad / Ginsberg blowing hot / Snyder blowing cool / Whalen on a long riff / McClure blowing high notes / everybody invited free / free wine / Rexroth on the big bass drum.

Best check with [Herb] Eaton about the wine. Do you have Rexroth's new phone and address? [Philip] Lamantia? [Michael] McClure? I'll try to find out if Garfias[1] will make Jap music. Other poets possibly also: Hackett; Tracy Thompson. Any other ideas? Neuri[2] might help (mimeo'ing etc.).

Warm in my little cabin tho it storms.

G.

PS. Any time you could send monies, a few bucks etc. most appreciated.

2. ALLEN GINSBERG [BERKELEY, CA] TO GARY SNYDER [MILL VALLEY, CA]

[*ca.* March 1956]

Gary:

Sorry to be so slow. This should stave off the wolf till the 5th (April)—and will send you more then. I got paid today—$10—I hope it reaches you.

I'm thinking of moving to S.F. since I am working here full time now till I leave.[3]

I'll be in Berkeley over the weekend. Walter and Ginny say the tapes came out fine.[4]

What happened after I left the party (18 Panoramic)? I had to work.[5]

Anything new from Kerouac? New poet in town from Black Mountain, Ed Dorn, married three kids, works at Greyhound, studied with [Charles] Olson.

Allen

EDITOR'S NOTE: *On May 15, 1956, Snyder set sail for Japan, where he planned to remain for an extended visit studying Buddhism firsthand in a Kyoto monastery.*

---

1. Robert Garfias. A professor of ethnomusicology at the University of California.

2. Neuri. A young woman whose name was Marilyn Arnold; at one point Snyder hoped to have a relationship with her, but nothing ever came of it.

3. Ginsberg shipped out with the Merchant Marine in June in order to earn some money.

4. The Berkeley Town Hall Theater reading was recorded and has been commercially released.

5. Reference here is to the party that was held in Berkeley after the March 18 reading.

3. GARY SNYDER [RINKO-IN, SHOKOKU-JI, KYOTO, JAPAN]
   TO ALLEN GINSBERG [BERKELEY, CA]

[June 3, 1956]

Allen Ginsberg, you are the Candide of the hipster world! It's not an ignoble role. When is your book?[6] Shall I order my copies from you or from Ferlinghetti? I want five anyhow.

I have an additional line for "America" for you—perhaps the last line.

> "America, what are you going to do to me for writing about
>   you like this?
> Are you going to snoop after me and let the air out of my
>   tires etc."

I'm too tired of repeating myself to describe this scene again. Look at letters to Jack [Kerouac], Phil [Whalen], Kenneth [Rexroth], and Locke [McCorkle] for varied impressions.

Poet Lindley [Williams] Hubbell,[7] in Kyoto now, is pretty good. Book published by Swallow called *Long Island Triptych* [1947] is full of goodies.

Listen man if you feel up to it will you write me a concise statement of your theory of beatness and its relation to vision, poetry, and America? and to sex? I am seeing new angles to this rough Zen-discipline shot; perhaps by reducing one's life to essentials of eating (barely enough) and sleeping (barely enough) and working (hard) and subjecting you to constant psychological pressure of meditation and interviews they are, within a controlled situation, making you thoroughly beat (Rinzai is the sect of the big stick whack)[8] and aware of what is samsara[9] and what one's body-self really craves, like food sex and sleep—and then makes that beatness flower into real insight—because in America all that's really sweet and creative now is coming out of the beat ones, i.e. you have nothing and become nothing and you create! Because what else can you create out of, but nothing? Like God. But beatness is a quality of the world that

---

6. Immediately following the Six Gallery reading, Lawrence Ferlinghetti, the owner of City Lights Books, had offered to publish Ginsberg's first book, *Howl and Other Poems*.

7. Lindley Williams Hubbell moved to Japan in 1953 and became a Japanese citizen in the 1960s.

8. Rinzai. One of two active schools of Zen in Japan; the other is Soto.

9. Samsara. The cycle of birth, suffering, death, and rebirth.

turns some people nuts, or to stone, or warps them, and for all the suffering men go through, precious little is learned—so the Buddhist shot and Zen in particular—is not to do away with suffering (an impossibility—in summer we sweat, in winter we shiver—that's all), but to make suffering flower into insight and beauty instead of dry you up and make you numb. Anyway I have these thoughts about poesy and about the hardness of Zen discipline and its way. I'll know more after I've gone through it, and brother I'm going to go through the real thing to judge from what they tell me. Miura Roshi[10] is considered one of the meanest cats in Japan. But let me know how you think. Also how you are writing. [. . .] I formally beg your forgiveness for my difficult behavior up north. I have those fits of solitude desire.

Write me,

Gary

4. ALLEN GINSBERG [USNS *Sgt. Jack Pendleton*]
   TO GARY SNYDER [KYOTO, JAPAN]

Tuesday 19 / June / 56

Dear Gary:

Sorry so short a letter after so long a time but will write soon at length to your very sweet epistle. Yow. I'm back in Seattle, now just leaving ship 4:30 P.M., June 19, 1956. Am working (and will mail this)—as yeoman storekeeper $5020 per annum and overtime on MSTS [Military Sea Transportation Service] ship—started a month ago with two weeks school at Fort Mason. My mother died last week leaving me feeling you and Jack are right, we all are short lived it's only a second before we fade, she left me surprise $1000—so I will be rich enough to actually travel and live for several years now. This ship a Victory freighter—goes nesting in Alaska in six weeks—to resupply the DEW Line [Distant Early Warning]—thru Bering Straits to Point Barrow and some way into the Beaufort Sea, the actual Arctic and glorious North Pole. Ice and the death of my mother—I wonder if I can see God in the white floes and brilliant black light up there? I work on the ship 6½ hrs a day and have 300 per month sent home automatically—should return and be fine (as

---

10. MIURA Joten Soko. Head of Snyder's Rinzai temple.

an extra hand for this project) in September or October this year. Jack left hitchhiking from Locke's yesterday I think—I'll leave a note for him at Homer and Joyce's—I gave him this address. Ship shuttles back to Beaver Point, Oregon, about five miles up mouth of Columbia River. Been there earlier this week—and I leave here tonight and return here to Seattle for the weekend, so maybe will see him. I have now eight hours to spend ashore before sailing again. The book is still in England[11]—so is [William S.] Burroughs who's cured of habit and taking my manuscript around to Barker, Treece, Fleece, Eliot, Speece, etc. I haven't seen final proofs yet, probably this month. I return to Frisco 28 June to read proofs, then head for Long Beach, see L.A., then return to Seattle for three weeks—wow!—then the Arctic. Anyway the book will be ready in maybe two months, I'll send them on to you. [Robert] Creeley and Martha [*sic*: Marthe Rexroth] are lovers. Kenneth has been flipping out—really so, talking extravagantly—even for so absurd a situation—too much to gossip about in such a short letter form. Anyway, threatening suicide, predicting hers, "He's not going to make a Natalie of my wife,"[12] weeping, holding my hand (or anyone kind enuf to come up and talk it out with him). He's unstable—but surely has reason to be—but he is unstable and strange. You would see. Great self pity—but also so extreme as to make me uncomfortable as if it were a madness and not some loveable frailty. I am reading thru Shakespeare on board, beginning to end chronologically. Went up and saw Marie at Gump's before I left, talked in afternoon, but she was busy. That night no so go, Peter [Orlovsky] finally made it with Gin, but couldn't come after all; same of Neal [Cassady]. Phil Whalen is the real *mensch* in that deal. I myself finally came across with her in Peter's presence. Sorry myself I needed you so on trip, I actually began by kind of loving you and pressured on the intimacy of the bliss of the red flower. But that's all over and we're disappeared around curves of the earth. Is there a secret mystery in Zen practice that explains the methods? How can I know? There is a mystery secret to me in heaven or earth and others may know it. If you succeed in arriving at any final level of Being let me know. I sent poems to [Lionel] Trilling, he called them "Dull." Dear Heart! He has a tin ear! And he complained there was no

---

11. City Lights had *Howl and Other Poems* printed in England.

12. The reference here is to Natalie Jackson, a girlfriend of Neal Cassady's who committed suicide by jumping off an apartment house roof.

"music" like I used to be able to write in school. Peremptory dismissal and brush-off letter he wrote. It really made me mad. Also, Ronnie the Hipster, a new arrival on the North Beach scene, stole $90 from my wallet at Peter's. Ha! Your manuscript—Creeley typed ⅔ of it, left town. Marthe has it to finish. When I return to S.F. 28 June I'll sew it up and get it mailed to you. I'll answer your letter soon. Has roshi[13] hit town yet?

 As ever, love,

Allen

5. GARY SNYDER [KYOTO, JAPAN] TO ALLEN GINSBERG [BERKELEY, CA]

[ca. August 20, 1956]

Dear Allen,

I just received your considerable missile. *Siesta in Xbalba* a delight to read again—better than I remembered it, very easy and swinging metric. Attached to left see two poems since America. There are several others which you'll see in time. But poetically I'm not trying right now, M&T [*Myths & Texts*] summed up too well and finished my thought, and now I must let happen and wait and new poetry will bud itself. But there is a Japan of old arty temples and a few stern monks and a Japan of would-be cat kids and big futility-camp intellectuals looking European and dour all over, and it seems like I must be the only person on this Island Empire who understands how both sides feel and could—especially those jazz-loving wild young ones—maybe talk them all together. It's not quite that bad. Monks from the *zendo* across the lane go downtown to hear jazz when they get a chance; but I get discouraged about the insensibility of Buddhists and (Japanese term) "après-guerre youth" to their mutual kick. Big noise in Jaypan [*sic*] right now is uproar about the middle-class delinquent students of Tokyo who apparently are found occasionally screwing each other. They are called *Taiyo-zoku* after a novel about 'em, "Tribe of the Sun."

 Well, now about your St. Francis, I don't quite understand why, but you seem to have a weakness for the Manichaean heresy, i.e. that spirit is pure good and matter is pure evil and the spiritual eye is acquired by sub-duing the physical eye (ear nose tongue body mind etc.). Because that's

---

13. A *roshi* is a Buddhist master and teacher.

where St. Francis and all those people are. And it is a total waste of time to approach discipline or willed spiritual oriented life that way. Drop the notion spirit anyhow. You have to take it back, one step farther, into the mind. That's where the problems that Xtians [Christians] attribute to "matter" have their root and where they are tackled—the flesh, sensuality, pleasure, sensation, etc., are all as pure and devoid of good or evil attributes as a chunk of granite or a seagull, and in Buddhist philosophy, are in the same class of phenomena as such—and that root's root is simply blind ignorant fearful craving, which darkens the mind and throws images all through the intellect and imagination and starts huge trains of psychological economics and warfare and intermental governments and counterrevolutions that weave in and out and are seen perhaps, in a jerk of the arm and more complicated behavior. And all this fixes itself in the intellect as ARBITRARY CONCEPTIONS, among which such ideas as spiritual, good, evil, the body, the mind, awakening, ignorance, craving, peanut butter, Rexroth, sunshine may be counted. Diamond Sutra great acid dissolving such, Prajnaparamita sutra a mental bomb which unfortunately requires that you supply the detonator, but still better than naught? Xtians wanted freedom liberation wake-up lightness, but didn't dig deep enough philosophically or practically to hit source (which is no-source) of human dull suffering.

That you can make weird and lightening things happen by physical austerities was enough real experience to keep them going, but they REALLY didn't have the cultural-philosophical background to understand what a real wisdom-search entails, so that Xtianity has a few bright spots, a few men who probably made it, but didn't understand why, and attributed their success to the wrong reasons. Take a good look at Indian philosophy sometime and see what a range of practices and ideas they experimented with, and the hells and heavens their saints have gone to in search of not only enlightenment, but all the interior landscapes that peyote and junk and wine and tea are but chinks in the door to. And on that base of practice and theory old Gautama golden-face built his little community of bo's, of which a few are still to be found. But to put down flesh, as such, is silly and unswallowable as practice. Certainly no part of ancient or modern Zen—which is totally silent on the matter of sex philosophically—assuming it to be a thing of individual taste and of no intrinsic relationship to one's wisdom or stupidity. To be hung up craving and suffering for pleasure is a drag indeed, but this ain't the fault of the body, it's the fault of your own vision and asceticism of Xtian type is like whipping your horse for eating the clover when you left the gate to the clover field open yourself and maybe on purpose.

When I said you needed discipline—which was quite possibly all wrong—I didn't mean quit masturbating or anything like that, I was thinking of a more systematic intellectual and meditational approach toward understanding your own natural and astonishing illuminations that shine through poems, and not falling into Demon and Angel traps except as myths and peyote-kicks, and learning thus cool and tranquil use of your buddha-nature and buddha-body as well as hot and frantic, not that former is necessarily better; that's all. Ah. Tell me more about the midnight sun. Maybe think about coming to Japan; I'll fix you up with a Zen Master right off for koan[14] study.

Gary

6. GARY SNYDER [KYOTO, JAPAN] TO ALLEN GINSBERG [BERKELEY, CA]

12:X:56 [October 12, 1956]

Dear Allen:

Four copies of *Howl* I ordered from Ferlinghetti came this week, I am carefully figgering where to plant those bombs. It looks real nice and I can't read it without your voice ringing in my ears and a vision of your navy sweater and Levi's and wine and frosty weather outside like in the Northwest. Of which place let me ask, did you ever get a clear view of Mt. Rainier and the Olympic mountains from the Sound or the Straits? There is no sight moves me more than the jagged Olympics floating above the islands and inlets of Puget Sound. "Baggage Dept. at Greyhound" ["In the Baggage Room at Greyhound"] a fine piece. I can see a solid intelligent style as a potential development out of the straight emotional sound of *Howl*—not to knock *Howl*—but it's interesting to think of Whitmanic lines being employed for a cool philosophy (as some of the lines in Greyhound carry) and not even Whitman got that far. Thinking of Whitman: "Starting from Paumanok"—ending at Carmel. Ponder that. Robinson Jeffers is the cynical, disillusioned incarnation of Whitman in this century. "What America did you have in mind . . . ?"

---

14. Koan. A Buddhist training story or phrase, a riddle without a rational answer.

just ask R. J., whose long line and philosophical twists and American scene is Whitman turned over and gone private and fierce.

I didn't say I took Zen as aristocratic did I? That's Mrs. Sasaki's[15] shot, and of course she's not right. What I suppose she's thinking is that the traditional Zen training as employed in Japan ain't for all types, which is true enough I suppose, and no Zen person here would argue that, but since in Buddhism there's a kick for everybody ("and to those to whom the Buddha and Enlightenment must not exist to be saved, the Buddha appears as non-existent and without Enlightenment . . ."). No one could say it's aristocratic. Even the meanest ole fruit-fly has the Buddha-nature, let alone us human flies. But without fear and trembling is exercising the Buddha-nature. Everybody hysterical mama etc. got a loving heart and a redeemable soul, but the hitch is hardly anybody knows how to bring it out, in themselves or in others. And this gap between the few who do make it and the many who could is what spawns systems and tradition to bring it off. But then they're all Enlighted anyhow. The function of a light-bulb is to get turned on. When a light-bulb's on it's got no shadow. Things that exist have shadows. Therefore a Buddha don't exist. (He makes shadows?)

Well sure maybe I could fix you up with a Zen Master in a couple years, and interpret for you in koan-interviews. And you could live awhile in a monastery and indeed you would weep and suffer, as very well may I, what with poor food long hours cold weather and no sex. But just how or when this will come off for me is very indefinite, as I see now the undesirability of staying under the wing of the Zen Institute beyond this year, and will be looking for employment after next May; perhaps shipping out for Europe from Yokohama. If I can get ships will work half a year or so saving money, come back here, and then try living in a place for a while.

I am beginning to really dig Japan and Japanese people now, seeing beyond their apparent looniness into all sorts of crazy-side-angled sense. If you really want to have a spiritual and physical ball, come just to see the folks and fuck Zen. I fall in love at first sight half a dozen times every time I go out. The girls are all magical radiant little Oriental goddesses of compassionate cunt—and you know that not a one of them snatches has got teeth in it, which is more than can be said for American gawky hairy

---

15. Ruth Fuller Sasaki. Zen teacher at the First Zen Institute of America.

critters with garden shears betwixt their legs and snakes for tongues. (I get carried away by language.) Anyway these Japs have a crazy formal-informal each-otherness and don't give a shit and well it's like I was sitting last Sunday in Daisen-in a famous old temple in Daitoku-ji compound talking with a 24-year-old Zen *bo* friend and drinking tea and a troop of sightseers came in from a sightsee bus to look at the garden and while they were doing this the little hostess-girls of the bus came into our little be-matted room, and from other trips there having known the *zendo* began to carry on the most hilarious unself-conscious friendly and not at all aggressive flirtations and brotherly-sisterly kiddings, and while he leaned over to write something one little girl said "hold still!" to him and also leaned over and grabbed a loose thread from his ragged blue robe and he held still and she carefully tied his threads and the point to me was, the feeling of the whole scene was weird because neither sexual nor non-sexual—for the Buddhist monks to the Japanese people there is no odium of world-rejection, celibacy, anti-feminism, etc.; and whereas for Occidentals a contact of that sort would be either consciously sexual undertoned or consciously a-sexual brusque, this was just a kind of mutual fearless warmth and ease and tenderness that could also mean sex or could not, but would lose nothing either way. And I get that feeling in Japanese personal relations everywhere I go; it has impossible (at first glance) forms of etiquette and language, but under that exterior—which the Japanese are not even conscious of, being so used to it—is a human receptiveness and availability that in Americans is generally put down deep inside.

Well here's just the tag end of a rollicking ballad I wrote last July:
This Thunderbolt is hard as Jewel
A swinging dink both hot and cool
The opposites are all congealed
and squares and fools will be revealed
By Whalen's calm and classic glance,
Allen Ginsberg's naked dance.
Write me from thy journeys, O Bard.
Gary

December 15, 1956

Dear Gary:

Gregory [Corso], Peter [Orlovsky], Lafcadio [Orlovsky], and me bussed to Guadalajara to meet poetess Denise Levertov, who is an excited pig-tailed gap toothed busy crazy mother who mutually digs and knows W. C. Williams and writes fine poems, with ellipses (unconsciously of the terms we used), and fine phrases too—not many at a time, but almost all good—and she dug us, we wandered around markets together. Like, a long nice poem watching her cat which in the last line magically disappears into a curtain of leaves, of the bush he's been playing with. Then thru nights and buses and trains and Lafcadio complaining and diarrhea, to Mexico City where I found Jack [Kerouac] sleeping in his bag all dresst in black sweater and hair mussed and unshaven and woke up in the morning at sunny 2 P.M. in a monk cell room of small apartment building. We got a lot high, climbed up pyramids, floated in green Eden gardens on gondolas, went down to whore streets and got clap (Peter and me from Peter) (and Jack no because he wisely used red protective squeeze tubes), walked late at night down grand streets all lit up full of tortilla and sweater stands and cheesy Mex burlesque and comedian theaters, ate big steaks cheap at expensive restaurant, listened to Gregory recite incessantly, he was always spontaneously scribbling in big 10-cent notebook, Peter talked to children, Lafcadio dawdled behind us on the street, I met the fairies and had big orgies, little orgies, not much of one really, found cantinas full of mariachi serenaders, Eisenhower was elected behind our backs, met a chic nowhere Mexican (passing for white) art dealer who had exhibit of Cézanne drawings, who put us down, visited archaeological museum and figured out the Calendar Stone and saw huge monstrous statues of Death, attended the ballet for 34 cents and sat in high upper balcony, floating anyway on tea [marijuana], and Jack and Peter danced wildly gracefully all the way up 13 stairways to the last balcony, an inspired Chaplinesque paranoiac modern ascent step by step each in turn, beginning at the entrance of the theater, finally we left Mexico City for $135 for four of us, in a car somebody driving to N.Y., Gregory stayed behind waiting for a money order to fly to Jarrell[16] and

16. Randall Jarrell, the poetry consultant to the Library of Congress, had invited Corso to visit him.

stay with him in Washington, D.C., where Gregory is now. We drove up drinking and bennies five days—oh! and I bought for $30 a French Morphee sleeping bag, 1½ lb. I think, mummy, light as a coat and size of a football, down, extremely mummy in fact, too mummy and don't zip all the way down, but very convenient to carry it's so small and light, will do, I tried it out in freezing weather in Texas night and was warm, but it don't seem long enough, my feet touched tip and were chilly (without wool sox tho)—it has a hood you tie under the chin. But at least I bought a bag.

Still trying to get your manuscript out here from Creeley who's sitting on it, Whalen and I finally both wrote him to send it on finished or not, so it will be done. Possibility of publishing chunks of it now here. We're in touch with [James] Laughlin and New Directions, he digs Jack and me, am bringing him *The Slop Barrel* and Burroughs and *Myths & Texts* (when I get it). Send me any new poems you want published, or those ready. Laughlin may do an S.F. anthology scene. Also Gregory's *Cambridge Review* is open, and Grove Press starting an *Evergreen Review*, publishing Jack and me, will bring him everybody else too, the editor, Don Allen, has a scroll, calligraphy, from Daitoku-ji given him from Donald Keene, so he was interested in you and is assembling S.F. material also. They'll be other magazines in Europe I think too. If you have any preferences what should be printed first let me know, I'm not familiar enough with whole long poem to know clearly myself. But, I mean, there seems to be a demand for material now. Also do you want anything done yet with Han Shan? Jack has a copy.

Best though, I saw Williams, talked for three hours with him, am to come back and read him ours, Philip's, and Gregory's poems, and Jack's prose. He can't read but is willing to be read to and was responsive to poems of Gregory's and mine I read him. Strangely, he dug "Over Kansas" airplane and the Joan dream (rain stained tombstone) ["Dream Record: June 8, 1955"] of mine more than long lines, which he also did like. So had big happy talk with him and will see him as often as I can before leaving and learn what I can—also he never read Lorca's "Ode to Walt Whitman" so I am to read that, a huge pleasure to do. Said he wrote little poetry and spent year rewriting 60-page short story about girl he knew who got murdered and asked him to write it up, she figuring in advance that something was going to happen, so he did on typewriter one letter at a time with left hand, right being paralyzed. He's not feeble, just a little waveringly, took me out to 2 P.M. dinner downtown Ruther-ford, his wife was fortunately out, then we couldn't get back in house, wrong key, I had to climb thru window to bathroom of his old Dr.'s office and let him in.

Here in N.Y., Jack, I stay at Paterson or Long Island with my brother in new house, he's married with new boy, I visited my mother's grave, saw my relatives, reading my father's book of poems, visiting poets and old professors and Negresses I knew, waiting to sail.

[Ginsberg has included a few of Gregory Corso's poems with this letter.] I threw in "Swindleresque Ink," tho it's not poem like the rest, I guess, because the phrasing is too funny. He wrote a lot, surrealist and wild, better than the book you saw, since S.F. visit. We gave a reading together in L.A., about 70 people from various sources on short notice, someone heckled him, I drunk began yelling take off your clothes and be naked to heckler and happily at long last disrobed myself all of a sudden—once for all I wanted to do it at a reading. Finally they "pre-vailed" on me to put them back on and I set off reading *Howl* again, about the best I ever did, real drunk and slow and Congo like, no emo-tional tears, just rhythmical power, so it wound up a great wild night, then we got drunker on champagne and sat on sidewalk and vomited all the way home.

Write what your plans are, merchant marine mail for me forwarded, once I leave.

As ever,

Allen

8. GARY SNYDER [KYOTO, JAPAN] TO ALLEN GINSBERG [PATERSON, NJ]

[January 8, 1957]

Dear Allen:

Well there you are finally finishing off America. Give my regards to W.C.W. [William Carlos Williams], he met me once at Reed [College] and read my poems and said some nice things to me—more encouraging than he even thought I suppose—and met me again at Lloyd Reynolds'[17] house in Portland, and I owe something to him for his good-spirit then.

---

17. Lloyd Reynolds. Snyder's English professor at Reed College.

But I suppose he forgot all that. I got back from two-week ball in Tokyo with my friend Jim Revard who is teaching there. (He says he met you at a party shortly before coming to Japan, somewhere near the Academy of Asian Studies, and got in a big argument with you about modern poetry about which he knows nothing, being actually just an escaped Osage Indian with a taste for side-wise snatch and I suppose, balls being alike everywhere and never quite as entertaining as they should be.) There's no use in describing all the whores, bars, dirty movies, sexual exhibitions (between girls with a giant two-way dildo), etc., I took in. Tokyo is a mad city of nihilistic workingmen who have no money and no hope so they spend what they do earn on millions of little bars and whorehouses while their wives sit home in frayed kimonos wringing their roughy hands in chilly rooms over feeble charcoal fires and weeping and the children bounce up and down in the street all day on pogo sticks trying to keep warm.

I enclosed a gloomy Tokyo poem and a bit on riprap and one other thing, samples of quite a quantity I produced this year in between zazens[18] and schools. I did one fierce meditation week at the Daitoku-ji monastery, 1–8 December with about twenty men, we all sat meditating seven days with only two hours sleep each night and the rest but for meals straight sitting. I came out high, bearded, wild-eyed, and laughing and crying at everything that moved. Couldn't even sleep for two days more.

Maybe I won't ship out this spring, I have a deal that I can go live in a country monastery where the Zen master (who imagines himself to be a tattered cloud) is a milk-drinking mountain hermit (five years on nuts and berries) haiku poet with a secret wife that everybody knows about in Tokyo. I can stay there virtually free learn lots about growing vegetables and have all the time to meditate I want. Meditating is the most. You just sit still long enough letting your mind wear itself down on itself and pretty soon the bullshit and camping and silliness of the intellect begins to evaporate and the brain and cock sort of come together in the belly and start laughing like a sharp-eared happy animal. So anyhow maybe I stay there awhile and then ship out for Europe and if you're still there then wow. When do you go? Where? etc. Jack too? Who else? Anybody heard of my manuscript yet?—if they show up, about them, *Myths &*

---

18. Zazen. Buddhist sitting meditation practice.

Texts stands as a whole thing, and I think very little of it can be broken out of place and used. But maybe. The other poems are all independent, and there are a few decent ones there. That manuscript has a lot of bad stuff in it too, it isn't to be considered a selection of my best, but a hodgepodge of all levels. *Myths & Texts* and a number of shorter poems would make a nice little book, that's what I hope to talk somebody into someday. Jack said Phil sent off "Berry Feast" to you—I hope that can be used, it's alright and I like it better as it grows older.

Go dig my Sis [Thea Bama], she's decided she's a writer now and been doing poems and stories. She wants to meet all you cats.

It's snowing off and on today. Nothing looks as great as big Buddhist temple buildings, surrounded by pine-tree groves and rock-walled creeks and long tile-roof walls, in snow. And the morning bell at 5 A.M. from the wood bell-tower come booming soft through the snowy flake pine woods and bent-over bamboo. [. . .]

O yes, at the country Zen monastery I began to write moonastory which is better, there's a just-arrived 28-year-old turtle-neck and bearded Paris boy who's come to join us Han Shans and tattered clouds. I met him, he's alright.

Don't catch cold, taking your clothes off in public,

Gareth

EDITOR'S NOTE: *A letter from Ginsberg is obviously missing here, so it isn't quite certain what the jolly news is that Snyder refers to in the next letter, but probably it is a response to Allen's assurance that the manuscript is safe.*

9. GARY SNYDER [KYOTO, JAPAN] TO ALLEN GINSBERG [PATERSON, NJ]

[*ca.* January 1957]

Dear Allen:

Jolly news. Glad to hear the manuscript of *Myths & Texts* is still with this world. N.Y. sounds fine. You boys are kicking up a regular storm. Phil said something about a *N.Y. Times* interview, what issue was it in? I'll look it up in the liberry here. I guess we all got leather coats. My sister guv me one for Christmas, mine is black and French. I was wearing it and my re-begun beard down in the geisha section the other night and four hoorhouses [whore houses] turned me away because I looked too fierce before I finally got somebody and then only because I talked real polite Japanese.

Listen, when you know what the scene is about Europe let me known, and keep me in touch, because when I was in Tokyo I went to Yokohama and found all about catching ships and it looks real easy right now on account of Suez making more tankers happen, so I might catch a ship and go to Europe late spring or summer. Never can tell.

Then when we're all in Japan at once we will go on walking trip through poetical countryside staying in thatch-roofed inns, drinking sake and fucking the maids carrying little packs like pilgrims poking into forgotten old temples, and issuing blasts at the stupid impossible pretentious intellectuals of this country and publish a joint Chinese-style anthology of aperçus and hike-haiku. [. . .]

Sleeping bag sounds excellent. Wear wool socks to bed when it's cold. Take care of it, use a sheet inside or pajamas or long underwear or something if possible to keep it clean. Dry-cleaning knocks about ⅓ of the warminess out of down.

Every day brings me closer to bodhisattva-hood[19] and the eternity golden milkyhood. Ol' Buddy / rasslin the bear / under the ho, under the bo, under the Hobo tree. Miz Sasaki says one time she solved one of her koans she went out and the trees were covered with jewels and everywhere she looked was giant lotuses and special music, just like Amida's Western Paradise.[20]

Here are some pomes.[21] The rolling heads song is NOT for publication but for amusement. "[Above] Pate Valley" is the pinnacle, in my opinion, of rip-rappy-ness being, as the Japanese has it, *putsu-putsu* (a word for things like mushrooms or pebbles or flowers, meaning sort of popping out severally everywhere at once) on numerous levels visual verbal and paraphysical and pointing out an artifactual conclusion of Chinesified irony echoing the two Tu's (Tu Fu and Tu Mu)[22] to say nothing of archeological accuracy, 10,000 years being the "conservative" estimate for Indian presences on your vast continent. Map is map.

---

19. A bodhisattva is an enlightened being.
20. In order to be reborn in Amida Buddha's Western Paradise, the disciple chants the Japanese mantra "Namu Amida Butsu" nonstop.
21. This was a playful spelling of poems that several writers in the group occasionally used.
22. Tu Fu (712–770) and Tu Mu (803–352) were Chinese poets.

Tell Jack, and your own soul too, that the "Lankavatara Sutra"[23] (recently re-published, Suzuki's translation) says about all one can say and in very elevated language with numerous Sanskritty stories, poems, images, and conceits. It requires enormous energy to read, but I now—second time—and making it something fierce on that old text.

Dig in title "Ballad of Rolling Heads" the sly almost imperceptible allusion to "Robespierre," ho ho ho.

Zazen is turning me into a thing. The "unconscious" is really just the body full of nerves and ideas of its own. Begin to perceive new interesting interior physical happenings so that sometimes they are happening outside and vice-versa. Idea is study the world as received rather [than] produced. Receiving reproduces.

Depending on what Grove [Press] says to some extent, if Sterling Lord,[24] or whatever his name is, says he's willing to take my book in tow, I guess there's no harm. I don't understand how those things work somebody ought to explain. Tell him or whoever it's the only copy for xts [Christ's] sake take care of it or get it in print quick. I really don't want to lose that stuff because I can't remember it all in my head.

Your strenuous efforts are appreciated, telling all those people and getting the book from Kreeley [Robert Creeley]. Thank you very much. Hello to Jack, tell him write.

Gary

[PS] Give my affectionate regards to W.C.W. [William Carlos Williams]

[Snyder includes three poems with this letter: "Map—Above Pate Valley—Ballad of Rolling Heads."]

EDITOR'S NOTE: *On March 10, 1957, Ginsberg and Peter Orlovsky took a boat to Morocco to visit William S. Burroughs. Jack Kerouac was already there helping Burroughs prepare the manuscript of* Naked Lunch *for publication. Allen and Peter left Morocco for Spain on June 11, intending to travel throughout Europe and visit friends.*

---

23. This is an important sacred text of Mahayana Buddhism.
24. Jack Kerouac's literary agent.

[*ca.* June 21, 1957]

Dear Gary:

God knows when this will reach you. Went thru Alhambra at Grenada—
great rooms full of Arabic designs got me hi just looking—then to
Seville, big cathedral, then the mosque at Córdoba and now at Prado
in Madrid—and on to Alan Ansen's in Venice, Italy. Guadalquivir at
Córdoba very ancient and timeless bridge—place of Lorca, Cervantes,
Averröes, Maimonides, and Góngora. This mosque 9th century [refer-
ring to postcard picture].

Love,

Allen

[PS] Living here is pretty cheap, tho Madrid costs for housing more than
other towns. Pete got hives.

EDITOR'S NOTE: *Nearly a year passed without any letters as Ginsberg
will mention in the following. During that time, he and Orlovsky had
settled in Paris, and then Peter returned alone to address family commitments in New York. Snyder had returned temporarily to California.*

April 2, 1958

Dear Gary:

Glad to hear from you, got your card, I wrote you a few letters, long
some, to strange address Don Allen sent me, but I guess they never got
to you Gary. Anyway I been here in Europe all this time, to sum up, two
and a half months in Tangier being Burroughs' slave typing up his manuscript and cooking for everybody, awful routine, good time there, met
[Paul] Bowles and Francis Bacon painter, took off with Peter thru Spain
and toured all great monuments mosques of Córdoba and Alhambra and
Toledo Madrid Barcelona then to Venice, stayed at [Alan] Ansen (friend
from N.Y.—Jack describes weekend in his house in *Subterraneans*) for
two months, more museums and more cooking, then trip with Peter to
Florence and Rome and Assisi, slept on grass and bugged the monks

hand in hand begging food and conversation, then back to Venice and
trip alone back to Rome and Naples and Capri and Ischia (saw Auden a
few nites and only argued lunacy), then with Peter again thru Vienna so
to see Brueghel paintings, then a few days in Munich, then here in Paris
got a room with cookstove gas and went sightseeing and settled down,
but didn't write much, then Amsterdam visited Gregory there for a
month, nice quiet Dutch canals and calm whore streets girls in windows
like legal mannequins, then back to Paris, goofed for a few months doing
nothing, then Peter left for U.S. to take care of brothers (and now has job
in my old Langley Porter type bughouse as attendant in New York City),
Burroughs arrived here (all full of new fine enlightenment, for him, all
his old evil Baudelairian ennui begone—he meditated for half a year
alone in Tangier and said he experienced first time the "indifferent
benevolent sentience at center of things"—sort of a late life crisis for him,
came to Paris to get last frazzles psychoanalyzed and has room downstairs, and Gregory went to Frankfurt where he contacted German poets
who commissioned him to make anthology of young U.S. poets, then
he went stayed with Ansen in Venice; now he's back and also has room
in this hotel—which is right near Place St. Michel, on left bank near St.
Germain center, my hotel itself only a few steps away from the Seine near
Notre Dame Ile de la Cité—great—tho I don't go out too much, lately, I
sit and loom and gloom and brood, don't know what's the matter, guess
I'll come off it sooner or later—too much poetry or self or publicity or
ideas about myself, hard to get out of, particularly as I was so involved,
self involved, well anyway hope I'm getting out of that, so then took a
trip to England, three weeks, slept on [Thomas] Parkinson's couch, visited Turnbull, Gale [*sic:* Gael], doctor near Stratford, and drove to Stone-
henge with Parkinson and wife, and made weepy BBC record, then back
to Paris been here a month or two getting restless and hope, tho broke
right now, to take off for Berlin-Warsaw, maybe Moscow, if I can get any
money. Bill has income so no starvation now. Never did really starve, just
ran out of money, so got fragments of loot from family or royalties or
records or selling books or BBC—actually have been getting quite a lot
of money in this last half year—almost maybe 70 a month or more—so
no real problems. I get royalties from City Lights, they sold about 10,000
I hear, so owe me another 200 this month, will use that and take off for
more travel—still not seen eastern part Europe nor Greece. After that
sometime in summer, July, will go back to New York City, rejoin Peter,

and figure out from there what next. Not written anything very great, that's bugged me, overanxious to please I guess and follow *Howl* up, obsessional, so just a lot of self conscious long lines about politics, horrid, some funny tho—I don't know, I have a lot of manuscripts. But maybe there's something left I'm afraid to begin typing it all lest it stink. Meanwhile I am about the same a little more withdrawn and frightened in a way can't smoke tea I get paranoiac and read the newspapers thru every day worrying about politics—they got cops with machine guns on every block here now, like Berlin 1934, after the Arabs, the Algerian war nobody talks much about but it's a big drag it's happening and the soul of Paris seems dead—frightening tho to walk out at midnight near Notre Dame and run into a black street full of thousands of nightmare cops with machine guns sitting smoking waiting inside huge Black Maria vans expecting some kind of military coup or Arab riot or student demonstration god knows what—shout in the streets here I keep feeling, run wild in the streets and you never know what would happen. America from here after year and half seems like your "This Tokyo" poem only worse, sort of unconsciously perpetuating a war, Dulles[25] spouting about saving world for white Christians etc., gave France half a billion dollars so that keeps the Algeria war going which is insoluble now anyway everybody so filled with hate there, newspapers suppressed here in Paris, Sartre magazine seized etc.—well a lot of bullshit but very oppressive so close up, I guess you got some kind of an idea traveling around the East—in fact what kind of an idea did you get I wonder about present history, seems to me America's taking a fall, i.e. all Whitmanic freedom energy all fucked up in selfishness and exclusion like a big neurotic paranoid that's about to crack up. Talked to some of the 41 U.S. students who made it thru Moscow youth festival to Red China, they shot all the junkies and prostitutes there and I read some Mao and Khrushchev announcements about literature, all brainwash party control—seems to be a different world. I sure would like to go traveling thru that red world and see what it's like. Burroughs very interested in Japan so, me too, I guess next world wander I head east—you any plans for going back there—or for that matter coming here? Jack writes you maybe off for hike tour with him thru West that sounds fine. But what happened, to you? Anything great from monastery? I saw some of your poems that Phil sent Gregory for the German anthology, liked them they're fine, some I'd seen before

---

25. John Foster Dulles was the American secretary of state at the time.

in N.Y., most in fact. Read thru Phil's again last night and they really picked me up, I was depressed I wound up feeling real great after finishing them including some new series called "Takeouts" he has . . . By the way, if can dig Ron Loewinsohn, he sent Gregory a whole mess of really good poems, amazing, I didn't think he'd so forcefully come up with out of his 20s or 23rd year, seems he has a girl and some kind of terrific great love match with her, and writes a lot, more or less isolated in S.F. says it's empty except for fairy poet clique he can't make, maybe true—sometimes he sounds a little like Whalen, but he seems, at least in poetry, very much an enterprising spirit and very alive. Also heard from [Michael] McClure who's changed somewhat for better, shipped out, read thru Jack's *Mexico City Blues* and flipped over them and got a room in the Wentley [Hotel], Polk and Sutter, LaVigne[26] there and Neal around there too says LaVigne, and McClure been writing weirdly and more free. How is Locke, and Sheila?[27] Give them my best. What's happening around S.F. now I wonder? N.Y. is strange, Jack and Peter write, everybody in the Village is giving poetry readings, lots of excitement, even [Philip] Lamantia there reading, all sorts of small clubs and bars, strange—I saw some of the poetry by young people tho it looks lousy, but with spirit. If you have manuscript you want to send out, there are a few places Gregory, Phil, Jack, and me have been sending to the last few months: *Chicago Review*, *Climax*, *Yugen*, *Partisan Review*, *Black Mountain Review*, *Measure*—John Wieners, interesting Olson type, in S.F. somewhere, Loewinsohn or Whalen or McClure know, I haven't his address. *Chicago Review* picked up on Burroughs with great enthuse, only place so far, *Partisan* and *Evergreen* both so far put him down. I left his whole manuscript with [Stephen] Spender in London for *Encounter*, who I think just lost it. Also gave a reading for 25 poetry types at Oxford—read pieces from everybody and they picked up, like at Reed.

So anyway that's the sum of me right now, not much, wish there were some Buddhists here to get drunk with. What your plans, you have any yet? Regards to anybody I know if you see them, Rexroth, Neal, etc. Tonight I go to movies see Rosselini's St. Francis picture,[28] never saw it in States. Saw Chaplin's *[A] King in New York* [1957]—did you in Japan?

---

26. Robert LaVigne was the artist who introduced Ginsberg to Orlovsky in San Francisco in 1954.
27. Sheila Williams was a girlfriend of Ginsberg's.
28. *The Flowers of St. Francis* (1950).

I hear you've been everywhere from Ras Tanura[29] (wherever that mighty name belongs to) to Okinawa, including Bombay—run into anything or anybody fiery or flippy? Or floop? Even. Flow! Write, I did write you— about two big letters they're lost in the Pacific somewhere—all about Fra Angelico and the cocks of Florence—oh yes, got high in the Forum at Rome, and climbed afoot Vesuvio and walked down twelve miles to Pompeii, I saw a lot of classical Europe got all hung up on painting for the first time—and also saw huge exhibits of the greatest all time painter I decided, Van Gogh—in Amsterdam—like a museum with 150 Van Goghs all at once. Plenty weed here, also lots of cheap excellent high quality heroin, sniffed an enormous amount and stopped when Burroughs came to town—he's kicked completely for the last two or three years after being on for a decade—so you see his whole scheme of things has changed a lot "I've told no one to wait for me" he saith, quoting [Saint-John] Perse. Had here, myself, a nice enlightened doll of an Indonesian girl was making it with, ach, but she found someone else last month—but anyway realized the future world's going to be colored yellow or brownish after everybody winds up all intermarried and happy—never really realized that before. Wrote one nice line over English Channel "the giant sun ray down from a vast cloud sun light's endless ladders streaming in eternity to ants in the myriad fields of England bearing minute gold thru smoke climbing unto heaven over London."

As ever,

Allen

12. ALLEN GINSBERG [PARIS] TO GARY SNYDER [CORTE MADERA, CA]

[July 15, 1958]

Dear Gary:

Leaving here in a few days and should be home (Paterson, N.J.) the 24th. (Friend says just like Burroughs, only 24, same education anthropology, horses, a Rothschild, tho offers him house north of Calcutta, I may go there next year.) Been sightseeing Chartres and Versailles the last days. Wrote Neal at San Bruno [prison] and home. Phil says he may make N.Y. around Xmas. I'll get job dishwash unless better scene opens than

---

29. Ras Tanura or Ra's Tannūrah. A Saudi Arabian port city on the Persian Gulf.

I know. Shipping slow, family sent fare. Hope your operation is ok. I'll write lengthier from N.Y. Found a weird short-form for poems—sort of irrelevant automatic images sandwiched in what I have out to say.

As ever,

Allen

[PS] Paris 14 Bastille Day—Dance all nite in the streets with firecrackers. Note reverse angel with stopwatch [referring to picture postcard].

EDITOR'S NOTE: *The letters from Snyder to Ginsberg from this period appear to have been lost.*

13. ALLEN GINSBERG [170 E. 2ND ST., NEW YORK]
    TO GARY SNYDER [?]

October 21, 1958

Dear Gary:

Got your drunk squiggly note from Vulture Peak. Sent you a (haiku?) yesterday. From V.P. ["On Vulture Peak" published in *Yugen*, no. 6 (1960)] the best I thought was from where section 5 camel winds up sublimed into mirror section 6 end, very perfect movement of thought thru the series of whale and seal tricks to disappear in the end. Don't dig rhymed parts so much, partly they sound like—like—oh like Donald Hall. Should "Vulture Peak" be silent as "a tomb" sans hard image tomb? By the way what's Vulture Peak a place, anyplace I know of?

I went up, by the way, thinking of you, to Hawk Ridge (before I got your poem) in Pennsylvania, a ridge on the Kittatinny range of the Appalachians—all the hawks and eagles of the N.E. hemisphere funnel down the skyway along the winds and gather in, where the wind-highway becomes narrow and passes over that peak near Hamburg Pa., as they have over the same spot for ages, to pass the mountain, swoop down following air currents to 100 feet of the ridge and pass on down to Peru. The day I got there was a balmy bright windless clear day, no hawks moving anywhere so I ate a red apple and went home. (Out there to give a reading at Muhlenberg College—first since I've been back—my cousin's boyfriend goes there and asked me to come so I did, refused a $50 fee and made them promise to buy poetry books.) (I was sweating and straining and wailing and took off my shirt and read "Bomb" [by Corso] and

Whalen's "Tantric Sermon" and went on for two hours till exhausted.) (Supposed to read December 5 in Chicago for Irving Rosenthal *Chicago Review.*) (Go there and spend a week first time in Chicago, I've always wanted to go there.)

Reading in Goddard's book,[30] and *Zen Flesh and Bones,*[31] Wang Wei poem, slowly accumulating reading that's all. I've looked into Zimmer[32] a few years ago and in fact re-remembered in dentist's chair some myth of a magic pool, I'll go back and look again. Took Peter to the dentist too last time and he got straight on what I'd been yattering about for the last month, in his own way.[33]

Main thing I've had happen is the withering way on the spirituality metaphysics longings I've clung to since Harlem[34]—tho I still don't understand how two such opposite absolute experiences can be reconciled—tho I don't try to reconcile anything anymore. I really don't believe anything.

I wrote to [Tuttle] Company asking for review books two weeks ago, and as postscript asked them if they knew of your work and Phil's and of Jack's [*Mexico City*] *Blues* and *Some of [the] Dharma* and thought they'd be interested. I guess you have their reply which is crazy.

Spoke to Don Allen on the phone today, he said—semi-definitely as he has said before—that Grove definitely planned to publish a book of your poetry, Whalen's, and also wanted to publish Jack's *Blues*.

(In addition several weeks ago I spoke to [James] Laughlin at New Directions and he said he wanted to see the manuscript and might. In addition LeRoi Jones at *Yugen* has a press [Totem Press] and wants to put out the books, too.)

Allen said he didn't think [Barney] Rosset (the owner) would be happy if you all published your poems with Tuttle and then, after, with him.

So then it's up to you and Whalen to decide where to publish, with Grove or Tuttle or elsewhere. I would guess you could get your complete works out thru Grove, cheap edition widely circulated, so that be a better deal; same for Phil.

---

30. Dwight Goddard, *A Buddhist Bible* (1952).
31. Actually *Zen Flesh, Zen Bones* by Paul Reps and Nyogen Senzaki (1957).
32. Heinrich Zimmer was a well-known scholar of Indian studies.
33. Ginsberg had been investigating the effects produced by laughing gas during his visits to the dentist.
34. In 1948 Ginsberg had experienced a series of visions while living in an apartment in Harlem.

So now I don't know what to do about Tuttle. I wrote Phil today too, same thing. Asked him to handle Tuttle, so everybody doesn't send them different confusing letters—and if a book does go thru, presumably let him edit it or assemble it. Unless you want to. I don't and am not equipped and Jack's got 17 other projects.

Mainly it's up to you and him, so please write him and figure out. Also might write Don Allen and ask him for definite idea when and if he'll publish your *Myths & Texts* and other poems in a book, what kinda book, how complete, etc.? So you can know what to do and tell Phil. All I'm afraid of is big 16-way correspondences all falling on my head. I'm messing around with too much.

In any case if you and Phil have nothing for Tuttle they maybe could have a book of Jack's like *Some of the Dharma*—prose meditations. Tuttle people seem very nice and quick.

Jack, Peter, and I went to see Suzuki[35] who was gentle and happy and gave us thick powder bitter tea, said America needed poetry, was glad it was here, wanted to see some. Send him manuscript we talked about your Han Shan.[36] By the way someone else is doing Han Shan he said. Mrs. Farkas of the Zen Institute here knows or knows of him if you want to get in touch. Suzuki showed Peter big picture of radiant smile on Han Shan and friend and Peter reflects back the same smile, Suzuki stared at him in goofy interest.

Also I'm compiling for City Lights—Ferlinghetti says he told you—a small anthology of Burroughs and Jack's and [Herbert] Huncke too, best prose. Bill's best routines, Jack's from Gothic *Visions of Neal* prose, a few letters from Neal, some of my poetry, Phil's and yours. That's all. Just perfect pieces for amber-preservation for future and to clear up present day bullshit by presenting a perfect handbook of high writing. Please make up 15- to 20-page selection for me of what you want included—anything of yours you wish—and send it to me. And any suggestions. Ferl [Ferlinghetti] asked me for a Beat Generation anthology including [Anatole] Broyard, [Norman] Mailer, etc. and I said no, but I'd put together the poems, prose, and documents that were sacred to me, for kicks. Preferably not material Grove will use for anthology but if the diamond parts are needed they can be printed in both places.

---

35. D. T. Suzuki was a Japanese author of books on Buddhism.

36. A collection of poems attributed to a mythological Chinese poet, translated as "Cold Mountain."

I hope this is not piling too much on your head. I have my hands full and want to get out from under as soon as this is done. But would like to leave behind at lest one pure unsullied culture text.

Love, as ever

Allen

[PS] 9th letter today—17 single-spaced pages so far so exhausted.

14. ALLEN GINSBERG [NEW YORK] TO GARY SNYDER [CORTE MADERA, CA]

[November 22, 1958]

Gary:

As Phil probably wrote you, Grove won't put out separate books for you and Phil (tho he may print Jack's *Blues* complete), but will be willing to print a book of all three of us. It may be long enough for Phil's complete works, and *Myths & Texts* complete plus some of your later poems; plus short section of later poems of mine, "Xbalba" and one or two other plus one new poem. I'm pledged to City Lights for a full book but [Don] Allen said it be OK if my part be token and give you and Phil more room anyway. Phil thinks maybe hold out for a book apiece for a while. That's good too. LeRoi Jones willing to put out books for you whether or not you take Grove offer. Or can dump rest on Tuttle. Or can try New Directions, I still advise that. I wrote above to Phil today. Read at Hunter College English Club and the advisor resigned in protest. *Chicago Review* winter issue suppressed and [Irving] Rosenthal resigned, my December reading there off. I'm writing new wild poem, continuing my mother's kaddish.

Love

Allen

15. ALLEN GINSBERG [NEW YORK] TO GARY SNYDER [MILL VALLEY, CA]

[December 7, 1958]

Dear Gary:

That's good, then, wait see. McGregor, Mr., at New Directions and Laughlin would like to see the manuscript too and might. Have Grove send them over or send them from you. I'd do it all, but there's now so many complications and I better retire. And as LeRoi must have written, he'll print a book too, if you want.

I'm writing a lot, long poem about my mother, narrative, ends in kaddish wail. Been hearing Yiddish *eli eli* funeral sounds and archetype rhythms and constructing rhythmic movements like them. Meeting a lot of Negroes here, first time, thru LeRoi Jones. Read at Hunter College and mad reading at Yale where began chanting at 300 Yalies. So busy. Dropt in at Zen Institute to look up Sasaki, but she was away. Jack drinking in town weekends, spent week at his house in Long Island when his momma was away.

Love

Allen

[PS] Dreamt of an eye in a black cloud. Line: Death is a letter that was never sent.

16. ALLEN GINSBERG [NEW YORK] TO GARY SNYDER [MILL VALLEY, CA]

[December 12, 1958]

Overwhelmed with letters, readings, and huge new poem [*Kaddish*], Hebrew chant mourning for momma, "Blessed be He who builds Heaven in Darkness!"—50 pages me in *gott*, prose, verse strophes, chants, wails, autobiog facts, asylums, rides in buses with mad Naomi[37] age 12—so using postcards for nonce, Blessed Gary. Fine about Grove. LeRoi will do book for Phil. You too? Don A. says he'll look round for book for you. I'll wait on my anthology (*Angel's Goofbook*, or *Sperm*) till dust settles anyway. Tell Hoodlatch send LeRoi poems. *NY Post* chubby sincere (I hope) reporter[38] investigating Beat Generation for 6- or 12-part series, reading everyone's books and manuscripts including *Zen Flesh*, William Carlos Williams, "Bomb," etc., be out in Frisco in a week, gave him yr address, so please spin the wheel, he wants meet McClure, [John] Wieners, you, and Phil, instead of beatniks. See my notes in *Village Voice* on Jack[39]? (Ask Ferl [Ferlinghetti].) Jack has nice healthy girl[40] who likes

---

37. Ginsberg's mother, Naomi, spent much of her adult life in mental institutions.
38. Al Aronowitz.
39. Ginsberg wrote a review of Kerouac's *Dharma Bums* for the November 12, 1958 issue of the *Village Voice*.
40. Dodie Müller.

to dance and paints good. Peter say Hello. I love you too. Goodnight from New York,

As ever,

Allen

EDITOR'S NOTE: *Snyder returned to Japan to continue his Buddhist practice and study, but letters from this period have been lost. By the time these letters pick up again, Gary had already married Joanne Kyger, a fellow San Francisco poet and meditation student. Ginsberg was beginning to plan a long trip that would eventually lead him to India where he and Orlovsky met Gary and Joanne and traveled together.*

17. GARY SNYDER [31 NISHINOYAMA CHO, OMIYA, KITA-KU, KYOTO, JAPAN] TO ALLEN GINSBERG [NEW YORK]

10.VIII [August 10, 1960]

Dear Allen,

A time for a note before we leave (Friday) for the Japan Sea. Joanne and I are going camping with a blackbeard young English potter and his sexy Swedish wife (who've been in Kyoto nearly two years; this is becoming shortly an orgy town I think), for two weeks, with Zen monk friend also going out to some islands in the Japan Sea to skin-dive and goof.

Drop out of the world six months you said. Good!

I'm glad you went there.[41] (Did I tell you about young Guatemalan who was here all last year living in the Daitoku-ji Zen monastery as a monk; looks like an El Greco type, with big eyes, his father is wealthy coffee planter?) How can Death get at the Unborn, go back before birth and look at death. Or look at death through a coffeecup or sharpen your pencil on it, protect the chair against death, don't destroy the chance of a boulder to life. Kali looks both ways. What does "no" mean.

Love lives by eating.

I saw all your pictures in the *Beat Scene* book somebody brought, your beard is beautiful and crazy grin too. Lafcadio is getting beautiful too. Is the scene as bad as Krim suggests in essay "Making It"[42]? Read all of

41. Ginsberg had just returned from a six-month trip to South America, where he continued Burroughs' search for the hallucinogenic vine *yage*.
42. Reprinted in Seymour Krim's *Views of a Nearsighted Cannoneer* (Excelsior, 1961).

"Aether" aloud to Joanne. I'd like to see it when you get your final draft on it (as I suppose I will in print somewhere) and am sending you, if I get it typed before we leave, "Bubbs Creek Haircut" first solid chunk of *Mountains and Rivers without End* to get done.

Everyday living IS the enlightenment and the insight. I tried to put the worlds / universes together a little bit that way in "Bubbs Creek," making them all, also, this world. "Aether" has the many worlds, "worlds without end, brothers" . . . have a cup of tea (if it don't sound corny).

I just wrote a review of a 3rd century BC Chinese poem (*Li Sao: An Elegy on Encountering Sorrows* by Ch'u Yuan) translation, for *Journal of American Folklore*, comparing it (validly, *en passant*) to *Howl*. Young anthropologist from Mill Valley via Yale in town, leaving next week for two years in jungles of New Guinea. Typhoon hits Japan tonight radio says.

Nobody can straighten American politics out because the people won't stand for it—how can the internal economics be put in order when everybody wants everything? Any sane monetary policy or farm policy doomed to ruin. Ditto by logical extension foreign policy. Bread and Circuses. No longer a problem of helping out American workers, but of giving up national comfort for whole world welfare . . . will America ever choose to be a bodhisattva? and wear blue jeans and sandals before the world and give away her property? The "orgy" has political and metaphysical significance. All we can do is shore up bastions for the future of the mind when Communism takes over and indiscriminately confuses the cures of economic suffering with the cures of illusion-bound ego and sees life through just one pair of glasses. I think. A month off and *sanzen* and zazen starts again, September.

Joanne and I send our love,

Gary

18. GARY SNYDER [KYOTO, JAPAN] TO ALLEN GINSBERG [NEW YORK]

1 November [1960]

Dear Allen,

Did you really go visit Castro like *Time* said? Langston Hughes denied it.

"Aether" was so much I couldn't bring myself to comment quick. Does "A Magic Universe" constitute a separate poem or division?

"Samsaric Consciousness." Not being, not non-being, not something else. "The mind turns in accord with / the 10,000 conditions; / The place of its turning is truly / mysterious" (part of an old poem; also a koan).

As for universes: Tsung Ping, the painter, speaking of a mountain scene said, "With every step it changes."

One week meditation at the monastery from tonight. Clear skies and persimmons. Joanne is off studying Japanese at a school, and out on the street a procession from some Shinto shrine is going by beating drums. Red China: "Work like an ox for children."

Gary

[PS] My best to Peter. I like his poems! and your beard / S.

EDITOR'S NOTE: *The Ginsberg letters from this period have been lost. A fragment from one appeared in Joanne Kyger's book* Japan and India Journals *(1981) and is reprinted here.*

19. ALLEN GINSBERG [NEW YORK]
    TO GARY SNYDER AND JOANNE KYGER [KYOTO, JAPAN]

November 9, 1960

[. . .] the great pronouncement finally came from an old lady Grete Bebering who second to Anna Freud is the Big Wheel in U.S.A. who raised her finger in the air and said: "What zees es, ees a varry courageous and lovely poetry—for what we see is the disintegration of the ego and the public experience of the primary forces of the Id, which is a terrible and awesome theeng to experience in the human beeing, for the purpose of the better experiencing of the beauty of our nature, and a more healthy reintegration of the ego—no wander the conservative forces in theese country experience such anxiety when in contact with theese man—he is a great poet," or some such speech she made putting down all the sociologist amateurs who were hung up with concepts of adolescent rebellion, etc. So the total result is all the symposium will be published by American Psychoanalytic Association. [Meeting of The Group for Advancement of Psychiatry: Symposium on Beat Generation]

20. GARY SNYDER [KYOTO, JAPAN] TO ALLEN GINSBERG [NEW YORK]

12.XII [December 12, 1960]
twelve-twelve (what Zodiacal significance I know not)

Dear Allen:

Good for you and Cuba. I don't trust the sentimental ex-Stalinist pro-Castro sentiment too much. God knows they needed a revolution there, but there are kids and there are men in this revolution business; I think Castro must be the former. Like, let him get aid from Russia and China if he likes, but be cool about it until his position is solid; bugging the U.S. out of its head serves no useful revolutionary function. And the excessive retribution-violence makes bad karma—"hatred is not cured by hatred" as the *Dhammapada* sez. But. Let there be beards in politics.

Poem:

A flock of seagulls
I HAVE THE MEAT!

(Joanne says that I don't need "A flock of.")

About what you're doing now with *yage*, etc. I can't think of anything better to work with than *Tibetan Book of the Dead.* Anagarika Govinda's recent *Foundations of Tibetan Mysticism* might help too; psychologically hip. "Afraid of traveling through cosmic cycles"—that's the trick point; the knothole, gate leading outside time is the moment, and that isn't approached through the vision-level of the unconscious, but at the non-dualism perception, neither I AM or AM NOT.—Dropping all the worlds at once. (The "three worlds" are past, present, and future; the "three realms" are form, desire, and formlessness) oh well. Just got out of Rohatsu four days ago (the one-week zazen bit) and am still swinging (in my way) Zen is magic man, because it's so fucking baffling simple and concrete and subtle, and won't let you fool nobody. "What color is the wind?" "Where does the rain come from?"—little "minor" koans. Not one "concept" in it all.

Am delighted with your success, victory, *Triomphe*—at the Psycho conference.[43] Makes me feel enormously tender toward the analytic vocation, which I usually put down. Maybe you can get all the mental hospitals to serve as secret hotels for wandering meditators and visionaries—

---

43. During the first week of December, Ginsberg had visited Timothy Leary at Harvard and spoke in front of a group of psychoanalysts there.

passers-through—sadhus in naked ash, eating the tongues of the dead. Joanne loves you too: [in Joanne's handwriting: (actually it's a bit more complicated than that)]

Love:

Gary

21. ALLEN GINSBERG [NEW YORK] TO GARY SNYDER [KYOTO, JAPAN]

[*ca.* February 28, 1961]

Dear Gary:

Leaving for Greece join Gregory first leg of Asia trip in two weeks so no answer letters well. Mushrooms are *psylocybe caernlescens var mazetecorum Heim.* Don't know if that helps. If you write Gordon Wasson,[44] he is expert and can perhaps give you Japanese data and references and varieties. Send him a note? Never got to Cuba. I'd be glad to work on book you suggest too. Sooner or later. LeRoi began such a project but I think it tended to bog down in his own intellectualism. Knopf wants such a book. But LeRoi gets too polemical-materialist. I'm still compiling notes on huge 40-page political poem-diatribe sort of surreal form; it gets to sound like Burroughs in fact. An area I haven't stepped into in writing before. Much political and mass media activity on drug reform growing now and I think something will happen by April. I'll write when I settle.

Love

Allen

EDITOR'S NOTE: *Another fragment from one of Ginsberg's letters that appeared in Joanne Kyger's book,* The Japan and India Journal *(1981), and is reprinted here.*

---

44. R. Gordon Wasson was an ethnomycologist and the author of *Soma: Divine Mushroom of Immortality.*

22. ALLEN GINSBERG [TANGIER, MOROCCO]
    TO GARY SNYDER AND JOANNE KYGER [KYOTO, JAPAN]

[*ca.* August 22, 1961]

"[. . .] Burroughs's cut-up method very similar (I guess) to koan method as a verbal-mind breaker." (Dr. [Timothy] Leary [is] returning with him to Harvard to continue experiments.) Burroughs has . . . developed a number of exercises to get out of his mind and body and into space, all mainly based on cut-up method—new book *The Soft Machine*—is really the most advanced—no longer writing or literature of any kind except secondarily—more a map of areas he says he explored and handbook of technique of altering conceptual consciousness. Harvard opinion is that "arbitrary conceptualization" is located in a specific brain area—cortex—and that the drugs knock out cortex activity and leave open brain. Thus the present world psychic struggle is a war over control of the nervous system. I see no way of writing at the moment since my original interest was something like mind transmission and present scientific research techniques have made great leap forward and perhaps by now obviated words. At least that's Burroughs/Leary's opinion. That is, any aesthetic thrill or awareness a poem can bring can be catalyzed by wires and drugs, much more precisely.

23. GARY SNYDER [KYOTO, JAPAN]
    TO ALLEN GINSBERG [ATHENS, GREECE]

4.IX.1961 [September 4, 1961]

Dear Allen,

GOOD to hear from you! Exciting letter and various news, listen man, the non-Western cultures have been doing what Burroughs is up to (part of it anyhow) for thousands of years: or been doing what the psychiatric-psychological researchers are just now studying, i.e. the dissociation of consciousness through techniques—and different levels of mental being—this is what the Comanche youth who fasted and danced was doing: or breath control, or countless native herbs, steambathing, looking at the sun, etc.—no wire or pill will ever put poet out of work, any more than it did in the past, in yoga India, say: because the wire or pill today is simply the equivalent of the ascetic technique in ancient times and other cultures . . . if one wants far-outness and insight through dissociation he NEVER DID go to a poet, he went to a man who could show him the drug or the best ways to dance, etc. . . . but the poet has another work, related, it is in language, it is not to be free of the word, but TO MAKE THE WORD FREE, sit down on the tongue of any man in the world (Joshu) (?)—and, to celebrate his insight, to sing, to tell, to push the hearer's mind of words far as it goes . . . but NOT to transmit mind, although he may sometimes do it by accident: his prime aim is to interpret? male magic language? something a bit else, I think. You Allen Ginsberg aren't great just because you're a see-er, but because you make it with the Muse too. At least I think the above. And passionately believe nothing will ever put poet out of business, he sees and he MAKES.

Also (side note) essential extra element in the full approach (say we call drugs, ascetics, yoga, etc., "shamanism") as in some of Hinduism and Buddhism, is element of conscious will to change, and to change something structural in the whole web of selfness, more than just exploring intricate by-ways of mind, to latch whole being onto mind and life there; a time-process.

Our plan at present is to leave Japan on Messageries Maritimes ship, *Cambodge*, about 12 December, arrive Bombay 31 December. Stay in India three or more months, depending on how money holds out. Return from Colombo also via Messageries Maritimes, visit monuments, ashrams,[45] a few people, and try and see some Tibetan Buddhist practice in Nepal, Gangtok, or Sikkim.

I thought about trying to give poetry readings in India at universities to supplement money, and by kind help of Ellie Dorfman[46] have huge list of addresses to write to. If you are interested in going in on this with me, I will draw up mimeograph letter saying who you are and who I am, and what poetry reading is, and send it around to all these addresses saying we will be visiting India and will give poetry readings to help defray our expenses while there . . . and see what the response is. Write me your answer to this proposal immediately.

I don't work for Mrs. Sasaki anymore because of huge fight with her;

---

45. Ashram. A community guest house for a spiritual pilgrim.
46. Elsa Dorfman was working for Grove Press at the time and later became a well-known portrait photographer.

Phil Yampolsky[47] and Burt Watson[48] also quit. I am still working with my roshi though—that has no connection. I feel much better about things. Have written two sections to *Mountains and Rivers* (you saw "Bubbs Creek"), second one is 15 pages long, "Night Highway Ninety-Nine." Am now teaching English. Lots of money teaching English. Will do that when we come back to Japan. You must consider returning with us, we will be keeping our fine big house here while we're gone. Much more I would say, yr last letter set Joanne and me both going . . . I don't know what to say about you and Peter parting, but change is usually right . . . my roshi said when the word comes out in a flash it's not a word, it's your true mental state; when you search for the right word, it will never be the right word.

    Love

    Gary

24. GARY SNYDER [KYOTO, JAPAN]
      TO ALLEN GINSBERG [ATHENS, GREECE]

17 October [October 17, 1961]

Dear Allen,

I pray this does get to you, wandering aphasick and melancholick amongst the Athenian ruins; it has valuable information in't. (1) Having heard from several people about my idea of poetry-reading in India, and having thought more of it, I had already come to something of the same feeling you had; why show myself off. Also: there seems no likelihood they would feel like paying anybody for readings there. And it seems that going thru the English departments of universities might be wrong; they are snobbish with their eyes on the English classics. An Indian friend, Urdu-speaker, who was in the Linguistics department at Berkeley, has written me much advice and a number of addresses. He says if you want to talk to people around universities, go to the Literature and Language department of the local language: i.e. Hindi, Urdu, Tamil,

---

47. Phil Yampolsky became a leading Japanese translator and Zen Buddhist scholar at Columbia University.
48. Burton Watson was a Buddhist scholar who worked on the translation team of Ruth Sasaki in Kyoto and did a number of East Asian translations for Columbia University Press.

Bengali, etc. department; they are more swinging and can tell you more. So I am thinking to let the idea lie; if we feel like reading someplace, or get a chance (free or for pay) and it feels right, OK. Not that I couldn't use more money, but there doesn't seem much chance for that anyhow. I have a lot of addresses from Don Allen and Ellie Dorfman of official intellectuals and literati, and some perhaps more interesting contacts from my above-mentioned friend, C. M. Naim, who is a poet in Urdu and English himself; at any rate we can look up people if we like. Also some Buddhist contacts (Mahabodhi Society; Lama Govinda).

(2) We have altered our plans a bit, after studying the weather tables, to disembark in Ceylon (in January while the south is still cool) and then to work north up the east coast of India to Calcutta. Roughly this would be our itinerary: Disembark 29 December Colombo off Messageries Maritimes ship *Viet Nam*; spend one week in Ceylon see Kandy. Then go to Pondicherry south of Madras, and stay a few days or a week in the Shri Aurobindo Ashram digging whatever meditation they do; see other S. India temples. Go on thru Madras and up coast; stop definitely at Puri and visit Konarak temple. Then proceed to Nagpur? stay a few days in Gandhi Ashram and talk to Gandhi movement?? Proceed to Calcutta and environs. Then go west, up the Ganges, to Bodh Gaya and stay a week in Bodh Gaya and vicinity doing meditation under Bodhi tree[49] and seeing ruins of Nalanda University, etc. Maybe stop at Santiniketan see Tagore University? hmm. Also, at this point, perhaps consider side trip to Nepal or Darjeeling for Tibetan Buddhist observations. Then to look at Benares, and go on up river to Agra (professor friend of Naim) and Delhi. From Delhi go to Hardwar, and plan to stay a week to ten days at Yoga-Vedanta Ashram in Rishikesh. Take walk from there into Himalayas and see view of Nanda Devi? Go on north following Himalayas thru Amritsar and Lahore to Rawalpindi and Peshawar in Pakistan, see Gandharvan Buddh art. Then train to Karachi and fly to Bombay, or fly from Peshawar to Bombay. In and around Bombay, and travel to Aurangabad for seeing Ajanta and Ellora. Leave Bombay around 31 March on Messageries Maritimes Company ship; or, if money holds out and visa can be extended, stay longer.

This is subject to change if I learn more: but I think the basic plan of get off in Colombo and re-embark to return to Japan in Bombay will

---

49. The tree under which Buddha attained enlightenment.

hold, otherwise I'd be traveling in the north when it's already cold, and going south when it begins to get hot, which don't make sense. Real heat is May and June: Monsoon starts June 1 in Ceylon, July 1 on the Gangetic plain. During monsoon season travel is impossible.

I guess my main idea in India, aside from just being there, is to experience several sorts of ashram, yoga practice and Tibetan practice; see Buddhist and Hindu art and temples; and commune with the Himalaya even from relatively far if needs be. But if I can I'll hike into them a bit.

Otherwise: I have learned. Claude[50] said he lived on $2 a day, including all transportation, while he was in India. He got bad dysentery, too. A friend in Tokyo traveled about India on $5 a day for him and his wife. You got to take water purifier tablets (halazone) and plan to eat lots of bananas and yoghurt, they're always safe. Never stay in a hotel. Railway stations usually have rooms you can sleep in. Dak Bungalows and Circuit Houses are in most towns and supposedly you can stay in these quite cheap, sometimes cooking your own food. EVERYWHERE you must carry your own bedding. Which isn't much more than a sheet-bag and blanket apparently. But they don't supply it outside of fantastic expensive Western hotels. Mahabodhi Society has Buddhist pilgrim rest houses many places, can stay for small contribution. Sleep on a wood bench. Ashrams are usually cheap. The Rishikesh Yoga-Vedanta Ashram is actually free, and all the yogins[51] sit around playing music in the evening in area of upper Ganges, and is crowded with weird ascetics of all types. Apply for visa early, the consulate here tells me. Get cholera shot and diarrhea medicine. God is close to dirt in India they say. That's all I can think of. Do you want to meet us in Ceylon? or where? (Calcutta maybe?) Sorry I can't talk about deeper things this letter.

Love,

Gary

[PS] Joanne says she'll carry on her dialogue with you in India. I'm reading Mircea Eliade's *Yoga: Immortality and Freedom* (1958) now. He says Indian holy men knew all the drugs, rejected them because use of drug or narcotic lacks the element of PARADOX somehow essential. hmm. What about Paul Bowles and Ceylon?[52]

---

50. Claude Dalenberg was one of the founders of the East-West House in San Francisco.

51. A practitioner of yoga.

52. Paul Bowles had a home in Ceylon and Ginsberg hoped to meet up with him and stay there. This never materialized.

25. ALLEN GINSBERG [ATHENS, GREECE]
    TO GARY SNYDER [KYOTO, JAPAN]

[October 21, 1961]

Dear Gary:

Moving slowly east—next address in a week be at American Express, Haifa, Israel. Peter now in Damascus, we probably meet up there November 1. I wrote you a few weeks ago, been in Crete since and saw Minoan castles and valleys, plenty shepherds bells again. So keep in touch—send me a card in Israel. I may go overland thru Persia if I have the loot, but hope to arrive Bombay by New Year. Everybody says it's expensive there because dysentery makes it hard to live native and there's no middleclass hotels. Having strange dreams and running around Athens cafés meeting European intellectuals now also again.

   Love
   Allen

26. ALLEN GINSBERG [ATHENS, GREECE]
    TO GARY SNYDER [KYOTO, JAPAN]

[October 23, 1961]

Dear Gary:

Yr prayers answered and letter of info. arrived day before I leave here. Next address American Express, Haifa, Israel. I'll answer yours from there—OK! I thought you were going to Bombay New Years! OK I'll meet you somewhere along the line with bedroll. I'll write Bowles and inquire about Ceylon. I have addresses of all sorts Indian gurus from Peter Mayne, a traveler. Thank god we don't got to read. I'll have to figure out where I'll be and meet you, so will write that later.

   Greek music and dancing is the loveliest outside of U.S. Blues I ever heard. Letter from Philip Whalen today too. Your trip sounds great. OK, I'll send this off.

   Regards

27. ALLEN GINSBERG [HAIFA, ISRAEL] TO GARY SNYDER [KYOTO, JAPAN]

[*ca.* November 5–6, 1961]

Gary, Gary, Joanne:

I did get your last Athens letter, I sent you card saying so, dincha READ
or get it? But nice to get another. I will definitely meet you in Ceylon/
New Years, but am waiting to finalize free or work-away boat from Red
Sea before writing you at length; which I'll so do in a week or two. Will
also then have heard from Bowles. Also got funny fairies' addresses all
over. Peter disappeared again but probably he'll come boating with me. I
leave for Tel Aviv tomorrow so can't write now. Note reverse site of many
Jesus Miracles.[53] Galilee lovely. You too.

    Allen

[PS] I heard from Phil. Jack wrote drunk card. He'd fly to India sometime
soon. Great no readings. I met [Buddhadeva] Bose[54] in N.Y.

28. ALLEN GINSBERG [ISRAEL] TO GARY SNYDER [KYOTO, JAPAN]

November 23, 1961

Dear Gary and Joanne:

I have your letters with itineraries but haven't answered except for postcard because my plans not fixed, and even now in some confusion still.
Peter here, arrived after huge Middle East hegira. We applied for visas
and immediately had trouble which U.S. cultural attaché is now straightening out, so that be OK presently I think. The Indians don't have repre-
sentation here except thru English so that doubles the bureaucracy, they
have to wire India for OK.

    Meanwhile we got about $300 between us or less, I'll get more from
U.S. when I get there, so looking for cheap or free boat; also movements
limited by Arab-Israel boycotts so can't go to Port Said now for boats
without side trips and new passports via Cypress or other where. So
still working on problem. If I can, will meet you as per your schedule in
Ceylon. I have all your addresses.

---

53. Reference to the picture postcard.
54. Buddhadeva Bose, a Bengali writer and poet.

So if I don't know definite plans I can write you in next few days before you leave Japan, I'll write you at above addresses to say how and where I'm going. See I don't have enuf loot to simply go there straight. Right now am trying to find out what boats leaving Eilat on Red Sea could take us nearest Colombo, but lacking right boat may have to head off via Djibouti or Bahrain. When I leave here I'll leave forwarding address so letters or notes sent to this Israeli address will be forwarded. Also when I leave I'll write you at India addresses so you'll know where to send me note if I land after you. This letter should get to you before 10 December when you leave. Israel is an interesting drag.

Buddhadeva Bose I met in N.Y. he invited us to visit [in Calcutta]. Also Professor Narasimhiah of University of Mysore visited me in S.F. and said to drop in. He is American Literature expert and likes Whitman and S.F. poesy.

I can't write Bowles from here straight because no mail service to Arab Morocco. Probably be a note from him for your and my name at Messageries Maritimes when you disembark, I'll write him via France.

I'm a little disorganized. Had (already) some colitis-bug up my intestines and been to doctors here to clear it up before I leave. OK—till later. I have both your letters so know where you're headed. I'll write you in any case to Colombo before I leave here—hope to see you there.

Love

Allen

29. ALLEN GINSBERG [TEL AVIV, ISRAEL]
    TO GARY SNYDER [COLOMBO, CEYLON]

[partial letter, *ca.* December 1961]

PS Some Subud-Indian-Russian friends from Tangier say the mother at Aurobindo's ashram is "wonderful and genuine, but that Swananda is phony and Hollywood."

The situation here is I'm waiting for $500 from *Playboy* I finally wrote for, so I can get a plane out of here with Peter. I have been hanging around, hopefully petitioning the bureaucracy to get me out of here! Via the only Orient oriented seaport they got, but all I've run into is four weeks of promises and static and I finally gave up. So I'm not sure what

route be cheapest and swiftest for us to go now. I would like to touch on
Ceylon first and see Bowles who's there—but that's the farthest point to
reach by plane from here.

And hate to blow all those greenbacks on a plane ride. Costs $250 from
here which is cheap. Or $116 to Teheran and then fantastic grueling trans-
India-Persia-Pakistan bus and train hurry hurry—what a damn fix!—all
the way to Calcutta or Ceylon. And—well as soon as I know my route
I'll write you both at Colombo and Calcutta. Maybe intercept you en
route—oh gawd!

Love
Allen

30. ALLEN GINSBERG [ACRE, ISRAEL] TO GARY SNYDER [KYOTO, JAPAN]

[December 20, 1961]

Dear Gary:
Things have been stupidly jinxed here for weeks, I'm stuck like in fly-
paper in this dreary joint. Can't get thru Arab states overland without
extensive passport hassles and trips to Istanbul; can't get boat out of
Southern Israeli port of Eilat. Waiting for money and maybe fly to Tehe-
ran or even India. I'll be late! Alas! But I'll be there within a month. Paul
Bowles should be in Ceylon. I sent him Messageries address, he'll leave
you/me/both a note there—contact him, maybe he has a house even. I
don't know where I'll land in India. Leave message for me in American
Express Calcutta, also leave a card with your itinerary in Bombay, and
another in Colombo. I am coming as fast as I can. I have your itinerary
which covers up to Calcutta January 15, is that right?

Love
Allen

31. GARY SNYDER [COLOMBO, CEYLON]
TO ALLEN GINSBERG [BOMBAY, INDIA]

29.XII [December 29, 1961]

Dear Allen,
Wrote you at Tel Aviv; here's a quick repeat of that if you missed it. We
look to arrive Calcutta @ 18–22nd January. Stay three or four days. Then

(depending on what we learn from them) go to Darjeeling/Kalimpong and back to Patna; then to Bodh Gaya; or from Calcutta direct to Bodh Gaya—Nalanda—Benares—Allahabad—Agra, etc., eventually to Delhi in the first part of February. Address there will be c/o American Express. Check with Mahabodhi Society in Calcutta. I'll leave more detailed itinerary with them when we leave. Take care! Boil yr water! Don't buy your rupees at the bank! (We got 7 to $1 in Hong Kong.)

Turtle love to Peter.

Gary

32. GARY SNYDER [COLOMBO, CEYLON]
    TO ALLEN GINSBERG [COLOMBO, CEYLON]

29.XII.1961 [December 29, 1961]

Dear Allen,

We got here cool and easy yesterday—sorry to see your immovability. We'd hop'd to see you sooner. Shit. Pox on the Jews and Arabs. We're staying at the "British Soldiers and Sailors Institute," which takes couples and is very cheap. Next door to YMCA. Went to great zoo and less impressive Buddhist temple today. Great tropical fruits. Leave day after tomorrow, the 31st, for Kandy—be at Aurobindo Ashram @ the 10th and thus to Calcutta @ 18–22 January; how long we'll stay I can't say (in Calcutta); will leave forwarding address and more precise itinerary with them. I suppose from Calcutta we'll go to Shantiniketan, (Kalimpong? Darjeeling?) Bodh Gaya, Benares—Sarnath—and on across stopping here and there, til we get to Delhi. (Which should be in the first or second week of February? Will leave additional info with American Express there. Joanne is fine. Food is pretty cheap. Try and buy your Indian rupees on the local black market, not at banks. Bank rate is $1 = 4.76 Rs; black market @ $1 = 7 Rs. once you get in India.) But be careful moneychangers give you full count. The Buddha didn't use money thank God. No sign of Bowles. Ceylon is lovely and cool and green.

Gary

33. GARY SNYDER [KANDY, CEYLON]
   TO ALLEN GINSBERG [COLOMBO, CEYLON]

Aurobindo Ashram 9.I.62 [January 9, 1962]

Dear Allen,

Your letter. The people here didn't tell me about your letter. I just happened to find it in the ashram post office. Information: 1. good place
to stay in Colombo is British Sailors and Soldiers Institute, next door
to YMCA—same street as *Ceylon Times* is on; close to Cook's. Beds
for Rs. 2.50 and 3.50 a night can eat cheap in YMCA cafeteria. If you
go to Kandy can stay for 3 Rs. a night in Visitor's Room at Boy Scout
HQ (actually a youth hostel room). Scout boss is nice guy; a Buddhist.
Straight ahead on road from Kandy Railway Station and then turn right
by big stone-walled market; wind along and across street from prison big
Boy Scout yellow building. German *bhikkhu* "Nyanaponika" in woods
back of Kandy writing Buddhist propaganda—interesting—locate him
with help of scoutmaster. If you go to see ruins of Anuradhapura can
stay cheap at Dutugemunu Pilgrims Rest—Buddhist run; leave 2 or 3 Rs.
contribution per night. Take bus from Anuradhapura railway station or
bus terminal bound for "old hospital" to get there. 2. Check black market
prices of Indian rupees in Colombo. If you have cash, might buy a few
in Ceylon because Indian official rate of Rs. 4.75 = $1 is not so hot. But
leave enough $ in your possession to satisfy Indian Customs; and carry
extra rupees in your socks or crotch. 3. We stayed one day in Madurai,
to see great Shiva-Shakti temple. Most all railway stations have "Retiring Rooms" nice beds—Rs. 8 for a double; Rs. 5 for a single and Rs. 2 for
each extra person in single room. Then we came to Pondicherry. Take
Madras train, change at Viluppuram for Pondicherry. Fantastic place.
They all believe that the MOTHER is a divine incarnation, represent-
ing a new step in human evolution; that Pondicherry is the center of
the power about to change the universe—not only by self-realization,
etc., but by actual objective transformation of the nature of matter—we
will be physically immortal—no sexes—glow with light—be in constant
contact. You should come see it. Mother is not seeing visitors now, but
every morning 6:15 A.M. comes out on her balcony to cast vibrations at
the 200-odd people waiting below. Stay at ashram, "Parc-a-charbon," Rs.
4 a day with meals. If interested write Mr. Madhar Pandit, Secretary, in
advance. We leave here the 11th, leave Madras the 15th, arrive Calcutta @

the 18th–19th, will expect news from you there. Not sure yet just where from Calcutta, probably Tagore's Shantiniketan a few days. We go slow; you catch up. Use third-class sleeping cars wherever possible.

Love,
Gary

34. GARY SNYDER [CALCUTTA, INDIA]
    TO ALLEN GINSBERG [COLOMBO, CEYLON]

10.I.62 [January 10, 1962]

Dear Allen (and Peter?)

If you stop in Pondicherry first go to "Bureau Centrale"—pay no more than 1 Rs. for two people plus luggage in pedicab from railway station (tip extra). Be sure and ask to meet K. D. Sethna—brilliant Parsi—poet—editor of "Mother India," wrote *The Poetic Genius of Sri Aurobindo*. Aurobindo wrote a sequel to the *Iliad* in "Quantitative Hexameters," plus theory of prosody—real 19th c. but also very learned. Aurobindo did volumes of purple poetry mystical and deep, but may have something. Sethna is fantastic—we leave tomorrow. (I told him about you.) (The mother is not a goy.)

Gary

35. GARY SNYDER [CALCUTTA, INDIA]
    TO ALLEN GINSBERG [MOMBASA, KENYA]

Calcutta 21 Jan [January 21, 1962]

Dear Allen!

I wrote a huge letter for you to Colombo, explaining everything about India, in faith you would get there! But it's no use from Africa. Actually Bombay would probably be a better place to come into. Our plans from here are roughly as follows:

24 Jan Calcutta—Gaya—Bodh Gaya
27 Bodh Gaya—Nalanda
30 Nalanda—Patna
31 Patna—Kathmandu

6   Feb Kathmandu—Patna

7   Patna—Benares—Sarnath

11 Benares—Lucknow

12 Lucknow—Bareilly—Naini Tal—Almora

16 Almora—Rishikesh

20 Rishikesh—Jullundur

22 Jullundur—Pathankot

23 Pathankot—Manali (high in Kullu Valley,
    Himachal Pradesh, Himalayas)

I figured to spend about 10 days camping and walking in the Kullu—Lahoul—Spiti regions—Tibetan monasteries and the easiest Himalayan high region to reach. Later in March or April would be better, but don't see how to make it much later. From Delhi it is one night train to Pathankot. From Pathankot all day bus ride to Manali. If you are extremely interested in seeing this bit, might meet us / me (Joanne may stay at Manali while I go out over the passes on foot) on the trail somewhere. Get "Kullu and Kangra" booklet from tourist office Delhi or Bombay for useful info. This bit needs at least pack and sleep bag and own food supplies; there are "Rest Houses" to sleep in. ACTUALLY you should figure to meet us in Delhi—we'll be in Delhi thus: March 7—leave Pathankot—Delhi stay in Delhi at the Mahabodhi Society Headquarters. ???? I don't know yet. "Lady Hardinge Serai" across from railway station is very cheap, I hear. *PS I just realized Delhi Mahabodhi Society probably has no rest house. So may stay in Lady Hardinge Serai, or Birla Dharamsala (Rest House) about three or five days. Meet Kushwant Singh and others. Around the 12th we'll HAVE to leave Delhi, traveling south thus: Delhi—Mathura—Gwahor—Thansi—Khajuraho—Sanchi—Ajanta—Ellora—Bombay. Bombay to Karli and back and leave Bombay 31 March. Time already closing in. We won't have much time for talk in India, so I guess we'll wait for you in Japan. Enough for now. Fare well wayfarer.

Gareth.

36. ALLEN GINSBERG [MOMBASA, KENYA] TO GARY SNYDER [INDIA]

[January 27, 1962]

Dear Gary:

Received your January 21 Calcutta note today. My boat sails February 6 and arrives in Bombay (via Karachi) February 15, costs 50 bucks deck passage, fine. My mail and money such as it be, and your letter, will be forwarded there from Colombo OK.

I figure according to your letter, you be at Rishikesh 16–20 February at Manali February 23–5 March, and Delhi March 7–12. I'm writing you a short note at each place now, one or all will reach you.

So I figure hang around Bombay a few days and go on and meet you at Delhi (or maybe even Manali if there's time). Tho Bombay to Manali trip immediately on entering India sounds hard. I see Pathankot on my map, but no Manali there even. But don't have bag and cookstove. I do have air mattresses and sheets tho, for warm outdoor sleeps. Anyway definitely by Delhi, and if you receive this in time and think it would be worth rushing up to Manali, send word and maybe we do that, keep Joanne company. But best not make such exact plans, maybe I be stuck a few days in Bombay broke anyway or have to answer letters piling up from Colombo and Tel Aviv the last months. Anyway definitely Delhi by the time you get there. I met a forest academy yoga at Gavin Arthur's[55] once. Been reading *Kim*, *Passage to India*, books by K. Singh and Narayan, Mahabharata, Ramayana, Gita, Vedic Hymns, Gandhi Autobiography, Jataka, Patanjali and Upanishads—have funny library collected in Indian stores here, old Dent Everyman books, Lin Yutang Wisdoms, etc. We took bus around Kilimanjaro, mostly hid in mist, up to Nairobi, living with Africs in black hotels eating cheap food, saw Jomo Kenyatta[56] give speech at stadium, Peter and I the only whites in audience of 20,000 shades, like some dreamy thing. Everybody courteous, tho I got my wallet with one of your earlier letters pick pocketed in crowd on way out. What are you seeing at such lightning speed thru these cities? I don't know most of the associations with the place names you mention except Gaya and Benares and Lucknow. Also we got kicked out of Tom Mboya's[57] wedding nite dance at 2 A.M. for not having jackets.

---

55. Gavin Arthur was an older San Francisco friend and astrologer.
56. Jomo Kenyatta became the first prime minister and president of Kenya.
57. Tom Mboya was a prominent political figure in Kenya, later assassinated.

I gather Bowles misinformed me about cheap living in India—lots great cheap Indian food clean hotels here and Indians tell me its same in India, so no problem as I'd thought.

I'll send essential info in this to Manali and Delhi at same time, to you, in case this fails to reach you.

Love,

Allen

[PS] We reach Bombay February 15, they say. *SS Amra*, British India Steamship Co. Send us info on Manali, anyway, Joanne, in case we arrive Bombay early and have time to get there. We might get to Bombay by the 17th. Bowles wife sick, so he never got to Ceylon—he'll come later he says.

37. GARY SNYDER [BIHAR, INDIA] TO ALLEN GINSBERG [MOMBASA, KENYA]

31. January, Nalanda [January 31, 1962]

Dear Allen,

Now have stayed four days Nalanda—ancient site of Buddhist Mahayana center 10,000 monks—see the 12-foot-thick walls and brick cells (one room each) still—also "new" Nalanda University nearby. (This is all very rural) with *bhikkhus* and students from all over Asia (nine Tibetan lamas) here. We been in their guest room. Last week Bodh Gaya; next to Nepal. Had good visit with Buddhadeva Bose in Calcutta and funny cranky young Bengali poet named Jyotirmoy Datta, who claims access to opium and hashish, but he may be bullshitting (he don't look that hip). Indians are SQUARE, Dad, even the nice intelligent ones. And they are all full of patriotism and progress and various sorts of "spiritual" values. "Hip" is indeed a rare new thing in the world, the next jump ahead on the dialectic, and literally incomprehensible to many intellects. Our previous itinerary still about right, except now I think we'll be in Kullu-Mandri region around 28 February–1 March, and back at Delhi around the 10th or 11th; to leave for Bombay around the 15th. We must try and see Ved Mehta in Delhi, he sounds interesting. I expect to have mail from you waiting at Rishikesh—but on present plan we will go through Delhi before Rishikesh—so write latest plans to me c/o American Express, Delhi. No alcohol, no meat—but India is worth all the trouble. Wow.

Gary

38. ALLEN GINSBERG [MOMBASA, KENYA]
     TO GARY SNYDER [NEW DELHI, INDIA]

[February 2, 1962]

Dear Gary and Joanne:

As I wrote you to Forest Academy and also Manali, we'll arrive in Bombay on February 15, thence to meet you in Delhi by the time you get this around March. I guess you got other notes. But this just in case. We saw giraffes and ostriches and zebras from bus here and sent huge skin drum to New Jersey. Saw Ramayana in the movies, Indian pix are great, the music high. OK

Later

Allen

39. ALLEN GINSBERG [MOMBASA, KENYA]
     TO GARY SNYDER [NEW DELHI, INDIA]

[February 5, 1962]

Dear Gary and Joanne:

I wrote you a week ago to Rishikesh, Manali, and Delhi (the last two, postcards)—then received your note of January 31 from Nalanda. As I said (in postcard which you probably have also)—we sail from here tomorrow on British India boat *SS Amra* to Karachi and Bombay—arrive in Bombay 15 February. I had all my Ceylon mail forwarded there—including I hope money from City Lites—we'll arrive with about $2 in pockets.

I figure from your letter you should be in Delhi around the 13th or 15th or 17th before going to Rishikesh? If all goes well, we should be able to land on the 15th, change money and collect mail and entrain the next day for Delhi and perhaps meet you there if you're there. If you leave there before we arrive, leave instructions for us at American Express in New Delhi, and we'll take off almost immediately to find you in Rishikesh (or Kullu), wherever you are expecting to be, or, if you receive this in time, send us a note to Bombay.

I don't know train schedules so I don't know how practical it is for me to say we'll entrain "the next day" but I assume it's possible, also I assume my mail and money will be waiting in Bombay. There may be many a slip (as usual) so better not wait in Delhi for us if we're out of earshot. But I will attempt to get there by the 18th or 19th. It's a 2-day ride?

So just leave instructions for us in Delhi where to find you. Both eager to get to Spiti areas, tho obviously we're un-equipped for serious climbing—have to improvise—perhaps stay down with Joanne. Anyway the day approaches, we meet, happily near Tibet or even Rishikesh.

I knew Ved Mehta in Oxford and N.Y.—give him my regards and say we'll be along presently, too. Hurrah, at last. Anyway, we do sail mañana. Have you ever read Shanhara (Sankara)? I'm still trying to get straight all the different Vedic—Hindu—Buddhist *devas*[58] and *nagas*[59] and *yakshas*[60] and interrelations between. But all this book learning seems to go in one eye and out the other. For reports on Africa see Rishikesh letter.

I should be getting last half year royalty check from Ferlinghetti, and Peter gets two of his veteran checks. So we may have enough loot to have a good time, and relax.

How was Kathmandu and Benares? You may get this after we've arrived in Bombay. But we'll go ahead to Delhi until we hear from you, in any case.

Love

Allen

[PS] How's the astrologers and planet's conjunctions' scene? Sad to miss Delhi on such a weekend!

40. ALLEN GINSBERG [BOMBAY, INDIA] TO GARY SNYDER [DELHI, INDIA]

[February 16, 1962]

[telegram]
Arriving Delhi Janata Express 11/45 Sunday Morn all magical. Allen Peter

---

58. *Deva.* Deity.
59. *Naga.* A primeval Hindu clan.
60. *Yaksha.* A nature spirit.

41. ALLEN GINSBERG [DELHI, INDIA] TO GARY SNYDER [DELHI, INDIA]

[February 19, 1962]

Dear Gary:

We arrived in Delhi yesterday and will stay here until we contact you. So far we're sleeping at the Jain Rest House. I left message for you at American Express also. I figure you should hit Delhi either before or after Rishikesh—on way back from Almora. So you might be here any day now? Send me word if you get this before I see you elsewhere or maybe you're already on way to Manali without stopping in Delhi? OK, that's the latest scoop known. Delhi water good so far. You got mail at American Express. I guess we stay here until we hear from you or find out where you are or maybe here we all meet. A train accident cut up a man we saw on the tracks.

Love

Peter and Allen

EDITOR'S NOTE: *Finally after all the planning, Ginsberg and Orlovsky did find Snyder and Kyger in Delhi and for the next two months they traveled together, exploring India. Ginsberg, Snyder, and Kyger have all published their travel journals from that period. In late April, Gary and Joanne caught a ship back to Japan from Bombay and Allen and Peter settled down for the next year in India.*

42. GARY SNYDER [ONBOARD A SHIP TO JAPAN]
     TO ALLEN GINSBERG [CALCUTTA, INDIA]

At Sea. [May 6, 1962]

Dear Allen and Peter,

We are supposed to reach Kobe on the 8th. Herein we summarize the salient features of the voyage: 1. Getting through Customs was fantastic—he didn't open a thing or ask for a thing—not even my camera declaration or money exchange sheet. Just stamped our bags and said that's all. "Medical Examination" meant looking for three seconds at the vaccination cards. We had a splendid meal for dinner with bananas and mutton curry. Actually lots of pork and beef roast, steak twice, etc. etc.—cheese for dessert, or ice cream; always fruit. Quite good. 2. In Colombo met with the Canadian High Commissioner, Mr. James George. In fact he picked us up in a big embassy car and drove us around, including Kelaniya Temple (Buddhist) in Colombo—we didn't see it before—which has interesting paintings, some about 300 years old, on the walls—and dinner at his mansion, very elegant. He started out as a Gurdjieff follower. Nice wife and children. They live in considerable style. He knows *bhikkhus* and swamis about Ceylon. 3. Singapore, I still think, is a drag. 4. Saigon Museum is quite good: Cham, Khmer, Chinese, Japanese, and Tibetan artifacts. The Mekong Restaurant, straight on the road to town about 2½ blocks after you cross the bridge on the way to the center of town from the ship, is good food not expensive. See the gibbons at the zoo. 5. In Hong Kong we had magnificent Chinese dinner—with Chinese wine bottle (tastes like medicine) and braised duck, sweet-sour pork pineapple beef slices and fried noodle—100-year eggs—at the Chunghwa Bookstore they sell mounted scroll reproductions (woodblock on silk) of southern Sung landscapes, Yuan and Ming painters—all made in Peking ($5–$10). The first turn up the hill to the west, up a stairway-sidewalk, leads to two nice restaurants, both on the left. I got a pair of lightweight summer Dacron-wool slacks made to order for 45 Hong Kong dollars in 24 hours and some wash-and-wear Dacron santans for H.K. $19. But be sure and look at the paintings. Ask for their catalog of their stock—it gives dates and dynasties, etc., in English. Enough.

Gary.

43. GARY SNYDER [31 NISHINOYAMA CHO, OMIYA, KITA-KU, KYOTO, JAPAN] TO ALLEN GINSBERG [CALCUTTA, INDIA]

[May 10, 1962]

My, my, all those naked bits and pieces of bodies.[61] Don't look much different whether they's detached or stuck on. Nice pictures. Will send some of ours when I get some developed; ain't got around to it yet. Shame about your notebook but here is a rundown of addresses: [here Snyder has attached a long list of Indian addresses].

Guess what I found when I got home? A check from the Poets

---

61. Ginsberg sent them some photographs he had taken of feet and arms cut from dead bodies.

Foundation for $500. Been here since February. So we don't have to worry about being broke or anything, in fact are planning to tour Japan as soon as possible. Got all my teaching jobs at the YMCA lined up right away. Joanne is gloating over her possessions, as I am gloating over eight mounted reproductions of great Sung, Yuan, and Ming paintings we bought in Hong Kong as I told you about. Printed on silk.

I am writing follow-up or parallel immediacy poem for Allen's America as Kali [published as "Stotras to Kali Destroyer of Illusions"], which is to say, Russia as Shiva[62] (all too obvious) and China as Ganesh; then one could complete modern mythopoetical prophepolitics by writing England as tired old Vishnu France as Rama and Algeria as Hanuman... Hare Krishna Hare Krishna do you remember where Krishna manifests himself in the Gita? It's horrendous; Margaret Randall went ahead and printed some of your stuff in *Feathered Horn* [*El Corno Emplumado*, no. 2] without permission "because you hadn't written." Peter, I will send you your Thirthankara pictures soon as I can, am going to take that roll down to get especially developed soon right away.[63] I think Joanne got the amoebic dysentery, she's still suffering. Philip Whalen is co-editing with [Richard] Duerden, new issue of *Foot*. Misc. grunge. Janine [Pommy Vega] is real pretty. [Alexandra] David-Neel's *Secret Oral Teachings* [in *Tibetan Buddhist Sects*] is a GREAT book, with absolute answers on some questions. Get it again!

Love

G.

44. GARY SNYDER [KYOTO, JAPAN]
    TO ALLEN GINSBERG [CALCUTTA, INDIA]

[May 30, 1962]

Dear Allen and Peter

Here are your miraculous cave photos. I'm trying to get Don Allen to use the standing one for a cover to *Evergreen Review*. Remember it was

---

62. Shiva, Ganesh, Vishnu, and the rest are all Hindu deities.
63. Peter had posed nude for some pictures that were taken in a cut-out stone niche in a wall.

Aurangabad Cave #1. Don Allen is real nice and since last July (especially) he says, "Extremely interested in Buddhism." Seems he was doing zazen two hours a day at the Bush Street *zendo* in San Francisco all last year. And wants to start sitting here with the Daitoku-ji monastery. I am about to write reams of bullshit about India, I fear. Joanne has been listless since we got back, but no real ailment. She is eating well and resting. I have lots of jobs now. I feel weirdly changed and ruthless and serious about certain personal matters, and prepared to be more drastic with myself and my *sadhana* from here on; also (paradoxically?) more relaxed and sexual.

Alan Watts is in Japan and is very turned on by it—has been taking lots of LSD and has a Shakti[64] with him, having left his own true wife. He says the future society will have to be one where there is total sexual freedom with tantric practices—children raised in groups, and people use LSD, mushrooms, etc.

All my Kyoto buddies have turned into hemp farmers.

There do seem to be two things going:

1. The individual working out his path by lonely self-enquiry and meditation.

2. A kind of social-sexual communal breakthrough, aided by dance, drugs, music, (meditation), etc. Now if we can reconcile these two and use them we can remake society utterly. (Cosmo-political project #1)

Love,

Gary

45. GARY SNYDER [KYOTO, JAPAN]
    TO ALLEN GINSBERG [CALCUTTA, INDIA]

[June 27, 1962]

Dear Peter and Allen if he's back,

I hope you get a great big *wang* that lasts forever and you can transmit it to all your friends, too.

I got lots of other good photographs but haven't had the money to develop them into real prints yet—when you come to Japan you can have a whole set.

---

64. Shakti. The female counterpart of a male deity.

I wrote a letter to [Timothy] Leary and somebody else answered it saying they wouldn't send me no psilocybin because things are tougher for them.

So here we are living in Kyoto about halfway through our local rainy season and Joanne is not feeling well today—we have two cats—I planting morning glories on a bamboo frame along the wall of my motorcycle shed-garage; reading all about India in several different thick books so as to put a round total grasp on the trip, and maybe write down the record of it all later.

Donald Allen of Grove Press has a new refrigerator and a most elegant bodhisattva statue installed in his traditional Japanese house with garden he's renting; he has a Japanese boyfriend already and he was going to start doing zazen at the monastery but then decided he'd better put it off because he'd just fallen in love. Cid Corman is reading Robert Creeley's new book, *For Love*, which is a hardcover book put out by Scribner's, because we all got together last night in the back room of a bar downtown and talked for quite a spell. There are a score or so of vigorous young poets with mossy skulls and Kwakiutl inflections at the University of British Columbia now and they are putting out a mimeo thing called *tish* which is an anagram.

Ai thought that *bhikkhu* at the Mahabodhi was creepy too. Hinayana[65] is arrogant.

Ganesh you gave me sits on my ledge above my desk and Tara is ensconced in a coven surrounded by worshipping Hanuman, Brahmin, and idolatrous bear. Listen, please get another *thangka* for me if you see interesting one and I'll pay you in yen when you come. Joanne sends her love and we are greatly interested in knowing if the monsoons are as amusing as people say, and also: be sure and get enough nourishment and vitamins because you really can get run down you know, it took Joanne two months to recover her strength!

Mahabharata (which I read finally) is wondrous great gas full of morals introcuntvertible [*sic:* incontrovertible] and beautiful images of wounded and battle, like flowers, chariots like clouds . . .

Love,

Gary

---

65. Hinayana. One of the early schools of Buddhism.

46. GARY SNYDER [KYOTO, JAPAN]
    TO ALLEN GINSBERG [CALCUTTA, INDIA]

[July 12, 1962]

Dear Allen and Peter,

Well now you must really be in the monsoon rains. We are having our own sort here. I wonder how it must feel? Give Bose and Datta our regards, sorry we couldn't have seen more of them. Allen must be vastly improved by all the spiritual benefits absorbed by hat *darshan* and presence at ceremonies—seriously, me studying the literature you (so kindly) sent I think that Sikkim must indeed be the place to go for Tibetan study, right now. Wonder what will come out of it?

Don Allen was about to begin zazen at Daitoku-ji monastery (I arranged it for him) but he "fell in love" at the last minute and said he couldn't come to zazen after all . . . the point is, and this is my only objection to homosexuality as it works on some people, that it takes precedence over everything else (he didn't have to quit zazen, he could have had his boy who is living with him now and is quite nice—and the Zen study too—but he doesn't want to put anything else first). Well that's my bitch at the moment. Don really is sweet, and really picks up quick on things Japanese. The vibrations are somehow just right for him here. Your gossip and information on all those monks and lamas is invaluable.

Well do try and mail the catalog of the arts and crafts Tibetan place in Darjeeling. And also the precise address of the young fellow who made your Wheel of Life,[66] perhaps I'll try and order one directly from him. How is the mounting on yours? If it is not mounted too well, I could have him send it to me unmounted and get it mounted here.

OK what's next indeed? What are you off to next? Lots of time left before fall and the end of monsoons. South India? or Benares?

Photographs are looking pretty good as I develop them up. The ones of the Kumbh Mela parade[67] though are all duds. Partly the funny West German film was scratched and partly the bad grey rainy day, and partly that I simply underexposed them. Nonetheless some can be used, but I don't think for an article.

When you guys come here you can select out all the pictures you want

---

66. The Wheel of Life is a traditional illustration of Buddhist teachings.
67. Kumbh Mela. Hindu pilgrimage parade of holymen held every 12 years.

from our set and have them made up. Something about India turned me on sexually—that's curious. Am working a lot lately writing, polishing, feeling good about it and also swinging with a great new batch of koans, from the *mumonkan*.[68]

Skin-diving (naked wives) (lots) next month, Japan sea vacation.
Love
Gary

47. GARY SNYDER [KYOTO, JAPAN]
     TO ALLEN GINSBERG [CALCUTTA, INDIA]

[October 15, 1962]
Dear Allen and Peter,
How are you now? Be sure and take vitamins and keep well! The English lama, Lobzang Jivaka, got sick and suddenly died! You must take care— we love you. So don't forget to come to Japan. David Ignatow wants you to send him some poems for a forthcoming William Carlos Williams issue of *Beloit Poetry Journal*. It don't sound like much, but Denise L. [Levertov], Robert Creeley, etc., will be in it, also one poem by me. Don Allen went back to San Francisco. We are having a great time these days. Cold out now too, and clear!! Wow!
Om Shanti
G.

48. GARY SNYDER [KYOTO, JAPAN]
     TO ALLEN GINSBERG [CALCUTTA, INDIA]

[November 15, 1962]
Dear Allen and Peter,
I hope you have shaved off your beards and cut your hair by now because we're all waiting to hear that you've volunteered for the Himalayan Light Infantry and will be shortly doing your bit for the salvation of the Vajra-yana[69] and the holy places of high-altitude Buddhism.

Everything at such a breathless pace. In response to your questions

---

68. *Mumonkan.* A collection of 48 Zen koans.
69. Vajrayana. Tantric school of Buddhism as practiced in Tibet and Japan.

and the letter of Lord Russell![70] I would hesitate to see it as an absolute statistical certainty that there will be a nuclear holocaust. That is not allowing enough to the natural intelligence of the men who are running the show in Russia and America. After all, they are very capable men and they are very aware of the risks. The trouble with them is what risk they're willing to run to preserve what they think they have.

To put it simply, if you believe in America as it is now or as it might become were there no Communist menace; if you value Christianity, the white race, the still relatively unpolluted mainstream of Western civilization, then it is not easy to be a pacifist. Because no matter what anyone says, I think that time, history, disarmament, and peace lead inevitably toward an internationalized mixed-race mixed-culture socialism. Which is fine with me. But if one was against this trend, no matter how scary war seemed, he would be committed in some respects to the use of force to help hold back time. In the recent Cuban crisis from the standpoint of preserving America, etc., Kennedy probably did the "best thing." Let go of it all and help South America go Communist (or Socialist)—send butter to Castro . . . sure, but the exchanges that will come out of this will be the end of any America we recognize now. Russia probably realizes that there is a similar threat in long term peace for them too, but they're readier for it. China is counting on it.

What would a war do for the reactionaries? They might just be able to knock out Russia and China, salvage themselves and grab reins of power, hold parts of the world down to colonial type status, and build up a real ruling class of white Christians. These guys are building fantastic bomb shelters for themselves while crying victory against communism, and they figure to come out ahead if not dead.

What does that mean to all us? It means that to the American reactionaries we poor folks without bomb shelters are expendable in their power-gamble. It also means that for those of us who are pacifists it is important that we are aware of the political implications of the non-violent position, and accept the fact that it implies an ultimate one-world socialism of some kind or other, let us hope it be benevolent.

I ain't against the total use of force *per se*, like Paul Goodman, I think

---

70. Ginsberg had received a letter from Bertrand Russell stating that nuclear war was a statistical near-certainty. This had unnerved Ginsberg and he wrote to several friends asking their opinion.

wars are bad but fistfights OK. I suppose from the Buddhist standpoint violence is just a form of energy, which could be channeled in the right direction (I'm starting judo lessons next week, to improve my grace and light-footedness).

So what should we do right now. I don't know about you but I ain't personally ready to come out of the corner fighting yet, take the State on, etc. World crisis will have to just wait a while for me to make my witness. If it's still here when I have seen through what seems my work now, I'll be "witnessing" as the Quakers say, without even trying, and maybe getting into trouble for it.

In the meantime take whatever *samadhi* that comes along.

Was glad to hear from you, whatever. Beginning to worry about you two. A fellow from San Francisco that stayed here a month or so, named Richard Dickert, is traveling on to India, and I gave him your names and Calcutta address. I like him very much, so will you.

Anyway you work out the trip, it is OK to Japan. Hope you really will be able to come for a longer spell . . . when does that make it? A year from now? I'm busy translating a recent Japanese poet who I find affinities with and reading still about India, which is in so many ways the breathing End. For meditation practice though, they've really got it here.

Your sadhu and ganja[71] scenes sound very nice, and curiously wholesome. I hope you lick Death yet, Allen. Rassle him down. Don't get lice or crud. Keep in touch. Joanne and I are trying to have a child now.

Love,
Gary

49. GARY SNYDER [KYOTO, JAPAN]
     TO ALLEN GINSBERG [CALCUTTA, INDIA]

[November 22, 1962]

Dear Allen and Peter,
Continuation, explication, and edition of previous letter. (1) a young man named David Winter will probably try and find you, if you're in Calcutta. He is connected with Timothy Leary and, in passing through Kyoto, laid some mescaline on me. I gave him your address. He wants

---

71. Ganja. Marijuana.

to try *ganja*, bhang,[72] opium, morphine, etc., but hasn't ever used anything except psilocybin and mescaline so far. If you see him tell him
that the letter from Leary about him came to me the day after he left
Kyoto.

Leftover answers. (a) There don't seem to be any Japanese Vedanta
centers. The Japanese don't go for that transcendental stuff. It's all transistor radios and a small car.

(b) The precise working of that koan is: Hsiang-yen said, "It's like a
man who's climbed a tree, and clenching a branch in his mouth is unable
to grab a limb or stand against the trunk. If a person at the bottom of the
tree asks him 'What is the meaning of the coming from the West' and he
doesn't answer, he is evading the question. If he answers he will fall and
lose his life. At such a time how should one answer?"

More on politics: "Give me liberty or give me death."—"You gits both,
boy."

(2) Last Saturday Joanne and I took 500 mg. each of mescaline; Joanne
got nausea which lasted all evening and all night until next day, very little
insight or vision, but a funny moment of involvement with one of the
cats and sense of wobbly identity; same with me for a minute, forgetting
she was she, etc. As for myself sat most of the night pondering; felt safe
against demons (which I realized are the demons and devils that live in
the world as insanity) with my beads in my hand and an arsenal of anti-
demonic weapons near at hand, like a sistrum, a conch horn, a *vajra*
bell, magic amulets, incense, a *zendo* whacker stick, and little sutra[73]
books. But as usual I felt they were somewhere there, existing, able to
threaten me on mescaline in a way they can't threaten me in ordinary
consciousness.

Then I had an interesting progression of thoughts about dragons: a
vision of writing, powerful talon-fisted being, and saw what the "Dragon
Emperor" (title of old Chinese emperors) meant, and that the dragon
means pure power, and the Chinese imperial system had a fantastic sense
of some weird transcendent utterly icy power. And the dragon is the same
as Shakti, and her "Serpent Power," of course. Then I recollected the
painting on the ceiling of Zen lecture halls, a great twist dragon gripping
the pearl of wisdom in one claw—and realized that he wasn't gripping

---

72. Bhang. A derivative of cannabis smoked or mixed in a beverage.
73. Sutra. A pithy summary statement of a longer religious text.

that pearl, he was held by it—Buddhism controlling the dragon—and saw motto of Zen temple as "WE TAME DRAGONS."

Then I thought about the symbols and thought of Buddhism, and saw it all as an enormous map of consciousness that developed through the centuries—the Buddha being a man who opened it up, through the center, the main enlightenment experience—and following generations of monks and philosophers pushing into that landscape farther and farther, naming things as they went, and making pictures and statues of what they saw. The bodhisattvas, the fierce guardian kings, etc., all stations and functions in consciousness—the bodhisattvas and *dhyana*-Buddhas, etc., all actually states and positions in the big wisdom mind which is called Buddha but can be sub-classified down. But exploration outside the wisdom mind too—other areas of consciousness which are governed by ego aspects, blind conditioning, instinct, etc. All of these have been covered.

So I had to think about the demonic, and evil, from that standpoint, and wonder what it was—and decided that within Buddhism consciousness from at least one standpoint you can see enlightenment as the perfection of consciousness, and its opposite as also existing—an insanity of ego and power. So evil is insanity, insanity of certain schizophrenic-paranoid types. And indeed schizophrenic people do seem to live in hell. The worst kind of ego-insanity mimics enlightenment in some respects—particularly the outward aspect of ease and self-confidence in the person.

So I figured out that the Mara demons and tempters and tormenters of the Buddha on his last night before finally making it were all insanity tendencies and ego pulls which are terribly more powerful when your mind is opened by trance or by drugs.

So I went on to consider, as an aside, that there may well be certain religious meditation traditions that get sucked into the wrong direction entirely, but having accepted it find it satisfying, and are thus insane but functioning. Like maybe some of the weird 18th century sadhu schools of shit-eaters and cannibals may have been.

Hinduism also is a map of consciousness, although perhaps not so consistently organized.

Anyhow the Buddha licked the demonic by calling Heaven and Earth to witness, whatever that means.

Anyway, as I sat there full of dope I also thought that at some point the demonic insane animal etc. realms are also illusory, and saw that that is what they mean indeed when they say a Buddha is "Master of the Three Realms"—he is a man who really can see all these things from all sides, the whole fabric. And probably drive insanity clean out of another person by just looking at him. Gautama did several times.

And I felt much solider than I ever have before on peyote, but not yet to the point where I can dismiss Mara and his followers as wraiths and spooks.

Let the Tibetan system help teach that too.

So, finally. I also decided that at least for me, no peyote experience has ever been enlightening. It has been illuminating, visionary, and of enormous benefit in understanding my own mind and the structure of consciousness, but I must say the basic central insight, supporting wisdom and understanding, as far as I have a little of it, came to me through zazen and general Zen practice, not through the mescaline. In the mescaline, that background both opens my mind farther and makes me understand better what is happening.

So I figure mescaline is a real consciousness expander, and shows one the CONTENT of consciousness, but it doesn't (as I say, for me anyhow) show the GROUND of consciousness, the content-less stuff of mind, self, which I know you CAN get a good sight of through Zen meditation. (I haven't found mescaline able to throw the least glimmer of light on koan.)

I guess, therefore, I must be suspicious of any claims to getting satori on these chemicals. (Another name for satori[74] is *kensho* which means "seeing your true nature." This ain't a vision.)

I'll be trying them again, also the psilocybin you gave me, and getting a Zen priest to try them. Maybe my view will change.

Toward the end of the night I set up my mandala[75]—which I haven't looked at much yet—and saw excellent sense in it; the roles which different figures were playing. Not the total middle meaning of the main figure though.

That's my report on that. Would like to have more mandalas to try and figure out cold.

Am on translating job now, of died 1933 poet named Miyazawa Kenji

---

74. Satori and *kensho*. Terms for enlightenment.
75. Mandala. A geometric pattern used to represent the cosmos.

(or did I tell you this?).

Cold wind from Siberia today. Starting judo lessons next week to keep me supple and used to being thrown about.

Om Shanti Shanti

Gary

---

50. GARY SNYDER [KYOTO, JAPAN] TO ALLEN GINSBERG [BENARES, INDIA]

[April 2, 1963]

Dear Allen and Peter,

Comme ça va? Allen when will you pass through Japan this summer and how long will you be able to stay before proceeding to Vancouver B.C.? Please you speak.

Cherries about to bloom. Windy and clear.

Gary

---

51. GARY SNYDER [KYOTO, JAPAN]
    TO ALLEN GINSBERG [BENARES, INDIA]

[April 21, 1963]

Dear Allen,

Your letter's length and meat makes up for gaps of time—especially glad to hear some firsthand view on war shit and poor old satyagraha[76] . . . I read article on proposed march to Peking, writ by Shankarrao Deo himself, which was published in English-language paper here . . . made me want to go join it myself for a few minutes. News in short is: a long cold winter and a lovely spring: Joanne and I traveled through the southern island of Kyushu for eight days, seeing it for the first time: I went on a week-long work-trip (businesslike rice begging to lay in stocks for the spring rainy season retreat) with the Daitoku-ji monks. It was moving to beg in mountain villages, in deep hat and monks garb, and get a quart or so of rice sometimes from the hands of old people in poor mud and thatch houses—to put in my begging bag—and realize the old-time rural faith that made them think it worthwhile to give to strange wandering

---

76. Satyagraha. Practice of nonviolent resistance.

monks—identifiable only as Zen—especially since there is no thing about merit and holymen here.

Now as to business: you must come here soon as you can, and of course you must plan to stay at our place. There's plenty of room, and it is within downtown by 20-minute bus ride, so you'll find it convenient. A month stopover en-route to a U.S.-type destination will prove no visa problem whatsoever. Why not leave serious sightseeing in Saigon, etc. til later boat trip at leisure and come straight on to Japan this time? June is good month here—not the pleasantest of all, since it is the Japanese equivalent of monsoon, which means light warm drizzles a lot of the time—but temples and gardens (especially) are best seen in that kind of soft green light. At any rate it isn't cold (as if that would worry you). And I think you will enjoy the change in diet and pace. You'll get a room all to yourself so you can arrange your thoughts or whatever at your own ease.

Blessings on Peter and the sarod.[77]

And hail to your direct and personal move in the rescue of the leper.[78] That is the simplest—and most difficult—way to get at suffering I guess, help out people who are suffering yourself. Ugh.

Joanne sends her love and anticipations.

Shanti,

Gary

52. ALLEN GINSBERG [CALCUTTA, INDIA]
    TO GARY SNYDER [KYOTO, JAPAN]

[May 25, 1963]

Dear Gary:

After various delays my ticket arrived and I leave here tomorrow. Despite your good advice I'm going to try to get to Angkor Wat, since I can fly there free. It may take me two weeks or more tho. Anyway, I hope to arrive in Japan by June 15 more/less. I'll write you when I am more sure. Send me a postcard with your address written in Jap characters yes? I

---

77. Peter Orlovsky had started to take lessons and learn to play the sarod, an Indian stringed instrument.
78. Ginsberg and Orlovsky had saved a beggar from starvation.

will be due in Vancouver around July 20 so that gives me a month in Japan.[79]

Peter staying in Benares singing with sarod. The beggar we helped got well, and his brother came (two days before I left town) and took him from hospital home in Punjab. His mama been crying for him all the while.

I'll send you any fresh details from Saigon. I saw Dick Dickert here, he's heading back home after a month working in a leper colony.

[Ginsberg has drawn a picture here, which he identifies as follows.] Design on Buddha footprint stone under Bo Tree, Bodh Gaya.[80]

Allen

53. ALLEN GINSBERG [ANGKOR WAT, CAMBODIA]
    TO GARY SNYDER [KYOTO, JAPAN]

June 7, 1963

Dear Gary:

Horrendous days talking to correspondents of U.S. network at Saigon—weird politics, I almost went helicopter to Mekong Delta and said ugh! But I saw Buddhist priests who were on hunger strike against government and U.S. giving half billion $ yearly police state. Now in Angkor Wat for a week and then I fly direct (say, June 12) to Tokyo and arrive any day in Kyoto. Never got your address in Japanese. I'll write.

Allen

EDITOR'S NOTE: *After stopping in Thailand, Vietnam, and Cambodia, Ginsberg arrived in Japan on June 11 and went straight to Snyder's house in Kyoto. There he spent a month relaxing and enjoying the Japanese life-style that Gary and Joanne shared with him. On July 18, Allen took the Kyoto to Tokyo train and prepared for his long flight back to Vancouver.*

---

79. Robert Creeley had invited Ginsberg to participate in a poetry conference in Vancouver, Canada, for which Allen was to receive an around-the-world plane ticket.
80. This drawing of three fish sharing a common head was to become Ginsberg's personal insignia.

54. ALLEN GINSBERG [TOKYO, JAPAN] TO GARY SNYDER [KYOTO, JAPAN]

July 21, 1963

Dear Folks,

Spent pleasant days, one nite up late late in Fugetsu—do's and lots of young creepy-pretty people. Saw museums and went to dreary party of fat middle-aged "American Colony" management—journalist—army types. Saw Ruth Witt-Diamant[81] also for an afternoon and evening. Also went to Turkish bath and got partial hand-job by pretty girl who washed me up and down—stumbled into that by accident last nite. KATO Mamoru[82] was a nice companion here and there.

Love, as ever

Allen

55. GARY SNYDER [KYOTO, JAPAN]
TO ALLEN GINSBERG [VANCOUVER, CANADA]

[August 1963]

Herez some letters that came . . . ay owpnd m bikuz ay figrd that thehr mayt biy sumthin uv intrest to miy in it tuw . . . az it tehrnd awt Peter did hav sumthing tuw sey tuw miy abawt thu redurdz. Haw duw you like this semi-phoneticized writing? Based partly on new U.S. linguists system. But my typewriter lacks symbols. Doing meditating and garden work this week. Garden looks real good now, no weeds. I should have fixed it when you were here. We (I and seven others) sent a letter to President Kennedy about South Vietnam. On basis as "Buddhists and friends of Buddhism." Also sent copy to XA-Loi and another to the fellow at Nalanda, Thich Thien Chau.

It was interesting and pleasant, etc., that you stayed with us and I think you created some good vibrations around here which are working out good karma still. What more can you ask?

Later

---

81. Ruth Witt-Diamant was the director of the Poetry Center of San Francisco State College.
82. KATO Mamoru was a friend of SAKAKI Nanao's and Gary Snyder's in Tokyo.

56. GARY SNYDER [KYOTO, JAPAN]
    TO ALLEN GINSBERG [SAN FRANCISCO]

[August 15, 1963]

How're ya doing?

Peter sent us a fine vocal Indian record, but he sent it in a huge wooden box airmail, the nut, postage was 40 Rs. We camped on the beach six days. Dickert says you were happy as a pig in shit in Vancouver.

Regards all

Gareth

57. ALLEN GINSBERG [SARATOGA, CA] TO GARY SNYDER [KYOTO, JAPAN]

[August 29, 1963]

Dear Gary and Joanne:

You must have given me some kind of permanent blessing because I seem to have come down into my body (and belly) ever since Japan and been wandering around in a happy rapture ever since.

The sensation of eternity of my Blake visions[83] turns out to be actualized through feelings of this body present—but feelings—mainly result of naturalization of belly breathing. I don't sit and meditate much tho. Before, I used to exclude women from my universe—discrimination—of feeling—and that blocked feeling caused mental splits. I wrote big hymns on train from Kyoto to Tokyo.[84] Stay in Asia did me a lot of good including Hare Krishna mantra[85]—but effects didn't really take place till I left Japan. Scene here—awful lot of suffering people—[Michael] McClure's lovely. Joanne, I made up with [Robert] Duncan (and [Jack] Spicer)—I'll write when there's more time.

Love

Allen

---

83. In the summer of 1948, Ginsberg had experienced a vision of William Blake that was seminal in his development as a man and a poet. In the years that followed he spent a good deal of time and energy trying to re-create that heightened spiritual awareness.

84. Ginsberg wrote an important poem called "The Change" on that trip.

85. Mantra. A sacred word or phrase that possesses special powers when used in prayer.

58. GARY SNYDER [KYOTO, JAPAN]
     TO ALLEN GINSBERG [SAN FRANCISCO]

[September 1, 1963]

Dear Allen,

Do you want your silk India shirt mailed? Where? I got a package forwarded from India—from Ferlinghetti—contains three *Howl* three *Kaddish*. I'll send these back to you, or, if you like and will give suitable instructions, mail them to kids here in Japan who you said you'd give books to. Like Kato and Nagasawa (who stopped by going back from Kynshu).

I have two new insights; one is emotional and the other scientific:

1. Niceness is a form of hostility.

2. A stream meanders because it swings. (I.e. not because there are "obstacles" which cause it to turn. This is true!)

OK

Gary

59. GARY SNYDER [KYOTO, JAPAN]
     TO ALLEN GINSBERG [416 E. 34TH, PATERSON, NJ]

[January 25, 1964]

Dear Allen,

You remember old SAKAKI Nanao? Well, Kato [Mamoru] was down and says him and Sakaki want to go to the U.S.—but Sakaki still don't have no sponsor and guarantor—you got any ideas how or who? They want to work and bum around. They are apparently very happy and lively, but tired of Japan. Some tanker company has promised all the free rides they want to Seattle, back and forth. Howr you? God is glugg.

Gary

60. ALLEN GINSBERG [NEW YORK]
    TO GARY SNYDER [KYOTO, JAPAN]

March 15, 1964

Dear Gary:

Forgive my long delay getting any word to you, there was so much to say I kept putting it off till I had leisure to write huge letter, and I got more and more involved in what was in front of my face when I got back. First, see, that whole stay in Japan was terrific, had a great effect on me, brought together and catalyzed and precipitated all I had been changing thru in India and the last night there with the three of us turned me inside out forever, decision to be or not to be, with all the hidden longings for girls, Joanne and you made such soft conditions of freedom / *abhaya* mudra[86] / fearlessness, both my feelings to you and her, I felt when I left, on train, sort of liberated, or at least a permanent understanding, how right all hearts were. On train to Tokyo finally in some kind of emotionally weeping exalted open state, wrote poetry again for first time in years. Have you seen that and recognized what it came from? Was in last *Fuck You* and printed in *Kulchur*, a long poem (written and published untouched on the train ride), "The Change." "In my train seat I renounce my power, so that I do live I will die." Came to Vancouver weeping and touching everybody, the softness lasted for several months—also in conjunction strangely with a lot of Hare Krishna singing to raise up my spirits when emotionally, or feelingly, dead. Too much to tell every change I went thru, anyway, a lot of old metaphysical problems disappeared resolved into dew, basic hell anxieties all gone, some kind of change of life precipitated that last night with you—"good karma in every direction." Yup, most of it's all there in that poem.

Also re poetry a new conscious understanding which is that if the breath in line follows the mantric-*pranayamic*-belly-breathing cycle the reader will be returned into his abdomen-belly, the sense of Self and Identity will be located back in the old bed of skin and its feeling, and cut out mental-worlds metaphysical confusion. The Kyoto-Tokyo train poem is sketch of that, I mean the breathing required by the poem to recite. The second line is in fact a big long long sigh "OH."

Here in N.Y., with Peter, still no resolve the sex confusions and

---

86. *Abhaya* mudra, the hand gesture of the Buddha immediately after Enlightenment.

timidities but at least I know where I am. Got cheap 35-dollar-a-month apartment four rooms—come visit stay in N.Y. free if you wanna visit— painting it up neat and clean this week.

I finished 100 pages *Kaddish* script[87]—*Kaddish* parts great but the added material about self is weak. More work. Also wrote 10-min. film script Buddha with Zapray third eye visiting U.S.A. setting things straight like superman. Ends burning happily in front of White House with China recognized in U.N.

I don't know what to recommend re Nanao Sakaki. I think more and reply in more leisure. I saw Paul Engle[88] from Iowa here in N.Y.—he had imported one Sunil Ganguli[89] from Calcutta who was one of the poets Peter and I hung around with, and is bringing Jyoti Datta here next year. Engle, when he heard I'd visited you, wanted to know all about you, he digs you, and asked if there be any chance your visiting them expense paid for a week or more when you're back in U.S.A. So you carry weight with him. He might be able to help Sakaki, you might write and ask. But it's a square scene and requires college degrees. However since main problem for Engle is transport money, he might work out some informal guarantor deal if Sakaki can get here on his own. The other avenue is Bonnie Crown, Asia Foundation, might inquire of her (I won't have time to ask for a month or more—just too loaded work). She knows you? Or your work, and could give advice and tips, maybe some guarantee?? I not had time for poetry since return, shot all my emotional load on people in Vancouver instead of paper and poems, alas, and then in Frisco running around two months and then here in N.Y. picking up old threads and family and apartments and then all different hells broke loose. First license department started busting all the non-commercial coffee shops, we formed committee been running around politicians' offices and ACLU. However the really great scene here's been in MOVIES, a gang of homemade young cats from Lower East Side making films orgies street scenes in lofts, I never saw such communal excitement since "poetry renaissance" days in San Francisco, something really lovely flowering, a Film Makers Cooperative—turning out mad weird movies and hiring

---

87. Ginsberg began work on a film script for Robert Frank based on his greatest poem, *Kaddish*.
88. Paul Engle was the head of the Creative Writing Program at the University of Iowa.
89. Sunil Ganguli became an important Bengali writer.

small theaters to show them. Last week they began getting busted too and police all over the joint and now maybe tonite one of LeRoi Jones' plays to be busted and raided. I'm in the thick of a fray; hot dog—big committee meetings—seems like some kind of emotional reaction in city government. Anyway a war's on—so I'm hung up in politics.

Kerouac in Long Island totally incommunicado saw him once. He's writing a huge epic probably his master work 1947–57 years with charts on wall and mother refusing visitors at door and nobody got his phone number cranky old fart but nonetheless seeing as I'm immersed in everything but poesy here I can see why. Still thank god I did write one great poem all that time away, just in time, on the train back to Tokyo after waving good-bye you. Have a ball in San Francisco, give my love to Joanne and my gloop too—hope things work out, what do you think will happen? (With you and her I mean?) Whatever happens I owe you both my soul, or flesh as it turned out. Key being the feelings are in flesh.

Allen

[PS] I'm recording Hare Krishna for Atlantic Records (they put out Ray Charles).

61. GARY SNYDER [AT SEA] TO ALLEN GINSBERG [NEW YORK]

[March 29, 1964]

SS Pioneer Mart (American Pioneer Lines) arriving N.Y. @ 18 April. I'm wiped. Stay with [Phil] Yampolsky a couple days, then go San Francisco. Am scheduled for readings N.Y. October will spend a month or so then. Don't want to get hung up seeing people, but do want to see you. Must talk about Nanao Sakaki: I spent two weeks with him Tokyo.

So.

Gary

62. GARY SNYDER [C/O CITY LIGHTS, SAN FRANCISCO]
    TO ALLEN GINSBERG [704 E. 5TH ST., #5A, NEW YORK]

[May 10, 1964]

Dear Allen,

Things were indeed not well here when I came—but they may arrange in a new and beautiful way yet. At the moment Joanne and I are in separate

North Beach apartments—only a block apart. She is being lady poet
moll Jack Spicer's crowd, but with a curious new self-knowledge. Love
conquers all. Will have the Sakaki poems ready next week I hope. San
Francisco is heavenly.

Love,
Gary

EDITOR'S NOTE: *Snyder and Kyger did not get back together but divorced
in October 1965.*

63. GARY SNYDER [SAN FRANCISCO] TO ALLEN GINSBERG [NEW YORK]

[May 26, 1964]

Dear Allen,
Nagazawa and Sakaki stuff looks pretty good to me. San Francisco is so
nice to live in. Joanne is someplace else. I guess it's better.

Am going to be teaching poetry at Berkeley this fall semester. Will
go New York in the spring. I'm surrounded by celestials who chatter in
Cantonese.

How are you and Peter? Did you ever make it with Sandra Hochman?[90] Did you find a girl to marry? And all.

Love
Gary

64. ALLEN GINSBERG [NEW YORK] TO GARY SNYDER [SAN FRANCISCO]

[June 3, 1964]

Dear Gary:
Received the translations and essay. I'll bring them up to Asia Society and
see what she recommends. Has Paul Engle contacted you? He could be
one to help, as far as arranging sponsorship. I'll make a copy of the (your)
enclosed and send to him.

No, but Sandra H. called us up for a party tomorrow night so mebbe

---

90. Although gay, Allen Ginsberg had girlfriends from time to time and considered having
children. Sandra Hochman was a longtime friend of Ginsberg's as well as a writer, poet, and
filmmaker.

I got something to report by the weekend. No girls turned up yet, but I quit smoking 45 hours ago and seem to have that habit licked so I suppose there's hope to jump for joy in the synagogue / *zendo* / cathedral / mosque some way or other. Gee I feel gloomy. I guess it's the cigarette withdrawal. Got drunk the other nite and high and began dancing so long and hard to Indian music I finally out-danced my capacity and wound up with three hours vomiting—heartbeat-burst breathlessness regretting I was alive at all it was so painful a body to be in. Recovered by now but quit smoking as result. Well I'll write soon. Happy freeways zoom and regards to [Lew] Welch, send Jack a freeway note.

Allen

65. GARY SNYDER [POSTMARKED EL PASO, TX] TO ALLEN GINSBERG [NEW YORK]

[June 24, 1964]

Dear Allen and Peter,

Don Allen and me staying at Creeley's a few days. We been visiting all the pueblos and sites we can. I see a new world coming, way off over the desert—sand painting is mandala. We got to make them quit logging by poetry. Dusty boots and sweaty clothes are sweet in this climate.

Gary

PS Will *Evergreen* do Sakaki??

66. ALLEN GINSBERG [NEW YORK] TO GARY SNYDER [SAN FRANCISCO]

[October 10, 1964]

Dear Gary:

Hastily, I got an invitation for expense-paid trip to Cuba to judge literary contest—January 15–February 15. LeRoi [Jones] supposed to go, probably Peter, and Jack Gelber.[91] Also [Norman] Mailer and [James] Baldwin invited tho probably they won't go. Also Jack Smith of *Flaming Creatures* movie is going. It'll all be legal, we get letters from *Evergreen*. *Nation* or *Esquire* sending us journalistically so no need for hassles with passports State Department—that be all correct and proper you be inter-

---

91. Jack Gelber. Writer and author of the play *The Connection*.

ested in going there too? (Expecting to make it a pacifist anarchist kindly good neighbor policy scene and not angry Marxist.) Let me know and I'll enquire. Marc Schleifer[92] arranging it all, be back in a week from Canada to consult.

All well here—I've had a couple pretty little girls making love to me-not wrote too much poesy—a few articles and some poems—I'll write more later. Meanwhile tonite rushing out to New Jersey to bar mitzvah a cousin tonite. Ed Sanders may come to Cuba too. Want to make a big happy phalanx (expenses paid roundtrip).

What's news? Later, soon.

Love as ever

Allen

[PS] Sanders' God issue[93] almost ready.

67. GARY SNYDER [479 GREEN #4, SAN FRANCISCO]
    TO ALLEN GINSBERG [NEW YORK]

[October 17, 1964]

Dear Allen,

Marc Schleifer called me too, about this. It is most attractive but the trouble is I don't see how I can get away from the university where I am supposed to be a full-time teacher for so long. Can I leave it open just a dab longer while I study schedules and make inquiries? Is it to actually be a full month? And of course I do want to keep my passport because I am going back to Japan.

I'll be reading in N.Y. on March 25 it appears; and then be on the poetry circuit April 5–20 or something like that. The university has been after me to teach the spring semester as well, and allowing as how I could have the time off to do the readings, come back here, and keep the job. It means useful money for me if I do, so I'm considering it.

Maybe you should come out and visit me this spring, if I do. I hear good things about your activities all the time. Things are exciting here; there is friction in some quarters (I am pissed with Stan Persky[94] and his

---

92. Marc Schleifer was the editor of *Kulchur* magazine.

93. A special issue of Sanders' *Fuck You: A Magazine of the Arts.*

94. Stan Persky was a poet and associated with Jack Spicer, Robert Duncan, and Robin Blaser in San Francisco, before he moved permanently to Canada in 1966.

bitchery so don't see people in that quarter much, but who needs those faggots) but most of the scene is a big flower. I wear Spanish boots, a gold ear-ring, dance the twist with young young girls all the time, and roar about on my big red motorcycle. To say nothing of secretly planning student riots. [. . .]

I heard you shaved your head and beard. I let my hair grow long all summer, but trimmed it back lately for the school shot.

Teaching is a groove, I have total freedom, and my poetry class is full of interesting hip young minds. And I have met a very keen man who has only been writing poetry about two years, my age, he served five years in San Quentin for armed robbery after the Korean war and read their whole library; a sharp sensibility (and a 20-year-old folksinger wife); his poems are strange and good. Gene Fowler.

Dave Haselton of *Synapse* magazine showed me your "May Day" poem, which is magical. I am going to have something in the same issue with it. He audits my poetry workshop.

All is not a loss.

How's Peter?

Love,

Gary

68. GARY SNYDER [SAN FRANCISCO] TO ALLEN GINSBERG [NEW YORK]

                                                   [October 22, 1964]

Allen,

Can't do Cuba I decided—lots of reasons—mostly can't spare the time. Motorcycling like a bird over swoopy freeways—and making up strange poems.

America is being born, like—Will be teaching at Berkeley until June, now—which means East Coast is to be a 3-week visit only. March 25— April 15. Love. To all.

Om Shantih,

Gary

69.   ALLEN GINSBERG [NEW YORK] TO GARY SNYDER [SAN FRANCISCO]

October 26, 1964

Dear Gary:

So much happening here I haven't been at my desk for a week. There was
a really interesting utopian group here developing the last months, Kerista, headed by a bearded Whitmanic fellow, they had a series of pads and
storefronts and everybody was naked and making it, little girls and 15-
year-old boys and happy teaheads and paranoid ex-amphetamine types,
but all bubbling happily New Eden and thinking of going to island (a
mistake I thought) all making it among themselves. Lots of pot mostly
but not much other unhealthy needle drugs. Then bam last week they
all (18 at once) got busted on dope and immorality charges. The overflow
nice rosy young girls were floating into my bed and that did me a lot
of good by gum so I know the Kerista group had something. Just that
they formalized it as an enlarged family and named it (another mistake
maybe)—but seemed to sound a future bell thru Lower East Side consciousness. Of course after the bust lots of confusion fear paranoia gossip.
But it seemed to me to bring right out into the open, in practice, what
everybody intuits—free love community larger family cells (they had kids
there too). I suddenly realize sex is repressed in kids from infancy on.
One baby girl two years laughing grabbed my naked cock, I got a hard
on, she held on tight awhile and then giggled and toddled off. I never
woulda got that near or dared naked bodies that much in my family 38
years ago, no harm. I been helping them find lawyers.

Fine you work here. I going to Cuba maybe a month and then be
right back no big scene just amicable visit. Maybe try to come west a
short trip this spring—like to anyway—We see. You got anything lined
up at Harvard yet? I go November 9–15 be guest at Lowell House give a
lecture and feel up everybody. Not doing much sitting but I regularly do
do mantra singing, getting better and better—and lots of belly breathing while walking sitting lying on buses, whenever I wanta get my mind
down quiet.

Send me card week before you get to New York City. Yes, Persky and
others are just too tight and prissy and no fun, in fact they don't seem to
get much fun out of pederasty even. I guess it's just fear/guilt, they sure
don't get much fun out of poetry even even. I wore beard a year here and
then shaved, saves anonymity on streets. I got tired of being stared at.

Lots of young girls here. I just lie back and don't worry anymore, whether or not I get hard-on, then I get one.

Oil blossom spreading then see down thru clear water is a classic construction I finally read David-Neal's book secrets oral yesterday.[95] Leary-Alpert rendering of Tibetan Dead book [*The Psychedelic Experience*] says similar thing, tho not so simply as she. It would take me a lot more quiet zazen to really still my mind to physically realize what they say. I'm rushing around naked so much.

I'm not writing much, tho I wrote one poem for Marianne Moore of all subjects. Someone asked me for her 77th birthday ["Little Flower M.M."].

Now we go dancing in Lower East Side took big ex-Polish club [The Dom] been turned into Beatles jukebox weekend dancing, huge happy crowds coming out of paranoid apartments to shake that thing. Some kind of millennium I hope—there's nothing else to do but make *deva*.

OK—Love to Phil, love to you, give Joanne pat on fanny for me,
Allen

70. ALLEN GINSBERG [NEW YORK] TO GARY SNYDER [SAN FRANCISCO]

January 10, 1965
Dear Gary:

[. . .] I'm leaving for Boston, today, testify Burroughs trial,[96] return Wednesday, yak on TV and radio Thursday on pot, then Friday escape for month vacation in Cuba, thence Czechoslovakia and back by March 15. Can reach me w/ Casa de las Americas, Habana, Cuba. February 15 or 20.

Allen

---

95. This is a reference to Alexandra David-Neal's book *Secret Oral Teachings in Tibetan Buddhist Sects*, which Snyder had recommended to Ginsberg a few years earlier.
96. William S. Burroughs' book *Naked Lunch* was the subject of an obscenity trial in Boston.

71. ALLEN GINSBERG [MOSCOW, USSR]
    TO GARY SNYDER [CALIFORNIA]

April Fool's Day [April 1, 1965]

Dear Gary:

Where'll this reach you? Got bounced out of Havana, landed in lovely
Prague and stayed a month, now for the last couple of weeks I've been
in Moscow and will go on to Warsaw and Budapest and London and see
you in Berkeley this summer. Got drunk with Yevtushenko and waiting
for Voznesensky to get back to town tomorrow.[97] Everybody real here,
it's absolutely amazing. Very slow and difficult to penetrate underneath
to some real life. I got St. Basil's onion dome and Kremlin walls outside
my hotel window and have filled up many detailed notebooks all thru the
last couple months. They got no answers here, anyhoo. Well hope you're
OK and wish you were here! I feel like Zeus walking thru Red Square.

Love

Allen Ginsberg

72. GARY SNYDER [KYOTO, JAPAN]
    TO ALLEN GINSBERG [1360 FELL ST., SAN FRANCISCO]

[November 11, 1965]

Dear Allen,

Are you OK? I heard about gall-stones or something from Martine.[98]
Coming back here was desolating—but beautiful, too; life is like living.
I went to the Noh play *Yama-uba* this afternoon—"old woman of the
Mts"—the one I described to you and Martine when we hiked up the first
day. Too much. Her staff has a garland of green leaves tied to it. How's
Peter and Julius?

Love,

G.

---

97. Yevgeny Yevtushenko and Andrei Voznesensky were two Russian poets who became close
friends of Ginsberg's.
98. Martine Algiers. A girlfriend of Snyder's at the time who went on a hiking trip with
Snyder and Ginsberg to the Pacific Northwest.

[April 29, 1966]

Dear Allen,

I'm gradually finishing the Milarepa.[99] Started from the beginning again. I finally caught up to where we last read from it—it was driving down from Shuswap Lake toward the Okanagan country—funny how those landscapes were evoked by the stories again—even the sheep up on the headland by the ocean where we stopped one morning came to listen.

It's a very useful book, all spring I've been reading Vajrayana literature and cross-reading, cross-comparing til I've come to understand what they're up to; what the language means. We passed right over several places where Milarepa was doing yummy sex yoga without even knowing it. Furthermore no doubt now in my mind that Vajrayana is great flourishing Buddhist dharma[100] for this age, given smoothing out and a synthesizing with Zen which really is identical with Mahamudra.[101] Only, be careful with Vajrayana, be careful with mantras, because if you don't treat them with respect they'll bounce back and blow your mind. As you yourself should know quite well, but some kids won't. Snellgrove's translation of the Hevajra Tantra [Snellgrove, David L. *The Hevajra Tantra: A Critical Study.* Oxford University Press, 1959] took me a full week to read—not that it's big. But checking the terminology step by step. Now, roughly, here's the four-phase bodhisattva path which is almost immediately available to a Western dharma.

1. Zen—i.e. a practice of *dhyana*—which develops *samadhi* power, applying this to

2. Love—and especially love-making, and all the vaster virtues that we understand by "love" but with one's lover you see, and turning this to

3. Art—i.e. one's work, or craft. So I'm a poet, but it should be the same for a mason or school teacher and thru that, one is

4. Action politically—i.e. this is the route by which one makes the social happen, correcting and reforming, revolution, so that people will be good to each other and nature, and come to have enough stock of good-humor, curiosity, faith, and *bodhi* to try

---

99. Milarepa. 11th-century Tibetan poet.
100. Dharma. The essence of righteousness.
101. Mahamudra. Buddhist method for understanding the essence and nature of mind.

1. Zen.

These four phases, I realized later, correspond in a way to the Four Vows.

Philip [Whalen] is very well indeed, moved to his own place and with a garden and two rooms. This place just naturally turned up one day, and it looked good. I'm going over to have dinner with the Shekeloffs[102] and Philip in a few minutes. Starting the 1st I go for a week to live in the monastery.

Martine is down at Big Sur being a Forest Beatnik or something—she funny girl, writes sweet sad stupid letters—there's no thought or plan there of her coming to join me anymore.

I can just imagine what you're into right now with all this LSD bullshit. Is it true LeRoi was in jail for carrying a pistol? Philip and I signed Tim Leary thing, too. I'm making Phil apply for a Guggenheim, who do you think—besides yourself—he should put down for references?

I haven't been making love much all this half year, maybe about five times at the most, three different women. Been too happily dug into my poetry writing and reading—with nobody to drag me back—to miss sex much. Now that the spring is here, it's all different though. Maybe I'll get a Japanese woman, they look better and better. Professor Chen Shih-hsiang is in town lecturing on Chinese literature at Kyoto University. He sends his regards. He likes you he says because when you sat in on his class with me and Phil you looked like you were really interested.

Well that is a big difference. Most folks don't seem to be interested in much of anything.

Laughlin[103] doing my next book, *Back Country*, it seems.

Om hum svaha

Hello to Peter!

Gary

---

102. Brian Shekeloff was an expert in Japanese folk and decorative arts.
103. James Laughlin was the owner of New Directions Books.

74. GARY SNYDER [KYOTO, JAPAN] TO ALLEN GINSBERG [NEW YORK]

[August 2, 1966]

Dear Allen,

I think it's very sweet of you to practice filial piety and I don't mean this sarcastically. I guess you don't do it for one's own father, really but for one's-self, to make the "father" in oneself possible, like you could even have a son.

People have sent me enough clippings that I realize you've had a busy year spinning the dharma wheels and lighting up your hair.

Yes, I've been meaning to do the Prajnaparamita [sutra]—almost completely over if necessary—to make a chanting thing. Take a crack at it. But the thing to use is [Edward] Conze's translation in *Buddhist Wisdom Books*, Allen and Unwin 1958, which gives Sanskrit, sentence-by-sentence translation, and total glosses.

Skandas. I'd say leave it in Sanskrit or literal, "heaps."

Avalokitesvara. "Down-glancing Lord."

Yeah, the basic self, a clear spring pool; mind-ground-water, same as trees. So the Sitka spruce thinks a bit one way (pointy needles, thin bark) and the Douglas Fir another ("I can live anywhere") working out different being-mudras according to where they're dancing.

Me, I'm coming back around 1 October stay U.S. till about January— be reading at Michigan in mid-November, Houston with Creeley and Duncan and Jo [Josephine] Miles at Thanksgiving. Meet Drum Hadley in Tucson and make a trip into the Pinacate Desert in Mexico again, early December. Want to come along? Betty Kray might fix me up at the Guggenheim in early November in which case I'll see you in New York.

Allen, I can't go to India next spring because there's still too much work to do here and the Bollingen thing[104] requires my presence awhile longer in Japan. I'd have to put it up to 1968 to do it, I guess.

Mrs. Jayakar[105] came to Kyoto for two days we had a grand time, took her to Daitoku-ji and she looked at all the monastery and talked for two hours, thru me, with ODA, Sessô Roshi, she asked real strong questions right out of herself, and the roshi gave her very straight answers. She dug

---

104. Snyder received a Bollingen research grant while he was in Japan and he had obligations to meet.

105. Ginsberg and Snyder had stayed with Pupul Jayakar when they were in Bombay.

him. Then we spent a whole day visiting places in Nara with a hired car. She's a great woman. Says we must come see her in India, indeed.

I wouldn't try using Suzuki's English Prajnaparamita; it's too choppy and not right enough. Must start with the Sanskrit, I'm convinced.

I still think for land the best buys are still up in Mendocino and farther north. Better chances of year-round water; trees and meadows mixed; land is cheaper. Tho it goes up. I hope to look some more at that territory in October.[106]

Here's my Vietnam karma—white-man blues, my own karma, too, poem. [Snyder has enclosed a copy of his poem, "In the House of the Rising Sun."]

And I'm glad Martine is hale and well; funny little girl I don't understand her exactly, but good-hearted. "Woman" (cf "wife") means "waveman" i.e. THE VIBRATOR. Antient Proto Aryan.

A garland of flower to Peter.

Love,

Gary

75. GARY SNYDER [532 THROCKMORTON, MILL VALLEY, CA]

     TO ALLEN GINSBERG [NEW YORK]

                                                    [October 11, 1966]

Dear Allen and Peter,

Walked across the Sierra straight off; from Giant Forest and General Sherman Tree to Mt. Whitney—slept on the summit windy full-moon freezing night—six days walking—then checked into San Francisco.

The dance-joy-costume-love-acid scene is too beautiful. I'm completely turned on by it. And total nakedness is taking over in Mill Valley too. I think our circumambulation of Tamalpais must have started more good vibrations than we dreamed. I dig, *camerado*, what you've been saying and doing this past year. Your *upaya* seems on the perfect balance. And it rather looks like Vajrayana is taking, quietly, over. The belated (a few decades) answer of the Dalai Lama to Artaud's passioned plea. I'll be in New York from November 3–8—reading at the Guggenheim

---

106. Snyder and Ginsberg were beginning to talk about buying some land together where they could build cabins and get away from the distractions of city life.

[Museum] on the 3rd. Where can I write or phone you? I'll probably check in at Yampolsky's first off. You like to try for a Prajnaparamita version while I'm in town? or out west later?

Love

Gary

76. ALLEN GINSBERG [NEW YORK] TO GARY SNYDER [MILL VALLEY, CA]

[November 29, 1966]

Dear Gary:

[. . .] Went up to Millbrook[107] with Maretta [Greer] and took a trip [LSD] with appropriate mudras mantras *mandirs* and mandalas and belly breathing, saw nothing but Krishna everywhere. I seem to be over the hump of fear I had. I guess it's the place to come back to via ritual that centers consciousness safely. Leary seemed like Shiva with his giggly Parvati[108] in his bedroom. They have a real ashram. A little confused socially but plenty of Indian dance and music and actual yoga there.

I'll be in California all January—running around giving readings. Date for Vajra Festival or Lightningbolt Festival or whatever[109] seems OK for January 10 or 12 by me and Leary and [Michael] Bowen.[110] Bhaktivedanta[111] wantsa do a turn out there in January, too.

Tenzin, it turns out, has a similar idea to us—a book of ritual which he's already completed from previously untranslated classic chapters of signal Tibetan texts—working with him, Geshe Wangyal[112]—we met him finally, a nice blissful old man in pants too big—anyway, he showed me the table of contents wants me to help shape it up labeled and framed for young seekers. We'll do some work tomorrow nite.

Tenzin said he figured it was probably our karma to turn on the Dalai

---

107. Timothy Leary had set up an unofficial research center for psychedelic drugs on an estate in Millbrook, NY.

108. Parvati. A Hindu goddess.

109. This event became the famous Human Be-In that took place on January 14, 1967, in San Francisco's Golden Gate Park.

110. Michael Bowen was an artist and leader of the counterculture at the time.

111. A. C. Bhaktivedanta, a Hindu swami who helped bring the Hare Krishna movement to America.

112. Geshe Tenzin Wangyal, author and spiritual director of Ligmincha Institute.

Lama literally when in India, he'll be there. That's a sort of mirrory thought to entertain.

Maretta [Greer] and Steven [Bornstein] and I went up to Columbia to help colloquium class discussion of Bhagavad Gita invited by Yampolsky, who said he was pleased by liveliness of it all.

Had supper with Wayman[113] and he's in contact with Tenzin. His wife may arrange some kind of Japan trip for me to read (maybe with Yevtushenko[114]) for pacifist organization there—next May maybe? You be there? I don't know if it's a useful project. She works with the peace group there and they said they'd like me to come (pay my own way) but they'll pick up expenses there. Couple weeks maybe.

Well OK till January. Call me if time. I haven't figured tune for four refuges yet, gotta hear the Jap a little more.

OK

Allen

[PS] OH! And I met a funny fellow with a cast in one eye who turned out to be C. C. Chan—Milarepa's publisher—had studied Mahamudra and six doctrines with him and a Chinee CHEN in Kalimpong—told him how we used the Milarepa book and he gave me a free copy.

"Wish 'em a good blowjob"—Peter's message

"I wish him *sunyata*"[115]—Maretta's message

77. ALLEN GINSBERG [NEW YORK] TO GARY SNYDER [MILL VALLEY, CA]

December 3, 1966

Two stanzas on Bodhi Mind by Tsong Khapa[116] from Lam Rin,[117] translated by Tenzin and Ginsey [Ginsberg] into English nine-syllable verse. Pretty closely following compactness and rhythms of original:

Four strong force streams completely carry

Hard reversing chain-bonds Action bind

---

113. Alex Wayman. A student of Tibetan Buddhism at Berkeley.

114. Yevgeny Yevtushenko. Russian poet.

115. *Sunyatta*. Emptiness.

116. Tsong-Ka-Pa (1358–1419), Tibetan leader widely considered to be the second Buddha by the Yellow Hat sect.

117. Lam Rin is a genre of Tibetan Buddhist literature, whose most famous work is by Tsong-Ka-Pa.

Ego hold of iron meshed entrapped
Darkness ignorant vast cloud all blind
World no limits borning to be born
Tormented current tripled endless,
On suchlike spacetime Mothers maken
More more thinking make perfected mind.

Gary: worked six hours to do this, literal root words ponied, then Tibet-sky repeated over and over to get rhythm, and then English adjusted. Not very clear actually but a nice first thing in regard to the fact that one could practically chant this monotone. Must try same with original Prajnaparamita—must get Sanskritist who can chant us the Hridaya [the Heart Sutra] in Sanskrit so we can duplicate the rhythm somewhat in hard English—doing the above made me realize—is heart sutra not origi-nally Sanskrit verses? Or is it prose snatches of a larger verse epic? How many and what kind syllables and tones in original and why not labor them into exact chantable English equivalent?

OK
Allen

78. ALLEN GINSBERG [NEW YORK] TO GARY SNYDER [MILL VALLEY, CA]

February 17, 1967

Dear Gary:
Enclosed the poem I said I'd send you for magazine. Back home for a few days before trip to Chicago East Lansing Detroit St. Louis etc. 10 days. Hectic in house but cleaning up mail.

COP Inc.,[118] on behalf of a list of poets may file an amicus curiae (friend of court) brief in support of Leary's constitutional appeal in his Texas pot case;[119] this be, not sure, either on professional artistic rather than religious grounds. I'll round up a dozen poets and have it done dignifiedly; Leary's lawyers will do the brief free. Do you want to be included? I'll try self Creeley Burroughs Olson Lamantia maybe [Robert] Lowell if he's out of bughouse—etc.

---

118. COP (Committee On Poetry), Ginsberg's foundation that he used for the tax-free sup-port of various projects.
119. Timothy Leary had been arrested for having a small amount of marijuana at the Laredo border crossing.

Not yet raised 6 grand but will next week.[120] Will see [Richard] Baker. Peter in good shape here, no crystal. So all is well. Hope this reaches you before you leave.

Love

Allen

[PS] Driving back into N.Y. the horizon at dusk a mass of smoggy cloud all blood red and Blakean, really impossible view.

79. GARY SNYDER [MILL VALLEY, CA] TO ALLEN GINSBERG [NEW YORK]

[March 14, 1967]

Dear Allen

Larry [Littlebird], Cece, and Thompson went back to New Mexico— she's white, and not allow'd on the Pueblo. Larry and I really connected before he left. Went to do archery one day. You write him—I know he'll want to see you.

Tomorrow night the Zen benefit reading. I leave @ the 23rd and am to participate in Tokyo readings and happenings on the 17th of April. Mahalila [Society] has a big new house at 34 Evergreen, Mill Valley. All is well.

Love,

Gary

80. ALLEN GINSBERG [NEW YORK]
     TO GARY SNYDER [31 NISHINOYAMA CHO SHICHIKU,
     KITA-KU, KYOTO, JAPAN]

[May 8, 1967]

Dear Gary:

In New York briefly, on extended reading tour. Enclosed find check for $500 for Mahalila Society purchase of the Maitreya *thangka*. I forgot if I said COP would also pay for mounting it in Japan, I think so. Let me

---

120. In 1966 Snyder, Ginsberg, and Richard Baker had begun to look for land in California to buy together. At first Gary preferred the area around Mendocino, but in the end Baker found property near Nevada City in the Sierras that suited them all. That land was to become Snyder's home for the next forty years. Ginsberg envisioned it as a place for retreat and eventual retirement.

know the further costs, shipment, etc. Did you bring it with you? I'm sorry I've taken so long to pay the bill but etc. it's all worked out.

There is a chance of my going to Japan June on a reading tour with Yevtushenko but I'm so over active probably it would be best if I didn't, Wayman's wife Hiddeko was arranging it via a peace group there. I guess I'll have to stay home all June and work.

I was out in S.F. for the 15th April Spring Mobilization—70,000 folks in the street, and filled Kezar Stadium—but in two hours only 15,000 were left at the stadium after uninteresting *Ramparts* speeches. Politicians drove majority away and no one represented the hippies on the stand.

Then spent 10 days with Larry [Littlebird] in his El Rito seclusion, shot his bow from the jawbone/cheek. Emmet Grogan[121] there also so we had chance to talk and I recorded and am learning Buffalo Mantra. The pueblo girls' initiation dance I saw was tremendous—falsetto clowns instructing girls "repeat after me—all you men and boys of the North, come to my house tonite and make love to me now that I'm a woman, all you men and boys of the East, etc."

Still chanting Prajnaparamita—headed for 10 days in Northwest— Portland Reed, Portland State, Western Washington in Bellingham, Oregon State in Corvallis, and Oregon University in Eugene. Got any instructions?

Love
Allen
Bom Bom Mahader!

81. GARY SNYDER [KYOTO, JAPAN]
    TO ALLEN GINSBERG [C/O ENGLISH DEPARTMENT, REED COLLEGE,
    PORTLAND, OR]

                                         May 14, [1967] Mother's Day
Dear Allen,
You sent me $50 too much—you had given me that much earlier. I'll send you a check for $50 at any address you consider reliable for the future few months.

The *thangka* is still in the U.S.—too big to carry on plane, and negative

---

121. Emmet Grogan. Member of The Diggers and author of *Ringolevio*.

reaction from Bowen to taking it off anyway. I presume Michael and Martine are storing it.

In Portland, Carol Baker, Charles Leong,[122] Lloyd Reynolds, and Jill and Gary Betts (the Seattle kids—who are now in Portland)[123] will all probably say hello to you.

Rexroth; daughter Mary; Carol Tinker his sec'y; Neale Hunter and Deirdre (just into Japan from two years in Shanghai where the Cultural Revolution finally wore them down) and Nanao Sakaki were all here staying in my house at the same time last week. Rexroth and Sakaki still here. Sakaki's group making two ashrams—one in the mountains, one on an island south toward Okinawa.

I'm getting a lot done, and hoping to be back to U.S. for good in about one year! I look forward to walks in the woods on our land, with you dear comrade. Give my love to Peter, and Maretta, if she's still with you.

Gary

82. ALLEN GINSBERG [PORTLAND, OR]
    TO GARY SNYDER [KYOTO, JAPAN]

[June 14, 1967]

Dear Gary:
Got your note on arrival in Portland, in fact delivered in Reed dorm. Saw Carol, Leong, Betts, Reynolds, etc. Had party at Carol's. I thought she lionized me a bit excessively and I wanted to relax rather, so wound up in bedroom discussing Chairman Mao with Charley L. Gave high reading at Reed in outdoor amphitheater joined group poets at Oregon U for peace etc.; scandal at Portland State becuz they published photo by Avedon in which I'm groin naked (covered by hand in meditation, other hand *abhaya*) on school paper front page, paper suspended, but not serious. Community forming there, with giant roller-bearing bouncy ballroom floor rock dance, I read there too for local SNAP (Society New Action Politics); had read to 4,000 in Eugene gym, and three-hour reading at Corvallis; then from Portland with Ken Kesey and bus and Neal [Cassady] babbling at wheel rolled into Bellingham met by 300

122. Charles Leong. A friend and informal mentor of Whalen's, Welch's, and Snyder's and a master calligrapher.
123. Jill Betts was a second cousin of Snyder's.

students at Western Washington, two days fiesta Neal, Ken, and me taught classes in junta (me constantly explaining Neal's babble as related to Joycean syntax in 20th Century English Prose course) ending in Jefferson Airplane's concert in gym next nite, us three M.C.'s.

Made enuf to pay off land, and cancelled all fall readings, I'll do nothing but home poetry meditation till next March. After couple months in Europe, I'll be at Spoleto July 4–9, see [Ezra] Pound; thence London all summer, till my father comes and three weeks with him London Paris Rome him aged 72 first time abroad. He wants to see Shelley-Keats' grave in English cemetery Rome. Maybe we'll go see Pope?

[Bob] Dylan long silent, spoke to him on phone, says his latest interesting song is "Dead to the World."

Regards to [Neale] Hunter, he called me a long while back and I was too preoccupied to be sociable. What's the scoop on China? Off track?

Spent two weeks in San Francisco, stayed with Haselwood and finally finished *Indian Journals* 200 pages for him to send to printer. Haight Ashbury—[Alan] Watts called me worried it's getting out of hand and no organization, we met with Thelins and Cohen and Ferlinghetti, they all had all sortsa plans sounded like they had energy to try at least, so didn't do what Watts first thought, issue popish bulletin discouraging invasion.

Had been with Larry [Littlebird] in El Rito and saw some terrific dances I hadn't thought extant on continent. Awesome initiation rite for girls.

Maretta in London with old boyfriend from India.

Hello to Phil. Dead tired. And too much mail to write decent letter.

All next fall home in N.Y.; then will read for COP next February-March; then plan more or less on Orient. But it's open. Can begin spend some time in Grass Valley build house or something if you're around. I guess we're sorta married, by that land. All's well in me, but N.Y. sure looks hot tight dirty and worried. Just too many people crowded together, too many messages coming in at once to pay attention to any single one. Tribal council forming here tho.

OK. Love as ever

Allen

[PS] Peter calm and at desk. Julius is talking since Napa where we found him several months ago. Dr. Eichman (*sic*) there (very competent doc) gave him effective combo shock pills and therapy.

83. GARY SNYDER [KYOTO, JAPAN] TO ALLEN GINSBERG [NEW YORK]

[June 25, 1967]

Dear Allen,

Here's a few very recent poems, especially note the CURSE poem ["A Curse on the Men in Washington, Pentagon"] which scared me when I wrote it (woke up in the middle of the night to put it in my notebook) but it seems right anyway. The lead mantra is a mantra "to cause large cities to tremble" from the Hevajra Tantra; the final imprecation is a chorus from a Cheyenne ghost-dance song, it means "we shall live again."

I've heard about the party at Carol Baker's from at least three sides now. Charles Leong is delighted out of his old Chinese Confucianist head that you kissed him on the cheek or something when saying goodnight outside a car or something. Altogether the Northwest trip sounds great. What's Kesey like? I suppose fate will cause us to meet sooner or later.

Just read (finally) [W. G.] Archer's *The Loves of Krishna* which straightens all that mythology out. And the poems of Vidyapati all about Radha and Krishna fucking, in the most elegant terms.

News from over here: *Psyche* magazine just had its fifth issue. Contains the text of a 10-page essay I wrote for *Ramparts* (not out yet) with Japanese translation by Nanao, called "Passage to More than India"—all about family, LSD, and tribe—and the whole "Renaissance" statement of yours, from the *Oracle* (who now just calls himself Naga) about love, metaphysics (Krishna), and politics which is excellent and original. By original I mean it clearly comes out of a strong thing in himself and is in no way a simple reflection of American hippie language. And a statement about an "ashram" the Bum Academy is starting in the highlands of Nagano prefecture. Three of us went up from Kyoto earlier this month and spent several days digging at a well, digging garbage pits, planting radishes, and putting a roof over the cooking area. My girl Masa[124] came up from Tokyo and cooked for everybody. Masa and I hitched from the mountains into Tokyo in giant dump trucks and went to look at Neolithic beads and pots in the Ueno Museum.

We gave a *Psyche* reading at a jazz-coffeeshop in Shinjuku, and then Nanao came on down to Kyoto and stayed 20 days; now he's at the island far to the south called "Suwa-no-se"—a 30-hour boat trip from Japan's

---

124. UEHARA Masa. In 1967 she became Snyder's third wife.

southernmost port, Kagoshima; starting another ashram.

Masa and I are going there for a month, from the 10th of July. About 15 people altogether will be at the island this summer and must build a shelter and start gardens there too. Bum Academy is very strong on hatha yoga these days, but walking is still the main meditation, plus dancing and singing and conch-horn blowing. Many conch-horns now. Lots more chicks.

Nanao and I took psilocybin together and went into a delight-and-gratitude *samadhi*[125] to the universe and the Goddess, and sang ecstatic devotional songs together for about three hours.

If you know anybody (or Foundation) that is set up to grant money for the arts outside the United States it would be interesting to see what the Bum Academy could do with just a little more money. Tell me if you have any idea. (I'm not asking you—you've got too many things out already. Somebody else.) An elder and experienced Zen monk recently took acid and was impressed, delighted, and educated he says. Made all sorts of connections between different levels and aspects of the dharma and the mind, he said; hadn't seen the relationships so clearly before, and especially the archetypal realities of god, demon, and bodhisattva-figures which he saw lots of and enjoyed very much. Said he found himself naturally making all sorts of mudras.

Hunter is in Australia now writing a book; then has an appointment to Berkeley in the fall for Chinese research and writing. So you well may see him.

I think I'll be closing things out in Japan and heading for Grass Valley[126] in a year or so; get all my stuff across the Pacific and then (after straightening out land and such affairs a little in U.S.) head for India. That's one idea, anyway. Like you, I'm open. It would be nice for us to get up on the land and camp and feel it out, and do a little building work together.

I have an enormous good feeling about that place; seeing it only one day, but it remains vivid and warm in the mind's eye. A good location.

Love to Peter and Julius;

Gary

---

125. *Samadhi.* Focus of a calm mind through meditation.
126. Grass Valley was an early name for the property on which Snyder built Kitkitdizze.

84. ALLEN GINSBERG [NEW YORK] TO GARY SNYDER [KYOTO, JAPAN]

[July 26, 1967]

Dear Gary:

Been in London—arrested for reading "Who Be Kind To" poem in Spoleto—opera *Bouffe*. Since here had great time at Poetry International for British Arts Council, reading as a team with 78-year-old Ungaretti, Italian friend of Apollinaire—nicest old poet I met since William Carlos Williams. Met Pound, silent just like Julius [Orlovsky]—looked in my eye tiny blue friendly pupils for five minutes, held my hand wordless.

Evening with Paul McCartney, and several evenings with Mick Jagger of the Stones—we plan to make a side of Hare Krishna together for next Stones album—what beautiful karma! Spent one nite watching Jagger, Lennon, and McCartney composing "Dandelion Fly" hairy new record at studio. Looked like three graces with beads and Persian shirts. They're all turned on and dig the Diggers and new Fresh Planet. McCartney—"We're all one." They got out of their fame paranoia this year—treated me like familiar holy phantom and all turned on yaketting about high soul—chanted Prajnaparamita to all, and all understood already—beautiful blue skies in London.

Now International Dialectics of Liberation—[Stokely] Carmichael angry and yelling, I stayed calm and kept chanting Prajnaparamita. Gregory Bateson says auto CO_2 layer gives planet half-life: 10–30 years before 5-degree temperate rise irreversible melt polar ice caps, 400 feet water inundate everything below Grass Valley—to say nothing of young pines in Canada dying radiation—death of rivers—general lemming situation. P. [Paul] Goodman sez welfare should save money by paying folks to live in the country. He has great ideas on rural reconstruction.

I'm making big TV British poetry conversation chanting scenes—wearing bright red satin shirt hand painted by McCartney—color TV-*Hari Om Namo Shivai*. Maretta here. Peter may come, and my father in one month, I'll take him three weeks London Paris Rome. Love to Philip—love to you. Emmet [Grogan] here too, organizing vast circus Hells Angels, Dead, McClure travel Europe.

Allen

EDITOR'S NOTE: *That fall, while in Italy, Ginsberg visited Ezra Pound. It was one of the high points in Allen's life and he must have described the visit in some detail to Snyder in a letter that is now lost.*

85. GARY SNYDER [KYOTO, JAPAN] TO ALLEN GINSBERG [MILAN, ITALY]

2:X:1967 [October 2, 1967]

Dear Allen,

[. . .] What a strange and lovely visit with Ezra. And all those blue sea views and mantras.

Philip and me and Masa and Julie (S.F. *dakini* staying with us) off to Manpuku-ji tomorrow for Obaku Zen Ming Chinese chants. Come! to Japan.

"Fresh Planet" maybe Lew's phrase? I'm not sure.

Om Ah Hum, love,

Gary

86. GARY SNYDER [KYOTO, JAPAN] TO ALLEN GINSBERG [NEW YORK]

16:XII:1967 [December 16, 1967]

Dear Allen,

I'm taking *sanzen* with the new roshi at Daisoleu-ji NAKAMURA Sojun—only @ 46. Quite a tough, detached little bastard. Only be able to work with him a few months—then must get busy with getting ready to return U.S.

G. [Gershon] Legman's pamphlet [probably *The Fake Revolt*] arrived and I think it's shameful, a real fink job under the guise of honesty. It's full of sensationalistic atrocity-mongering and distortion; wild swings at almost everything and what shows behind it is a sick old Mosaic-Jewish prudishness and old left sentimentalism. A hired goon writer from *Time* would have been more objective. So, what I'm saying is, you and others shouldn't take it lying down. Legman has sold out here, and deserves to be told so. You can forward this to him if you know his address. (Not in the U.S., I believe.) What business have these pricks who never learned anything except out of books and have never been in the West, in the desert or mountains, got talking about what's happening anyway? Boils on their asses.

How's America? I saw you and Spock-sensei[127] got arrested. Phil is

---

127. Ginsberg and the noted pediatrician Benjamin Spock were arrested for protesting the Vietnam draft.

back staying at Bill Brown's—and other friends from Asia side are now
in Bay Area, including Neale Hunter (after two years in Red China) and
an Italian anarchist couple who were part of Rainbow Cape in Kyoto
and are now forming a tribelet in San Luis Obispo. Love to Peter, Julius,
Maretta, Lafcadio,

Gary

87.   ALLEN GINSBERG [NEW YORK] TO GARY SNYDER [KYOTO, JAPAN]

Jan 11, 1967 [*sic:* 1968]

Dear Gary:

Been back for over a month and already sucked in to sit in with Dr. Spock
(went to court and no fine or sentence in jail. Ferl in S.F. with Joan Baez
spending two weeks in can) in front of Whitehall, reciting "Pentagon
Exorcism" in court, manifesting for LeRoi Jones with other poets, etc.
etc. It's nerve-wracking in a way—uneasy sense of unbalance of States and
growth of actual military/police state—seems realer than I'd anticipated,
unless I'm overwrought—the violence more on surface, and more and
more incidents of crackdown injustices etc. I dunno, it's like a game that's
gotten more nightmarish.

Have been at least able to stay mostly at desk for several weeks and
almost finished preparing poetry manuscript for City Lights. Should be
done this month.

I had read Legman's pamphlet—in one ear and out the other—last
summer and sent him a few notes and postcards trying to "correct" this
or that impression—but it didn't irritate me much, mainly because his
yakking did bring to surface in my mind same worries as above first
paragraph—the sense of a real authoritarian threat from government
already established, and lack of any alternatives but black power urban
violence or withdrawal to Neolithic countries die while the tide passes
over cities. Legman is irritating in suspicions that hippie führer will
arise, that's kinda insulting. But I don't have time to get distracted into
polemics and Legman, I'd rather spend hours on poesy. Actually I don't
know any answers to give him and've half forgot what he was polemicis-
ing about.

. . . anyway I quit smoking around Xmas and my head too goofy and
unstable to consider anything as unmusical as his prose for long enough

to understand it much less reply. I got happy with yr reaction to his pamphlet tho, I'll send him a Xerox. I had pleasant postcard exchanges with him—summer—his temperament a little like Rexroth.

New Dylan album out—Nashville twangy poesy, elusive intentions but very calm . . . I think surely LeRoi Jones was framed with those guns by the way. That's what's interesting. Can't figure what's real or unreal about his violence, sometimes it seems justified necessary, other times just another karmic threat-tide. I'm not making sense so I'll shuddup. Heard from Phil, he sent me *shikaku* etc. I'll be in S.F. this summer maybe.

Xx as ever

Allen

[PS] Marriage comfortable? Julius is real talkative and alert now.

I've been doing research on economics of military industry. It's the largest single business in America—employs one out of 10—7,000,000 people. "The business of U.S. is business." "The medium is the message."

88. ALLEN GINSBERG [NEW YORK] TO GARY SNYDER [KYOTO, JAPAN]

[January 13, 1968]

Gary:

I forgot to ask, in last letter—I sent you a $500 check May 8, 1967 for Mahalila *thangka*, did you cash that? My records are a little mixed up so am checking. Can you send me a note?

Since I wrote you I passed by New Directions and got and read *Back Country* all through last night—most immediately affecting set were the four poems for Robin solid as old classical Chinese poetry for presentation of that particular archetype desire ghost—Billie Holiday karma. Thinking a lot about "presentation" concreteness since seeing Pound and *Back Country* is wonderfully dense with that specific Thusness. It's like a piece of sculpture, almost a solid object. Completely readable book, good to give teenyboppers for sensibility and training. I see how you're organizing psyche-thematically, but it would be also interesting to see a chronological graph of these returns to the same places in the mind. (One way doing it would be loose leaf book page numbered as you have it now, with specific dates of primary composition noted on each piece so you could shuffle it about in thematic order, and back to chronological order.)

Photo of Masa U. [Uehara] on back cover first I've seen of her—she looks vigorous and cheerful and sane—pleasurable face to see. You did fine. You both look experienced and healthy and well adorned.

Listening to tapes of Pound pronouncing his broken lines I hear a vowel music slower and more conscious than anything we're doing, but something real that could be added to William Carlos Williams ear practice. Pound pronounces slowly individual vowels with usura the lines grow thick—grows is pronounced with same weight as line and thick (as distinct from inattentive da de da unaccented de grows which would be hangover 19th century accentual pronunciation for me if I hadn't heard tapes—Pound says daa daa daa line grows thick, three long heavy judicious vowels).

I'm listening a little deeper lately to slower music than I did. OK-Phil says maybe he'll go build cheap geodesic dome in Grass Valley—I'll encourage him.

XX Allen

[PS] Whalen mentioned possibly building cheap geodesic dome in Grass Valley, I said groovy.

89. GARY SNYDER [KYOTO, JAPAN] TO ALLEN GINSBERG [NEW YORK]

January 15, 40068 [January 15, 1968]

Dear Allen,

Your letter just came to me with news and energy in hand so right away. The date (above) is based on "Tribal Reckoning," taking the rough estimate of the earliest cave-art and Magdalenian carvings—as 40,000 years ago—as a sensible beginning for this Epoch. The new newspaper that Sakaki and cohorts in Shinjuku, Tokyo, have just brought out, *Buzoku* ("tribe") is dated by tribal reckoning. The newspaper is almost as good-looking as *The Oracle*. I'm sending you a copy by separate mail. Most of it is in Japanese but for a short piece with English and Japanese both by me, and a thing in English by Nanao.

The subculture here is flourishing daily and with great healthiness. Like, everybody keeps pretty clean and there's very little grass, almost no acid, and no body ever heard of amphetamine. The latest *Oracle* has my brief account of the Banyan Ashram of last summer. I still think you would find it a restful and creative thing to do this year—come over here and join us farming and fishing—no newspapermen, no literature—in July and August. Not a car or a road on the island. No electricity at the ashram.

Nanao and Nagasawa have become real leaders, in quiet and dignified ways. Nagasawa and his girl Piko are leaving at the end of the month for India—maybe they'll eventually make it through Europe and to New York, and on out to California. The tribe, which calls itself the Harijan now, uses my house as a stopping place. As many as nine kids camping here overnight—digging the Indian music, looking at books and magazines—getting a bath—and talking about things. Some of them as young as 17, and very smart. Thing about Japanese kids is, they have good manners, are neat and cooperative, honest; so that they are no trouble at all to have falling in and out.

My book *The Back Country* is finally finished—just got a copy yesterday—and will be for sale soon I guess. An essay, "Passage to More than India," was accepted by *Evergreen* and should be out soon—I hope it answers Legman and a whole lot of other nits by showing the historical threads and forces, and the anthropology, of what's going on. Just finished another extended essay too, "Poetry and the Primitive." Am going to gather all sorts of short pieces from the last 13 years—including old reviews of Jaime de Angulo's *Coyote Tales*, etc. and publish it, under title *Earth House Hold*, "Technical Notes and Queries / to Fellow Dharma-Revolutionaries." Either New Directions or Four Seasons or Coyote.

As you may have heard from Dick Baker, Dick Werthimer our lawyer and our old buddy Claude Dalenberg have also bought in on the Montezuma Ridge land (that's the real name of that ridge). It's really keen to have a sharp lawyer in with us. Provides all kinds of warm security sense.

A man I became very close to in Kyoto—Franco Beltrametti, his wife Judith, baby Giona, now in San Luis Obispo teaching architecture at the polytechnic college there. He's brought up as Italian Anarchist Kid—Buddhist sense, tantrism, very smart and gentle—may come up and join me and Masa on our land; I mean his family and ours might combine for practical and friendly reasons. He's a licensed architect, now busily studying American Indians in California, and started a course for his students on "California Indian space concepts" . . . contact him if you get west c/o Dept of Architecture, Polytechnic College, San Luis Obispo.

Tassajara[128] seems to be doing extremely well. Dan Welch is one of

---

128. Tassajara. Buddhist retreat center in California.

their solid leaders now. They'll produce a number of people with good zazen and discipline capacities who will be capable of carrying things a step beyond the narrowness of Japanese Zen—all sorts of foundations for the new community being laid. In the meantime America may go all shit to hell; but the "neolithic countryside" may be precisely the survival power we need to sit out a fascist takeover, or a major economic depression, or total decay of the cities into violence. I don't know what to do about the Negroes tho except show them the tribal African sense connection with American Indians, let us all join as Indians and forget both white and black; Red Brothers . . . Levi-Strauss *The Savage Mind* is a fine book. If LeRoi really was framed it's shitty. Yet the same karma. LeRoi should do a Gandhi in jail; meditate and build up spirit-power; turn it to his own growth.

Marriage with Masa is really superb; I never knew (this sounds corny) what "love" was before. She's the best thing I ever did. And she's going to have a baby in mid-April, as I may have told you, which is fantastic and exciting. Working hard now at getting back to California by next December. Taking *sanzen* with new Daitoku-ji roshi—he's tough and funny.

Love
Gary

90. GARY SNYDER [KYOTO, JAPAN] TO ALLEN GINSBERG [NEW YORK]

18:I [January 18, 1968]

Dear Allen,

Hey, put my name on the COP thing for LeRoi if you run it off again. I've been thinking a lot about his situation—saw the snide article in *Time*—and strongly suspect he was framed (only: why didn't he say so in court?).

Thank you for strong good words on *The Back Country*. Now on to new things!

About geodesic domes: It's hard to let anybody put up anything more permanent than a tipi until the land is divided—and certain agreements on where to drive cars, which trees never to cut down—are made.

Furthermore I, personally, think geodesic domes are ugly and don't fit well into a woody landscape. Others like Dick Baker or Kriyananda might agree. I'd say encourage Phil to camp up there—even put up a tipi or frame tent—but after getting Dick Baker's advice on location, water, etc., do no permanent structures yet.

Not that Phil will ever do anything concrete anyhow. Soon as I get back next fall I'm going to go up there and really study water and land-use and figure out how to best use it and help Dick divide it sensibly.

$500 check received and cashed = $50 was returned to you as per debt.

I'll write Phil anyhow.

91.   ALLEN GINSBERG [NEW YORK] TO GARY SNYDER [KYOTO, JAPAN]

[January 22, 1968]

Dear Gary:

Both your air letters received as you got both mine, and note from Phil, "I had long talk with Dick Baker by telephone and I can't see how anything can be done with that real estate. Swami Kriyananda has water now. Baker says that the introduction of hippies onto the scene might prove the beginning of a disastrous invasion of hippie hordes rushing into the layout hoping to be near you and shitting all over the lot and burning down all the elephants, etc. Maybe I'll get a visionary gleam if I go see it all." So wrote Phil. I'll be out there this summer and you be there fall to figure out apportionment and ecological security, it'll be there for him (Phil) in long-range, meanwhile tipi if he wants. I don't think there's much to worry about elephant-shooting hippies tho as I won't be making a fuss about the area.

If all goes well I think I'll try to spend some time on West Coast later summer-fall. My father wants to visit in summer so I promised to show him around San Francisco. Maybe settle the land with you around, then later if done with manuscript take off for India. Rec'd *Indian Journals* proofs from Haselwood today—several hundred pages plus drawings and photos should be pleasant book. You got any key photos you want printed in it by the way? There's not too many entries about our trip, but odd photos might not be out of place—any good [Kumbh] Mela? I threw in all the interesting snapshots I have with little captions, maybe 30 or 40.

Enclosed statement by Roi [LeRoi Jones], sent from his lawyer. He did and witnesses did testify to his being beaten and not having guns in trial. Just that all-white jury believed the cops. I spoke to his father and wife and they assure me he didn't have guns. But trying to get to Roi by phone I get no return call, and an angry secretary who finally said Mr. Jones busy anything you have to say can communicate by mail.

I'm going out on reading tour in two weeks, take in $10,000 for COP (or more) 20 readings (ugh or more)—last two months. Then summer mebbe with my brother's family short Mexican trip then to S.F.

Prose book sounds useful. I've assembled all my prose also and Random House publish it when I edit it down. It's a fat fat book—I wrote a lot—to be called *Manifestos Essays Interviews Prefaces Introductions Letters* etc.—composed of Xeroxes of several dozen texts scattered published over 10 years. Laughlin be glad to get your book I'm sure. Glad Dalenberg around.

You sound fine just keep temper like you told me. Baby good news. Dylan emerged this weekend with little beard very humane with Pete Seeger and Odetta and Arlo Guthrie and Jack Eliot and folksingers to give concert at Carnegie Hall sat together on stage no prima donna despite hysterical clapping of audience for him and all sang evening tribute of Guthrie folksongs, odd return of cycle Dustbowl company spies reminding me of city breakdown and CIA futurities and the old radical spirit a little sad (This [machine] kills Fascists) but odd sense of cycle return of that anti-authoritarian humanity tradition—surfacing again now that military clampdown seems creeping up. Nice to see all the hippies in bells at concert applauding "Union Maid," union this time the community (in my head) rather than UAW NMU.

[Thomas] Parkinson called passing thru N.Y. says he and Rexroth think things get worse.

Saw Beatles' Maharishi here last nite, he wants pyramid-club-type meditation half hour morn and eve, but's very vague about the State, said [Lyndon] Johnson and their police know more than he does about what they're doing. I shocked everybody around by warning him that same folks were worried he was a CIA plant. He took it in good stride.

OK. XX.

Allen

[PS] Best to Masa. Continuing M-I [military industrial] complex research and got underground newspaper on it now.

92.   GARY SNYDER [KYOTO, JAPAN] TO ALLEN GINSBERG [NEW YORK]

22.II.40068 [February 22, 1968]

Dear Allen,

Here are a few photographs I had fried up by the man. Not much, but maybe of some use. None of my Mela photos are worth reprinting.

Phil and Claude went up the land—Phil says it looks great: Kriyananda has a fine deep well and a redwood water storage tank. I think there is a danger of un-wanted visitors cropping up there—let's think of Montezuma Ridge as a quiet and private community and organize giant ashrams elsewhere. Someplace to go look at the sky from. Speaking of such, I'm about to think about MONEY. I want a whole lot to pour brown rice, nails, kerosene, etc. into our Japanese ashrams.

Franco [Beltrametti] figuring to look for near-the-ocean land in Calif too.

Any suggestions for a good American Sanskrit Chinese name for a boy? (We have a girl's name.) The state of the nation may, it occurred to me, actually cause us all to go on the warpath. Hmm. I am busy figuring out how to manipulate basic Occidental myths in our favor. (If it doesn't look encouraging I'll go on the warpath.)

Love

93.   ALLEN GINSBERG [CHERRY VALLEY, NY]
       TO GARY SNYDER [KYOTO, JAPAN]

[July 8, 1968]

Dear Gary:

Kept putting off writing because I had so much to say, so I'll be brief. I bought (or am buying) a farm upstate N.Y., isolated 2000 feet up near Cooperstown, surrounded by State Forest—70 acres and old 8 room house $9,000, spending a few thousand more to fix up for the winter. Peter and Julius been up there several months, Gregory Corso and his girl, Barbara Rubin pining for me (ugh!) (ouch I mean) and a young competent film-maker farm couple [Gordon Ball and Candy O'Brien]. We have 3 goats (I now milk goats) 1 cow 1 horse (chestnut mare for pleasure) 15 chickens 3 ducks 2 geese 2 fantail pigeons, small barn right size, nearby a friendly hermit [Ed Urich] been up there sans electric since

1939 teaching us how to manage and what to repair. More kibbutz than commune, very loose, but the place is getting organized, Julius has work to do and speaks, Peter's mostly off meth and calm. No electric, now hand pump, we're digging well up in our woods so as to have gravity-fed running water. 15 acres of woods one side, the other sides all state woods permanent—pine, oak, and maple, etc. Got lotsa books on flowers. Table is meatless, we eat fish tho. So that's started. Will also build simpler place sooner or later in California land. Visited Tassajara finally one nite.

Local (U.S.A.) sociopolitics confusing. This yippie hippie be-in shot in Chicago[129] has been a big drag since undercurrents of violence everywhere (state and street Black Mask etc.) make peaceful gestures seem silly. Yippie organization's in wrong hands sort of. Would like to get out or redirect it to some kind of prepositional New Nation Confabulation, but I don't have time.

Finished proofs of *Planet News Poems 61–67* for Ferl, and *Indian Journals* for Auerhahn Haselwood. Next, collected poesy volume and collected interview/essay/manifesto volume to compile—all work's done except editing that.

Received photos you sent in December. I met Franco [Beltrametti] with Philip W. in S.F. last month.

Skandas Snyder??? Sounds Norwegian (poor l'il Skandas). Well let's see, a name—lets see the body of bliss first. Other gossip—I'd spent ¾ hour with Robert Kennedy discussing pot, ecology, acid, cities, etc., a month before he started running for Prexy and died. Peter/meth big karmic problem. Gave up (drifted off) sex with him to take off pressure if that was it. Lightens our relations a lot.

I'm driving to Mexico with brother and five nephews [*sic:* four nephews and one niece] and sister in law, two weeks and thence to S.F. again meet my father and show him around two weeks—then likely back to the farm—maybe trip out to convention Chicago and back, hole in for several months.

Wrote one fantastical poem about being screwed in ass with repeated refrain "please master"[130] which really got me a little embarrassed, but read it at last S.F. Poesy Renaissance big reading and it turned out to be,

---

129. Ginsberg was involved with the planning of demonstrations scheduled to take place at the Democratic National Convention that coming August.
130. "Please Master."

as usual, universal, one hole or another, one sex or another. Really amazing year after year I stumble onto areas of shame or fear and then catharsis of community awareness takes off the red-cheeked bane.

How's fatherhood? Babyhood? I wrote Kapleau[131] and he sent me his Prajnaparamita translation—he chants in English monosyllables, one of the Tassajara senseis or roshis is a Sanskrit expert, we can check out with him on your next trip here. Any plans? OK.

Love, as ever

Allen

[PS] I keep straying on mental anger warpaths, and then come back to milking the goats.

94. GARY SNYDER [KYOTO, JAPAN]
    TO ALLEN GINSBERG [CHERRY VALLEY, NY]

20.VII [July 20, 1968]

Dear Allen,

Ah, summer is on us with full heat now, the rainy season let up about four days ago. Good feeling. Interesting news about your place. Sounds like a superb buy.

Since I'm going back in October with all household gear and books, I'm thinking of looking for old farm up Mendocino way or such to rent or buy myself, need a place quick to put books in and to write and study in, I want to finish *Mountains and Rivers* in the next two years. Sierra land, like you yourself see it, a later thing to use to build on simply.

Will buy VW camper and travel widely the Far West, Canada, and Mexico—doing natural and social "fieldwork"—if too much static in travels and studies willing to adopt beardless anonymity so as to get work done inconspicuously.

Yippie thing does seem kind of irrelevant at the moment—though revolution as theater (or play) and street-drama-guerrilla tactics may work a little later better.

Read [Regis] DeBray and was mostly turned on to idea of self-sustaining independent guerrilla camp in mountains—"The guerrilla controls the territory his feet take him over; his base of support is his

131. Philip Kapleau. Buddhist sensei who established the Rochester Zen Center.

knapsack, in the early stages" as transformable into non-violent cultural-guerrilla mobile bands and secret fixed camps in U.S.—like our farms and communes—but perhaps doing as DeBray says really staying out of the cities and issuing liberation magazines from the country, or hidden radio station doing very high straight talk and music. All you need is to win the support of the local peasants eventually. Hmmm, that sounds less likely in Iowa or Alabama.

Baby's name is Kai, here are some photographs.

I've got another book coming out this winter too—from New Directions, to be called *Earth House Hold* prose collection with recent essays and early journal notes combined.

Development in Tokyo: Five friends busted there—Japanese—for possession of 45 g. grass, a political move actually by government—but an excellent lawyer has taken up their case and the very case of the marijuana law in Japan (imposed by MacArthur occupation, when they didn't know nothing about it) and hopes to make it a constitutional-legal major case, right now, before public has any opinion one way or the other on it. Also wants to bug the U.S. government—which it would if Japan changed the grass law before anybody else. Lawyer group wants contact—advice—information—from U.S. lawyers and groups acquainted with problem—especially medical, technical, and legal. All information to go to: Mr. Sunami.

I went up to Tokyo last week, met (found, via a left-wing professor friend) Sunami and his group, explained the history and situation of the hemp laws to them—to their astonishment—(they, like all other Japanese intellectuals, assume it's like opium)—and apparently convinced him. Gave him a xerox of your *Atlantic* essay (conveniently located it at the American Culture Center in Kyoto) and am having Shig [Murao] airmail him a copy of *The Marihuana Papers*. So that's where it is at the moment.

Let anybody you know who should be told, know; and pass the address on please.

Fatherhood is like having a Zen Master in the house all the time. Talk about dignity, demands, non-verbal communication; and a mirror held up to yourself. And thoughts about karma. And koan: Where did KAI come from? The same clear original face—ah.

Did the five-day *yamabushi* sacred mountain ridge-running (up as high as 6,200 feet) pilgrimage route last month. Saw wild deer, heard monkeys, virgin oak forests with grass underfoot like Merlin and little Arthur woods—and tasted *yamabushi* sacramentalism—they really make the whole outdoors their temple (fire-ceremonies are held in dry river-beds, or at the foot of cliffs) and scorn the need for special buildings.

Grand once-in-a-year fire ceremony, the Master of Ritual, a tiny old coyote-man; mostly surrounded by billows of smoke as he stood in front of pyre making mudras and chanting—200 *yamabushi* chanting around it in a large circle—and throwing bundles of sticks into the flames saying "take this, take this,"—meaning my own stupidity, anger, dullness, greed, 108 defiling passions, etc.—for me the fire did indeed transform—at one point, when they started beating a four-foot dharma drum and all the *yamabushi* started chanting the Prajnaparamita Hridaya together, to the rhythm of rubbing their beads so it sounds like rattlesnakes rattling—buzzing—like in the communion, the fire became the body of Vairochana[132]—the real presence—for a while, and afterwards I felt I had been burned clean.

I still feel cleaner than in years. Like mental warpath stuff.

Next week to Suwa-no-se island for a few weeks. Masa will have to stay in Kyoto with Kai.

See you soon. Please do what you can toward helping the Japan hemp case.

Love,
Gary

95. GARY SNYDER [KYOTO, JAPAN]
   TO ALLEN GINSBERG [CHERRY VALLEY, NY]

7.X.68 [October 7, 1968]

Dear Allen,
I know you've been busy because I read about you in *Time*, I think, from Chicago convention; and other reports. I had my ear against this tiny transistor radio, on Suwa-no-se island, in the middle of a typhoon wind and rain night that was tearing off the roofing of the cowshed in great rips in the dark, thru the static and noise picking up English language from

---

132. Vairochana. One of the five transcendent Buddhas.

Okinawa military radio station—hearing live the convention voices and shouts. And the anger and frustration about the streets.

Well I'm pretty definite now, sail November 16. I want to ask you about your foundation. The ashram at Suwa-no-se is doing so much good work (we were up every day at 5 for zazen; work in morning and evenings, midday siesta—and yoga asanas for an hour as the sun set) and on such a tiny amount of cash that I'd like to give them a solider chunk of aid than I've been able to so far. If I did, something like $500 maybe, it would be good if I could legally tax-deduct it with proper proof. To do that, it occurred to me maybe I could donate a sum of money to COP and COP could give a grant to the Banyan Ashram for the same sum. How would that be?

I was down there six weeks. Masa and Kai stayed in Kyoto. We were rooting out more stumps and clearing additional garden land—about 18 people, almost all men; three or four of them 18 and younger and shoulder-length hair and little dandy touches that made them look like Shonshone braves—cutting timber on the mountainsides and carrying the logs down; squaring the logs with adzes toward building a proper house this winter; exploring and fishing from the "Gabo" little boat with an outrigger and paddles they bought this spring from an old boat builder in the Amai islands; planting sweet potatoes, clearing trails, and hearing lectures (by me and by Nanao) on yoga, Zen, Vajrayana, the Rinzai-roku, and astronomy.

I was on the crater one morning—up for a view of the world—and looking in, when it mildly erupted and with tears in eyes gasses in lungs delighted in rocks rising slowly up, arcing, and falling back in again. Purple, black, red, and white smoke and steam mixed and braiding upward, and diving in dangerously heavy seas, spear fishing at the edge of the coral reefs alone, got all turned over by big surf and hit on the head on rocks and for a while didn't know where I was going to end up. A little caress from the great goddess to let me know she means it.

And we ran short of food because the typhoon weather kept the boat from coming; so had great meals of edible acorns gathered on the mountain mixed with barley gruel and a kind of rhubarb-type wild plant called *Fuki*.

The ashram worked out its four points of practice: four *"gyo"* (practices) *sagyo, shugya, angya, yugyo*:

1. work (gardening, cooking, etc.)

2. yoga (zazen, asanas, study of such) and mantras

3. wandering (as they do when hitching to and from island, and other times; or walking about the island on foot)

4. play (which they take to be dancing, singing "free song," drumming, drinking *shochu* or mind-benders, and making love)

and they practice the old Zen rule, "No work no food" literally—if somebody wants a day off to read or meditate he fasts for that day. It's nice. I did for two days. As it is, there's about five free hours midday and after dinner is free, too.

Talking with Drum and Diana Hadley about possible trip into remotenesses of Baja California in February.

I've felt bad and wanted to tell you so, about the *thangka* I got you to buy. I feel unhappy about it because I don't think Michael Bowen will ever put it to an "ashram" use but considers it probably his own private property, and I am afraid I was sort of conned by Michael and Martine; and then turned around and got you involved in it. I was thinking about that and several other bad things I did in life, like the time I tripped you in Seattle, O! Forgive me! and let's see, being such a nuisance when I visited New York last bringing all sorts of girls to the apartment and generally acting like an opera singer or something. And also (since I'm into it) being selfish about Martine on the trip up north, I guess I was in a dumb monogamous mood at the time but it would have been more proper and *dharmic* to have been more open and playful, all of us.

Baby flesh, baby mind, is charming and dignified. Any being that starts as a baby can't be so bad—humanity has a good chance. I been changing Kai's diapers. (On the island, standing on a boulder looking all over the hills and down over the pasture and bamboo thickets, I suddenly saw, scarily, "Everything out there, grass and bush and tree, came from a SEED.")

U.S. headquarters address will be my sister's new place [in] San Anselmo, Calif.

Tokyo marijuana trials just starting, I'll let you know how it comes out.

With all the troubles in America it will be nice to be back. Come out west and be with us a while.

Love,
Gary

96. GARY SNYDER [KYOTO, JAPAN] TO ALLEN GINSBERG [NEW YORK]

22.II [November 22, 1968]

Dear Allen

I forgot to say—in the letter with photos—anything you dig up on Japanese business collusion with American military industry we'd like to see. And anything else you might have—that would be significant for the Japanese people, to translate and use in forthcoming issues of *Buzoku*.

Talking about the "war path," O well, the craziness and violence of the scene is infectious. The dharma is indeed outside of all that, I was remembering as I walked to the post office—the enormous beauty and peace of the universe—against which Vietnams or Johnsons or anything else is a tiny turbulence—not even unharmonious—Ah,

G.

97. GARY SNYDER [SAN ANSELMO, CA]
TO ALLEN GINSBERG [CHERRY VALLEY, NY]

28.XII [December 28, 1968]

Dear Allen!

I got back to America a few days ago to hear you crashed![133] People tell me you should be home by now so I'm sending this home to you—but whatever / whichever, git well enough soon enough to get together. Were Peter and others OK? Do you have any advice on buying (I'm thinking of it) a VW camper after crash experience?

Met Keith Lampe here—interviewed for *[Berkeley] Barb*—he's all concerned with whether to join White Panthers—I told him for me, no violence. He says you are holding firm on that, too. I think good, must work—I see more and more—as Gandhi insisted—from a truth level—even if it doesn't offer short-range gratification.

Will send check for Banyan Ashram grant when you are more well—it will take a visit to N.Y. Sumitomo Bank to shoot $ > ¥ for Japan comrades.

California seems OK—violence fantasies and gun-practice mostly

---

133. At the end of November 1968, Ginsberg was injured in a car crash at the Albany Airport.

Berkeley whites apparently (I mean left-wing violence). Blacks are something else. I respect their karmic need for this trip. Otherwise—am staggered by actual immorality of fat careless affluence everywhere—see personal responsibility—to show having less, like finally and naked sadhu—"it can be done" proof necessity. Masa doesn't like the comfort of sister's home—no smells of earth, no chill of cold morning air. Am buying a wagon and moving farther out soon as can!

Love

Gary

[PS] Keep touch, love!

98. GARY SNYDER [SAN ANSELMO, CA]
      TO ALLEN GINSBERG [CHERRY VALLEY, NY]

24.I.40069 [January 25, 1969]

Dear Allen,

Your place looks chill and frozen and the kerosene lamp in the photo makes me think of Kenneth Burke who they say wrote by kerosene light into the '50s.

In another letter I'm sending the check should go to the Sumitomo Bank (or other Japanese bank with branches in both N.Y. and Kagoshima) in New York and be made into a draft for the amount, payable to: Nanao Sakaki or Banyan Ashram, Suwa-no-se Island, Japan. Check with someone at the bank, of course; but I believe this is the most efficient way to get the money to them.

It looks like we won't be around for your visit in February. Thea [Gary's sister] will take care of Kai, while Masa and I drive (in our brand new "Lotus White" VW camper) to Tucson to meet the Hadleys and go on the trip through Baja California. I went and got good books on desert ecology and Baja history yesterday. Seems a great place for big birds and grey whales. Masa and I leave January 28—back here by third week of February. Perhaps paths will cross somewhere—Tucson? Phoenix?

We've got a small apartment in San Francisco lined up: will move in there when we get back from Baja. A temporary thing, prior to (1) finding a big country place to rent, or (2) going ahead and building something on the Sierra land and moving up there. Kriyananda (Don Adams or whoever he really is) shows an interest in developing a big "center" on his portion—which I find a little disturbing. But apparently Dick Baker and Dick Werthimer the lawyer worked out a "maximum density of human use per acre" plan which Kriyananda agreed to and which holds us all down to a set limit (which, as I recall, seems more than enough). I must go talk to Dick Werthimer about all this. After Baja will go up there and camp for a while—see how it feels for living.

I bought (with Lew Welch's advice and aid) an older Winchester 30-30 carbine—and have strangely gotten into the study of cartridges, gunpowder, fire-arms. Not as a "revolutionary," but as an extension of my *sadhana* under Fudo with his halo of flame and sword and noose—to understand "The Weapon"—and sulfury super-yang gunpowder flashings—the clangs and sulfurs of dwarfish forges and volcanic furnaces—geology—planet heat and smithing. Also, as Paleolithic yogin, must try hunting again—eat venison and acorn bread in the Sierra.

By October I'll be settled enough to bring Nanao to America for a visit. I'd hoped to do it April. He is: Japan—as you: America. Secretly. Has become one of my most important teachers. Second only to ODA Roshi.

Phil is not at ease here—practical things like money and transportation—the solve simpler in Japan. I don't want him to go back, but there's nothing for him here, unless his forthcoming Harcourt book brings in surprising money—or one of us says "come live with us"—which I won't do, because it doesn't help Phil come to terms with life/death nitty-gritty self-help truth. He'd need that to really stay and survive in U.S. Ohh, I don't know.

We'd like to come visit you—maybe in the fall? Spring and summer are for the West—Far West.

Keep in touch with me via this address—when I get back I'll have newer place, maybe phone. Hey! Wayman's book is out: *Fundamentals of the Buddhist Tantras* (The Hague: Mouton) and it is utterly enlightening. What precision, clarity, psychological hipness. Actually entirely a translation of text by leading disciple of Tsong Khapa.

Me with a bad cold—yes, the body is transitory and given to pains and disorders.

And I notice, living on a ship three weeks and with my sister four weeks, that I feel distinctly different (and less clear) on this rich diet. Food makes a difference in mental and physical states after all.

We hope to spend time with you soon. Around campfire.

Yours in the Eternal Dharma and radiating grace of Vairochana, etc.
Gary
PS Saxton Pope, the UC doctor who was a pal of Ishi and used to go bow-hunting with him—his long out of print book—*Bows and Arrows*—re-issued by UC Press paperbacks.

PPS Problems of running a big primitive place are ¾ solved by having a few ashram members who know how to work and fix things, and feel it is their thing, too.

99.   GARY SNYDER [2131 B PINE ST., SAN FRANCISCO]
      TO ALLEN GINSBERG [CHERRY VALLEY, NY]

16.III.69 [March 16, 1969]

Dear Allen,
Too much to talk about in a letter. A month in Baja with Drum and Diana [Hadley]—now living in the city. Yesterday to bi-annual Sierra Club Wilderness Conference, with Keith [Lampe]—heard numerous scary facts from sharp young scientists—knowledge of approaching horror far outstrips any imagination to deal with it—beginnings of some talk about radical conservation tactics. A strong feeling for all this is beginning in the young around here—but they're ignorant. Should push for radical "GREEN STUDIES" courses on every campus.

   Love,
   Gary

100.   ALLEN GINSBERG [CHERRY VALLEY, NY]
       TO GARY SNYDER [SAN FRANCISCO]

[April 20, 1969]

Gary:
Sorry slow answer: I'll be one day in Portland a week after you (April 23 to read for *Resist*) and 24th at Gonzaga in Spokane—then a week ([April] 26–May 1) in Tucson. Will end up mid-May back in N.Y. after Little Rock, Ark., and Nashville, Ten.

   A week ago left side of my face paralyzed with Bell's palsy, usually lasts five weeks or months, not forever.

Have you seen Irving Rosenthal and his commune now several stable years old? A really oddball commune, half gay. But a real family. He wrote and asked about "farming" some of our Sierra land. Haven't answered him yet. I don't think the land is farmable though possibly an acre of it is. If you have a chance please drop by visit him and talk it over. I haven't answered him yet and will tonite, explaining I want to keep the place mostly untouched and it'd be probably too hard to farm. But as it is poetry retreat land, I wouldn't mind his commune making some careful use of it.

If you haven't please look up my interview *Playboy* April last few pages. I've been working on *Look* magazine people feeding them suggestions for ecology-crises issue, and a poem too. "Shit brown haze to the horizon." And "Smokey the Bear Sutra."

I forgot if we discussed the image but as the color is as of dung-brownish over L.A. and as it's literally waste products of machines, the smog is robot-shit quite literally.

Has Phil gone to Japan March 28 he said?

U.S. left and right full of hysteria and perturbation, overcrowding and unnatural emotions and outages. Underground papers also tending toward bullshit rhetoric (i.e. tonight read in *Berkeley Barb*, April 4–10, p. 5, "Camejo's Cuban Caper: It Blows the Mind" column 5, last three paragraphs, "Camejo also rapped favorably about the crushing of the hippie movement in Cuba . . . live high . . . without working . . . prostitution with foreigners . . . all hippies rounded up . . . Cubans agree . . . and don't smoke pot." That's all doubletalk like the '30s—it's outright persecution of fairies and literally hip friendly new-conscious cats they're apologizing for: Liberation News Service has an odd party line on this. I.e. "Smash the jails and free pot prisoners in the U.S.A."—"Smash pot smoking hippies in Cuba don't want to work and fuck foreigners." This is of no great account, just that I've found myself confused staying here so long reading all these wildly poetic sympathetic anti-pig proses that finally it don't look in focus anymore, a lot of its imprecise nose. (Unprecious noses?) (Imprecise noise.)

"Green Studies" would "professionalize" (Paul Goodman's term) the academy in a nice (pragmatic) useful way.

Saw your interview in *Barb* and wrote note to Lampe. He's followed everything for years so could fill you in on all radical theatrics since you've been gone.

I'll be traveling till May 21 and then done for good this year, maybe stop these heavy reading tours. I'm on a cane and half palsied now, better quit before I turn into C. Aubrey Smith.

Yours

C. Aubrey Smith

[PS] What's your itinerary? I'll see you here or there summer maybe.

I sent $400 to Nanao thru proper banks—went downtown New York, Sumitomo Bank and cable transferred money to Nanao Sakaki, c/o Ban-yan Ashram, etc. All OK. Done over two months ago or longer. Sorry not to keep you posted earlier. But it's all OK.

Visiting Philip Kapleau April 22 to chant with his group some reli-gious/poesy conference.

Best to Masa and young Zenroshi.

101. GARY SNYDER [SAN FRANCISCO] TO ALLEN GINSBERG [NEW YORK]

[*ca.* April 1969]

Dear Allen,

I had a few glasses of wine last night and called you, but talked to Peter pleasantly instead, you were in New York he said. He sounds on the phone like "Wolfman Jack" the celebrated Los Angeles disk jockey (whom we picked up on the Jap transistor in the depths of Baja Califor-nia desert wilderness).

Just back from five days in Santa Barbara; visiting mother and show-ing grandchild to her; reading poems at dawn on Buddha's birthday in front of mountainside Chumash Indian caves with paintings of dharma wheels inside, of red hematite ore—also evening reading on campus, Lew Welch and David Meltzer there. Brother Antoninus read one night, I was disappointed by his posturing and staginess, it's an old guilt-and-sin and authority drama he's presenting.

Before going to Santa Barbara Masa and I camped on the Sierra land three days.

Kriyananda has been going straight ahead regardless of the land-use agreement he signed (I'm sure you must have seen a copy of this) which specifies that any member of the "corporation" must consult others before cutting down many large trees or building many buildings, etc. and has done a lot which looks fairly junky to me but Werthimer is going to come down on him and it may slow him up a bit. He has grandiose plans for a large community, which is very much different what he told Dick Baker originally.

I had some talks with Dick in Japan, and the other day with Werthimer about the land, and here's how it stands:

1. The land is held jointly by the "Bald Mountain Land Co." and is in Dick's name. It has not been surveyed, so there is no precise way to delineate "whose land is whose."

2. A land-use plan was drawn up by Dick, very rough, but I presume you've seen it. It says each person holds acres like shares, and in terms of land use no more than two permanent houses per 12 acres (not including work buildings and sheds outside of main dwellings) and maximum temporary use of land no more than two people per acre—i.e. you or I could have up to 52 people as guests each. And no logging or farming or construction without consulting the group and adjusting it to everybody's needs and the main thing, Preserving the Wilderness Quality.

3. I agree with Dick's plan for the most part, in any case it is only rough and subject to everybody's agreement. Kriyananda has plans to exceed the scale in buildings and in people, I'm afraid.

4. SO, in fact here's what I think will happen: Kriyananda must be written off and left to go his own way. But the rest of us can work together and use the land in a delicate way. When I see Werthimer next I'm going to propose the following, and I'd like to hear what you think: that the rest of us—for some time at least—genuinely hold and use the land in common, all of it, as "our park." Thus anyone wishing to camp or put up a structure could do so on any part of the whole land. Roads to construction sites be temporary, and after work is finished, roads be returned to nature; and that the whole park be closed to automobiles. Car park area at some convenient place on the land at the entrance and trails from there. Any water development—well digging, etc., should most efficiently be a group enterprise. Other things may work out best as group enterprises also, when the time comes. Like a bathhouse.

5. So, offering Irving Rosenthal, or anyone else, use of the land seems ill-advised at this time. (It isn't farmable anyhow except perhaps in the meadow, and that would take a bit of thought and study, because the meadow is so nice as it is.)

But also, if somebody were to farm the land they'd have to live there; and to live there they'd have to build things, maybe cut trees, use water, etc.—and none of those things have been thought thru yet by the rest of us. ANY land use should be thoughtful, and any use by guests or friends should be thoughtfully supervised—and we haven't looked at that bit of land that's been loaned us enough yet to know what to advise.

6. Masa and I will be camping and living there fairly regularly from late May on—so I'll be able to report on the summer water situation and other things, later. We are planning on getting a tipi and living in that, maybe part of next winter too. So why don't we plan to get together soon—all go up there—camp for a few days—or live with us?

7. In the fall we will experiment with the black oak acorn crop and try and make acorn flour.

8. Eventually may build real house—geodesic domes or something—and live there permanently as base camp.

My skedyul [schedule]: Portland Ore 16, 17, 18. Norman Okla April 23, 24, 25. Iowa City April 28, 29. Michigan April 30, 1, 2, 3. Colorado May 6. Utah May 8. Then home. Latter May perhaps to Los Angeles a few days to look at Peruvian exhibit.

Summer, partly on Sierra land, partly traveling I'm not sure where yet, maybe S.W. for summer Indian dances; and one high-country Sierra backpacking trip.

I'm terribly sorry to hear of your PALSY? How weird. Connected with auto accident? Meditate and concentrate to thaw left side?

I saw your *Playboy* interview which is so precise, and on the highest levels I thought accurate, charming, beautiful, and to me illuminating. Also your prose style is exciting. Or, in this case, talking style.

I guess I'm about to really sharpen my push down to American Indian soul / Ecology knowledge / Buddhist wisdom, poesy.

Love,
Gary

102. GARY SNYDER [1 CAMINO DEL CANYON, MILL VALLEY, CA]
     TO ALLEN GINSBERG [CHERRY VALLEY, NY]

[September 18, 1969]

Dear Allen,
New address—in the woodsiest part of Marin County—to winter the winter and move in spring to the Sierra land which I've called KIT-KIT-DIZZE after the most common little plant up there. How are you dear

brother? Thanks for sending *Look* [magazine] my way, I think I reached
him a little. I was walking 10 days with Nanao (who lives with us) in the
high Sierra and saw the ancient bristlecone pine and Indian petroglyphs.
It will be elegant to read with you. I'm in Ohio afternoon of Friday 21
November. Where can I find you to visit maybe Saturday–Sunday 22–23
November?

Love,
Gary

103. GARY SNYDER [MILL VALLEY, CA]
     TO ALLEN GINSBERG [CHERRY VALLEY, NY]

8.X.69 [October 8, 1969]

Dear Allen,
Scheduling: maybe 22–23 November, I'll stay with you at your apartment on 10th Street. I'll be arriving Friday the 21st, I think—perhaps go
first to Phil Yampolsky's for one night—or something. On the 25th I have
to do something—on the 26th—a gig at Columbia—some class. 27th up
to December 2 is open. Thanksgiving weekend. Maybe we could go up
to your farm then? December 2—Trenton State. 3 and 4—Princeton.
5—Buffalo—and home.

Doing a big ecology benefit reading at Berkeley—Pauley Ballroom—
tonight. Brautigan, McClure, Howard McCord (who's staying with me
right now—a keen man)—Lew Welch—Meltzer—etc. reading. Money
goes to 1. Ecology Action and 2. Ecology Center.

I wrote some new poems, too.
Gary

104. GARY SNYDER [POSTMARKED ST. PAUL, MN]
     TO ALLEN GINSBERG [CHERRY VALLEY, NY]

[November 2, 1969]

Another boy GEN origin, vigor, born 1 November early—but strong (I'm
in Minnesota) (Masa is in California and is well). See you soon.

In Beauty,
Gary

105. GARY SNYDER [MILL VALLEY, CA]
     TO ALLEN GINSBERG [CHERRY VALLEY, NY]

14.III.40070 [March 14, 1970]

Allen,

I did like you said and telegram'd Leary's judge. And told Alan Watts and others.

Please do give Masa a call if you get a chance when you're out here. Any chance of visiting Kitkitdizze this summer or fall? I feel that getting our roots down, knowledges developed, in country regions, is really beautiful and essential right now. I'm away, March 29–April 26.

Movie with David is looking really solid now. Constructed well.

Love,

Gary

106. ALLEN GINSBERG [CHERRY VALLEY, NY]
     TO GARY SNYDER [NEVADA CITY, CA]

May 30, 1970

Gary:

In rush thru hundreds of letters returning to farm, will write later. Spring planting here and I've traveled so much so hard so tear gassed I want to stay here in one place as long as I can, finish Blake project type poems and find my own body rhythm outside of airplane drone in my skull.

All well I'm absolutely happy.

Love, more than ever,

Allen

107. ALLEN GINSBERG [CHERRY VALLEY, NY]
     TO GARY SNYDER [NEVADA CITY, CA]

August 24, 1970

Dear Gary:

Home on farm since mid-May, I'm finally catching up with masses of unanswered letters a year old, and cleaning desk.

Have been continuing organ practice and can now notate and play and sing melodies and chords simultaneous; so been setting new songs more elaborately than before. If you didn't receive the Blake record (and also *Indian Journals*) send me a card.

Wind-charger's now set up here on platform next to the ram house, with batteries and a solid state inverter set down below frost line in ram house, and wires leading to remote switch in house by radiophonotape machine units. And it all doesn't work.[134]

At least not in summer, we're told winter winds much more ample will provide plenty of electric. As it is the batteries just run down slower than before. We may have defective batteries. All these kinks to be ironed out in the next year, by then we'll have some workable system to produce 400 watts' worth—400-watt litebulbs. Using neon lights you get brighter illumination for 20 to 30 watts by the way, if electric's scarce. Meanwhile, if you're interested, you can run TV or minor electric equipment off car or golf cart batteries. I'll let you know what we work out.

I wake every morning totally depressed, 4 or 5 A.M., Leary and [John] Sinclair[135] in jail in my mind, the weight of sustaining the farm heavy in light of apparent continuing disintegration of social order. Vast garden crops coming in, and we'll have canned 100 cases of vegetables (corn peas string beans etc.) enough, really, for winter survival, I'm amazed to see—by the end of harvest. Great organic garden this year, third year of Gordon Ball's experience and study—also planted orchard of fruit trees and permanent strawberry and asparagus beds on hill above house.

I got $12 sleep bag and sleep out under stars in full moon now—stayed out for Perseid meteorite shower last week.

Not getting much literary writing done but now recently converting 4 A.M. depression energy raw consciousness of disaster into articulate notes in notebook at bedside, so it lightens my mind load and in a few months I'll know or be able to read back and see what's bothering me.

Ferlinghetti got invite 13 readings Australia next May so I said I'd go along (as I was invited) if the money was all right, and spend a month down under. Thence see Bodrubadur or Polynesia or Philip Whalen, return via India Persia take time. I think I need to go around the world

---

134. Ginsberg's farm in Cherry Valley had no electricity and here he mentions one in a series of attempts to create their own power.

135. John Sinclair. A Detroit poet and activist who was arrested and sentenced to 10 years in prison for giving an undercover agent two sticks of marijuana.

again (like pulling a chain—"I think I need to go to the bathroom again") . . .

Don Allen phone today said you were starting your house walls, beams and rafters and roof must be in? What's happening? In brief, send me a postcard.

The cities—I went to Yale Panther Rally May Day and saw Genet, he gave a great "commencement" speech which I got a copy of and prefaced for City Lights to publish, tear gassed there chanting *om a hum*. Then to Washington May 9 and tear gassed there singing plain *om*. Have been immersed here ever since, walking in woods and sleeping recovering from city shock—catching up with paperwork.

O! I got one psilocybin Mexican authentic mushroom (silk-smooth purplish cap) and ate it—with Maretta and others—tastes fine unlike peyote or any other preparation—absolutely easy, natural, not a trip, i.e. no departure from any normal custom, you just eat some food, soma-esque food, but basically just regular body food that tastes like ordinary Jap dried mushroom if you soak it halfway and chew it—found myriad tiny fish making ripples in the green backwater behind the beaver dam, frog sitting haunch in mud, head stuck out looking around the woods where we passed—walked six hours all over neighbor's hills and found old woods familiar and neighbor lake set in valley below reminiscent of Tolkien landscape. First such experience since 1967 and just about imperceptibly smooth transition from quotidian activity and percep-tions. So all's well there. Collecting fly agaric here as per Wasson's *Soma* book but won't try till I find expert.

Saw Sakya Lama last spring in Seattle—he said "Marijuana? O that's fine"—but hadn't tried LSD. Saw Trungpa Tulku and had long happy high talk, sang and chanted. He demonstrated proper *phat* sound—a "hike!" in back of throatskull like a soprano baby shriek, very lovely.

Maretta Greer here, back from street sadhu begging *sadhana* year in Rawalpindi—she wants to go back and settle in Ladakh. Very good shape, meditates and does mantra quietly all day like the Sakyapa[136] old man did, she also reads extensively now, got herself together quite neat, everyone remarks on her beauty and quiet demeanor, and she helps out here and there with gardening or canning or curry cooking—we take long silent walks in woods. Ray Bremser and wife and babe here almost half

---

136. Sakyapa. A major school of Tibetan Buddhism.

year. Peter strong and marvelously straight compared to last year—he don't drink smoke or speed—I don't smoke now also. Practically no sex also—all dem vegetables. OK luv, regards to Masa and kids. I hear you're overproducing your scheduled *Changes?* Well I guess we'll have to colonize the sun.

As ever

Allen

108. ALLEN GINSBERG [WASHINGTON, DC]
       TO GARY SNYDER [NEVADA CITY, CA]

October 12, 1970

Dear Gary:

Met an energetic Kundalini Baba Swami (Muktananda Paramahamsa) and began getting back to regular sitting an hour each morn—in fact spent four days sitting in room doing nothing all day but getting back into sitting. Finally. Am on way reading tour beginning Richmond, Virginia, and week in New Orleans.

That swami will be around Bay Area October 14–30 with Richard Alpert (Baba Ram Dass)—so if you're in town please do check him out—his people know of you. He'll be lecturing all over area. Nice Indian. OK.

Love

Allen

109. GARY SNYDER [NEVADA CITY, CA]
       TO ALLEN GINSBERG [CHERRY VALLEY, NY]

17.X [October 17, 1970]

Dear Allen,

Thanks for note on Kundalini Swami. Am still busy on house and will continue to be so until December. During the winter quarter (January–February–early March) I'll be at UC Riverside teaching; and then east for readings in mid-March mid-April month. In June, Masa and I are going to Japan for one month. I'm working on a book on Hokkaido (Japan) wilderness (with a photographer) Friends-of-the-Earth. After next June we will be quietly here, or out in nearby deserts and mountains.

House-warming party sometime early December. Ten of the people who camped and built the house here this summer are buying 117 acres adjoining our north border and will eventually have a small community there—in harmony with us. The wild grapes in this region are luxurious and flourishing, along water-courses; making jelly. And making manzanita cider a lot. Wrote three poems this summer. I guess your farm is all weather tight for the cold now.

Love,
Gary

110. ALLEN GINSBERG [CHERRY VALLEY, NY]
     TO GARY SNYDER [NEVADA CITY, CA]

[November 9, 1970]

Dear Gary:

Home after odd journey Virgin Islands (petroglyphs on St. John's Island 1000 AD Arawak, invaded by Caribes from South America menfolk kilt [killed] and Caribes married their women; then Columbus' first move getting water apparently was to kill a few hostile Caribes so's he could put ashore). Antigua poor—Bermuda 200 businessmen and Rev. Billy James Hargis and hardshell Rev. Carl Macintyre—New Orleans huge French Quarter bigger than North Beach Greenwich Village combined—Boston Tufts reading ending *Om* and five minutes quiet silence. I'm still sitting pleasurably one hour a day mornings mostly.

I'll probably be in California mid-April to mid-May (teach a few days at Davis College nearby Grass Valley so see you then). March April I'll be in and out of East so we'll probably cross paths.

I may go to Australia May–June and then spend time in Orient afterward so not impossible I can come to Japan while you're there if there's any reason. I thought of dawdling in Java and wandering islands toward India—or Hanoi—or China?—I dunno.

Things quiet on farm, Lafcadio here now too with Julius. Peter in good health and recovering from speed years with lovely girl Denise [Feliu] who works with him in fields and helps with his brothers. Maretta here, lonely. Gordon says hello.

I have all sorts of documents accumulated indicating (proving really) that CIA is responsible for opium traffic in S.E. Asia (wherefrom 83% world's illegal opium comes, not Turkey as mythologized).

Also doing a survey of repression of underground press for PEN Club, as they can prepare a "white paper" on U.S. Police State tendencies. Lots of paperwork. Started 30-page "Ecologue" (bucolic poesy about our pig "Don't Bite Me" now 100 lbs. and white and friendly) pigs are emotional. Peter's recent indulgence.

Visited [Louis] Zukofsky and played piano and sang, his wife sets his songs, and heard Charles Reznikoff read first time, clear eyed 1920s vignettes, city life.

Letter from Leary a little bombastic optimistic free but glad he's out, I suppose he got fed up.

[Jacques] Cousteau says 40% ocean life gone in the last 20 years! *NY Times* editorial says world's oceans be dead as Lake Erie by 2000. Nobody seems to take it literally. Enclosed Adirondacks overcrowding report.

I feel good, the sitting is peaceful privacy. A few little body *samadhis* but not much more spectacular so far as far as Kundalini fireworks.

Love to Masa,

Allen

[PS] Bolinas poet gang sounds interesting.

111.   GARY SNYDER [NEVADA CITY, CA]
       TO ALLEN GINSBERG [CHERRY VALLEY, NY]

                              12.XI.40070 [November 12, 1970]

Dear Allen,

Here's this SPEL ["Spel Against Demons"]; I thought you should see it. What do you think?

We had a good meeting with Kriyananda and got the by-laws altered to provide a definition of a hermitage; a limit on the number (48)—and a top population limit (of residents) at Ananda—of 50. He's a creep, but he can be dealt with step by step.

Living in the house, five workers still with us, doing the finishing of the interior. Will be reading in the spring, East Coast in mid-April. Studying (as much as I can) anthropology and Tibetan Buddhism; eating lots of venison.

Love,

Gary

23.XI [November 23, 1970]

Allen,

Here's a somewhat more accurate version of the "Spel"—a few changes. (Change: plowed under / to plowed back.) How does it strike you? (We're so happy working this land and being at this elevation.)

But I guess I'll have to join the fray in another month or so; much study I want to do, Tibetan, American Indian, Biology—I'll be East Coast reading March 9–April 17. Maybe you can come up here at the end of April? We'll all be here; a good chance. We're all learning Indian sign language now. Very elegant mudras.

Love
Gary

SPEL AGAINST DEMONS

The release of Demonic Energies in the name of
            the People
      must cease

Messing with blood sacrifice in the name of
            Nature
      must cease

The stifling self-indulgence in anger in the name of
            Freedom
      must cease

this is death to clarity
death to compassion

The man who has the soul of the wolf
knows the self-restraint
of the wolf

aimless executions and slaughterings
are not the work of wolves and eagles

but the work of hysterical sheep

The Demonic must be devoured!
Self-serving must be
            cut down
Anger must be
            plowed back
Fearlessness, humor, detachment, is power
Knowledge is the secret of Transformation!

Down with demonic killers who mouth revolutionary
slogans and muddy the flow of change, may they be
Bound by the Noose, and Instructed by the Diamond
Sword,
of ACHALA the Immovable, Lord of Wisdom, Lord of
Heat,
who is squint-eyed and whose face is terrible with
bare fangs, who wears on his crown a garland of severed
heads, clad in a tiger skin, he who turns Wrath to
Purified Accomplishment,

            whose powers are of lava,
        of magma, of deep rock strata, of gunpowder,
                and the Sun.

He who saves tortured intelligent demons and filth-eating
            hungry ghosts, his spel is,

NAMAH SAMANTAH VAJRANAM CHANDA
MAHAROSHANA SPHATAYA HUM TRAKA
HAM MAM

November 23, 1970

Dear Gary:

I guess we'll crisscross paths again, but anyway I'll be in San Francisco till early May probably. When you get final itinerary later, sketch it out. I'll be in California probably last three weeks of April.

Continuing to sit daily an hour, very reliable. How long each morn did you sit? 3–5 A.M.? in Japan. Oh well, when I see you I'll ask you about sitting.

The poem's sentiments I do approve of, but the image of "hysterical sheep" is an abstract one I think. "Stifling self indulgence in anger in the name of" is too long and generalized, as are many sentences lines 1–23. "must" may be too overused, can place the sentences as injunctions like, "Quit messing with Blood Sacrifice" or cease messing. "Must Cease" does sound like stylization/parody/usage of the revolutionary rhetorical device so maybe has a place.

From Knowledge on it's all OK. I think it'd be interesting to nail down the specifics (Weathermen? Panthers? Tribe Yak? Army Math Center? W. 11th St.? Hoffman? Rubin?) of blood sacrifice, self indulgence, etc. to be effective as poem would need images transplanted from explosions or cities to specify the release of demonic energies (trashing of libraries); blood sacrifice (accidental bombslaughter and cop death mistakes); self indulgence (use of creep mantras like pig).

Where'd you find get receive that mantra?

Maretta said "gee he's angry."

The idea of such Spel is important and "courageous" and I definitely approve despite the fact I get mad enuf to wanna see U.S.A. blown apart finally—but should be nailed harder down to fact.

I wrote Leary, *Nola Express*, and spoke at Buffalo recommending one hour daily sit on ass. But meanwhile the oceans be dead as Lake Erie by year 2000?

Love

Allen

114. GARY SNYDER [NEVADA CITY, CA]
     TO ALLEN GINSBERG [CHERRY VALLEY, NY]

30.XI.40070 [November 30, 1970]

Dear Allen,

You've seen by now the later version of "Spel" I sent you—to answer your objections briefly—I leave it abstract in the main part to touch on peoples' own leanings—too easy to pin it down to specific events—then everyone who wasn't there can say "I'm blameless."

Me myself I imagine shooting up pigs sometimes, so I must exorcise these things.

The poem is NOT against revolution, or deliberate and careful violence, but against the release of the Demonic. Which is a kind of self-indulgence; a believing that "because it's a human emergency karma can be set aside."

Images are not used, to allow Achala as an image to have the full stage. Achala = Fudo, the patron of yogins and *yamabushi*. I get this mantra as a *yamabushi*. It is also the mantra I gave "Smokey the Bear" reading him as a form of Achala (who in turn is a form of Vairochana).

"Spel" isn't, I think, as good as it might be, but the intention was genuinely magical and I referred back to Fudo several times in the writing of it. Ah well.

Kitkitdizze: Two people—Zach and Bruce—still with us, working, doing miscellaneous interior finishing. Great rains a week now. Today I was out strolling in the storm, saw two does, one four-point buck, just a few hundred yards away. Weather hasn't gone below freezing yet.

Did I tell you ten of our summer crew have gone together to buy 117 acres of land just north of our land, right on the border. I should say, nine of the summer people and the tenth is David Padwa who will build a little retreat there.

We didn't get to do any gardening—but did gather much manzanita berry for cider—wild grapes and ate up two deer this year. Very moving, the whole trip with the deer.

On January 29 I'm doing a one-man benefit in Berkeley for the Tibetan Meditation Center—Tarthang Tulku. They have Martin L. King High

Auditorium. Where will you be then? Any chance doing it together? A worthy cause!

Love,

Gary

and love to Maretta!

115. ALLEN GINSBERG [CHERRY VALLEY, NY]
     TO GARY SNYDER [NEVADA CITY, CA]

December 26, 1970

Dear Gary:

Lew Welch wrote he'd talked to you and wants to buy COP Inc. land. I had him and Phil Whalen in mind when I bought it actually, sort of a small poetry ashram, with idea of spending some time there myself on and off later years.

I don't have the Bald Mountain rules here. Can I give (as grant) Lew one third of the land, later give Philip one third of it, and keep a third for COP use? Or is that too many buildings? That may be. Hard to plan ahead decades, which this involves. What's your advice?

Should I send copy of "Spel" to Liberation News Service? They asked me to scout for poems desultorily. This way "Spel" be spread thru underground papers widely. It also fits with recent Bernardine Dohrn[137] manifesto review of misdirected violence and isolation of Weatherman, so it be useful.

I'll be at Davis College April 27–28 and thereafter be free so will visit Kitkitdizze. Great.

I still don't think hysterical sheep is accurate—tho admittedly I've seen few sheep—(I've never heard of sheep slaughtering and executing) maybe—hysterical two legged men or something mammal like that. Still the "Spel" is necessary so its alright magic, I do hereby approve. x [his mark]

Can't come January 29—going to wedding in Far Rockaway, Barbara Rubin marrying hip orthodox Jew with full ceremony.

Call me up collect when next you're at a phone. I'll be here till January

---

137. Bernardine Dohrn. The leader of the radical Weathermen group.

4 or 5, then in N.Y. for a week or more. We can figure out how to give Lew some land from COP so he can have his own territory. That way also he'll be able to use his few thousand savings to build with. I'm assuming that, as he wrote, the move is OK by you. I also have to OK it with Peter and trustees of COP.

I've seen Sonam Kazi here (in New York City) for about 12 hours steady talk and singing—helped translate one of his teacher Dudjom's *sadhanas* and learned new mudra (purification) and took *wang* for *Om A Hum Vajra Guru Padma Saddhi Hum*. He doesn't use *Omee a Hum*—just *Om A Hum*. I notated his wife's tune. He told me please spread the mantra, teach it, I said OK.

Maretta getting more helpful round house after Peter started screaming at her she wasn't a saint she was lazy.

OK, Love

Allen

116. GARY SNYDER [NEVADA CITY, CA]
      TO ALLEN GINSBERG [CHERRY VALLEY, NY]

31.XII.70 [December 31, 1970]

Giving land to Lew and Phil a beautiful idea, only problem perhaps a resistance from Bald Mt. Association to subdividing. What about giving land-use to Phil and Lew, with written promise of same for their lifetime (protecting interest in cabin they might build) and arrangement for them selling interest in house to us if they decide to leave for good? Also informally arranging that they pay share of taxes, but land ownership remains with COP.

I'll talk to Dick Werthimer about this and other possibilities. Also am or have or will phoned you—will plan to attend Davis reading and drive you up here when done!

Love,

Gary

PS Where can I get copy of Dohrn interview? Your thing in *Barb* on Leary precisely correct.

117. ALLEN GINSBERG [CHERRY VALLEY, NY]
     TO GARY SNYDER [NEVADA CITY, CA]

January 11, 1971

Dear Gary:

Enclosed copy of Dohrn Weatherpeople statement.

I haven't seen *Barb* piece, probably taken from interview in *New Orleans Nola Express*, I've sent for copies of original and'll send you when arrive.

Be sure to send copy of "Spel Against Demons" to Liberation News Service c/o Nina Saberoff—and one also to *Nola Express*, c/o Robert Head or send me a dozen. If you wanna send one to Leary—address Hotel Mediterranee, Room 23, Elle d'Jamilla, La Nadiaque, Alger, Algeria.

Yes, talk with Werthimer and see what can be done to give lifetime land occupancy guarantee to Lew [Welch] and Phil [Whalen]—though owning title would be the most secure-feeling I imagine. I'd like to reserve ultimate place for myself somewhere on land, with small garden if that's ever possible, but maybe giving entire piece to Lew and Phil would solve Bald Mt. commitments. I could forego my or COP title entirely, that is, I suppose, if necessary. I mean I'd like to make their possession secure for them. Ultimately I may dissolve COP as a burden. IRS is checking us out now, as they did Don Allen's Four Seasons [Foundation]. COP is built very securely legally all along, I think, so there should be no major pressure from government. But you never can tell, these days, etc. Anyway find out the options, and if possible talk to Lew too to explain technical necessities. Your arrangement outlined in letter not at all bad, probably workable.

Going to Detroit for three days raise money and court testify re jury selection for John Sinclair. Then back here for weeks.

Allen

118. GARY SNYDER [NEVADA CITY, CA]
     TO ALLEN GINSBERG [C/O CITY LIGHTS, SAN FRANCISCO]

[May 10, 1971]

Dear Allen:

Here also Lew's site-description and request. I cancelled the Japan trip
and book. A questionable project. So will be right here to look after you
if you come back again—please do—bring Lawrence [Ferlinghetti].

Love,

G.

EDITOR'S NOTE: *The above was attached to the following letter from
Gary Snyder to Dick Baker, which explains in detail the land association
agreement.*

Dear Dick,

In answer to your latest; yes, I do feel it would be appropriate for Ananda
to deliver whatever monies it realizes for the two incense cedar that were
felled into a Bald Mountain Association fund.

As for your ideas about buying Ananda out; it's a good idea, but not
entirely practical. At least at the moment it doesn't seem so to me.

Allen was here, and we had a meeting with Kriyananda and two
of his helpers; the meeting was quite cordial, and at that time I said
to Kriyananda that if he would allow the agreement to be changed to
lower the limits on population and structures, I might be able to vote
for allowing the craft shop, on the basis that the craft shop plans be sent
to us, with description in writing of what power-sources are intended,
what crafts would be practiced, how advertising and marketing would
take place, etc.

Kriyananda is loath to have any lowering of population levels, but I
personally would insist on that. He asked me, what would I suggest, and
I said I would think it over.

He invited Allen and me to attend a meeting of the Ananda Community (meetings to which he isn't going these days). Allen and I went,
and there were 21 or 22 people there: the meeting was presided over by a
person named John Novak, called "Jaya" and everyone present was asked
around the room what he had to say. When it came to us, I said I would

talk about the craft shop and then I read the agreement aloud. Everyone was shocked, somewhat apologetic, and all said they'd never realized that there were such limitations and responsibilities on their use. Some expressed full agreement with the intention and spirit of the agreement. This seems to be another case of Kriyananda's sloppiness, which is either devious or stupid, I'm not sure which.

They all agreed to meet at 3 P.M. the following Friday (May 7) and walk out their own land-boundaries, and begin to formulate some land-use policies in accord with the agreement. I couldn't go, but at 3 P.M. my right-hand man, Zac Reisner, went up there to join the walk with them. Nobody was there at 3. Zac rounded them up, a few, and "Jaya," who claimed to know where the corners were, said he would join them later, but never showed up. No one had a compass, so Zac showed them what a compass was, and how you walk a line with it. Nobody had ever seen a map of the area before, or had heard of the geodetic survey quads, it seems. On walking the line, they noticed that the boundary on the north is only three feet from the corner of the craft-shop, and runs right through somebody's geodesic dome. A large permanent tipi is well over in BLM [Bureau of Land Management].

Allen and I went on a rather thorough walk, and noticed the following (this was on a different day than the boundary walk).

Geodesic domes—7
Tents and tipis—15
Wooden hermitage structures—9
Trailers—8
This gives a total of 39 domiciles.

Now, here's what I would tentatively propose: We change the agreement to read, on

POPULATION: 5 residents per 10 acres.
Giving Ananda a total of 30, giving us each about 12.
HOUSES: 1 single-family dwelling per 8 acres (or equivalents)
Giving Ananda a total of 7, giving us each 3.
HERMITAGES: I would say 3 hermitages equals 1 single-family dwelling. From what I've seen of his hermitages and what sort of presence they make in the woods.

In the case of Ananda, I'd say his complex of Temple Dome plus office equals 1 single-family dwelling, and the Commons plus kitchen equals another single-family dwelling. Subtract 6, then, from 21, which would be the total number of hermitages for Ananda. The Craft Shop, if allowed, would be the equal of another single-family dwelling, so subtract another 3 hermitages. This leaves Ananda with 12 hermitages.

Since they have 9 hermitage structures, and 3 more domes (Kriyananda's, Mr. Hanl's, and a third one going up) that gives us 12. Which is exactly the limit I propose. NO MORE BUILDINGS. This is lenient, as those geodesic domes of Kriyananda's and Hanl's, and the new one, with refrigerator, propane, generator, stove, and whatever, would qualify as single-family dwellings in most places.

That leaves us with the problem of 15 tents and tipis, and 8 trailers. Some of those tipis would qualify as permanent structure hermitages.

If Kriyananda can't accept these limits, it would seem to me his plans are truly at variance with the spirit in which we all bought this land together, and he indeed should move elsewhere and prepare to sell his share out. I suspect some of the residents of the retreat might agree.

As for his guest program, he should be able to work it out in terms of what already exists. As it is, the total-land-use limit of two persons per acre (a total of 120, for him) is already threatened by his Sunday Church crowds, which approach 200 he says. That's a lot of cars on the road.

Of course if Kriyananda and his people lived more sensibly—didn't heat with oil, cook on propane, heat their domes on nice warm days, run their refrigerators during the cool season, etc., they'd have far less need for cash, and might not need a Craft Shop so much. Surrounded by thousands of square miles of forest land with down dead wood, they are dependent on fossil fuels. Ugh.

Allen has gone back to San Francisco; yesterday we had a magical visit from David Monongye, a Hopi Elder, who sang for us and blessed the house and land. Enough.

Love,

Gary

EDITOR'S NOTE: *On May 23, 1971, while Lew Welch was staying with Gary Snyder on his land, he suffered a severe bout of depression. Welch disappeared into the woods with a gun, leaving only a farewell note behind. His body has never been discovered.*

119. GARY SNYDER [NEVADA CITY, CA]
      TO ALLEN GINSBERG [1801 WOOLSEY, BERKELEY, CA]

[June 7, 1971]

Dear Allen,

Lew is supposedly alive—tho not known where—word came thru Sheriff's office. Keep an eye out in the city. Maybe he's monstrously drinking.

G.

120. ALLEN GINSBERG [BERKELEY, CA] TO GARY SNYDER [NEVADA CITY, CA]

June 28, 1971

Dear Gary and Masa:

I'm still wrapp'd up in brown tapes—living in Berkeley. Should I not send Lew Welch his grand? but where? Your poem on Coyote/Ananda gets better with the weeks. I'll come up again before I go. Saw Phil with Don Allen at phone and spent day in Bolinas—he's in charming and healthy mind, strong—no worry. I love you as always. I been perfecting Vajra Guru tune and voice.

Love,

Allen

121. GARY SNYDER [NEVADA CITY, CA] TO ALLEN GINSBERG [BERKELEY, CA]

6.VII [July 6, 1971]

Dear Allen,

Since we don't know where Lew is, and he isn't doing any building, I don't see how you can send him a check. The only evidence we have that he's alive even is the bank's word he was in there.

Exquisite hot clear days now. Too many visitors over the 4th—hoping for a few quiet weeks of work and then a High Sierra trip.

I've had word from Bob Greensfelder[138] that you are wondering about trading land or something. If you decide you don't need this land, I

---

138. Bob Greensfelder. A classmate of Snyder's at Reed College.

myself—or Dick Baker and me together—would just as soon buy your shares and thus keep things fairly quiet at least for the time. But my fond hope is you'll want to build your secret retreat or library or whatever up here. You should spend a few weeks here and get into this area. The surface is not romantic or postcardy-pretty, but there is a lot beneath the surface. Takes time.

Blessings

Gary

122. GARY SNYDER [KITKITDIZZE, ALLEGHENY STAR ROUTE, NEVADA CITY, CA]
TO ALLEN GINSBERG [C/O CITY LIGHTS, SAN FRANCISCO]

17.IX [September 17, 1971]

Hail!

We had a forest fire nearby after you left—14 acres burned—haloes and wreaths of Fudo Flame as we stood Smokey the Bear–wise in the path of the fire with our shovels and duff-hoes digging fire-trails til the heat would actually make us flee, and start digging again. It was on our neighbors', the We'pa's,[139] land. After it's all over it doesn't look so bad—good thing, probably, took out a lot of slash, and didn't kill more large trees at all.

I write to suggest that if the COP has funds and wishes, it might consider a little grant to Gisen Asai. I came to understand in talking with him that his organization gave him travel funds to and fro Japan, and an absolute minimum living expense. He is somewhat disappointed, and feels rather constrained, wishing to be able to travel more freely in the U.S. A few hundred dollars even would help. I myself am going to make special efforts to aid him and take him places—but not, after all, on three-week poetry reading tour, as ultimately too tiresome—we'll go together in December to see Sasaki Joshu Roshi in L.A.—and maybe to see Chögyam Trungpa[140] together—etc.

Week of September 20–27 I'll be in Bay Area staying at Greensfelder's

---

139. We'pa. A Nisenan (Southern Maidu) word for "coyote," the original people of the area.

140. Chögyam Trungpa. The Tibetan Buddhist teacher who became Allen Ginsberg's spiritual teacher in the years that followed.

in Mill Valley and working with Zach Stewart on enclosed vigil at Grace Cathedral. I don't have any idea where you are.

Also I wonder if Bonnie Crown at the Asia Foundation might be able to give Gisen a little help. I'll talk to him next week and see if he might be willing to give a talk on Rinzai Zen or something if we went off to New York together.

Fall winds blow thru the pines. The well-water stays cold and sweet though the air hot and dry. A sense of cooling-from-here. A doe was seen down in the meadow by the *zendo*.

Reading Yampolsky's translation of *Zen Master Hakuin: Selected Writings*, just out from Columbia. It is very clarifying and fresh and helpful for me; swept away a lot of cobwebs; returned me in a way to my own best and central practice . . . that of Zen, "Seeing into your own nature." Hakuin is delightful, not only blunt and energetic, but grandmotherly and with freaky tastes sometimes.

Love,

G.

123. GARY SNYDER [NEVADA CITY, CA]
     TO ALLEN GINSBERG [C/O CITY LIGHTS, SAN FRANCISCO]

29.X.71 [October 29, 1971]

Dear Allen,

The great meadow west of here, and adjoining woods, are up for sale by the owners, Brophy. They came to Richard's yesterday. They would prefer to sell to us non-developers—but must sell it soon (22 heirs are waiting for their bread). So Richard Sisto is to be secretary of an effort to get some people together—several groups, or various individuals—to buy it. 197.6 acres in two parcels—one 137.6 acres; one 60 acres—they are asking $250 per acre which is a fine price.

We are contacting you, Tarthang Tulku, the Zen Center (some people there want country land)—and some people Richard knows, first. If you have any interest in this write Richard direct c/o Bodhi hermitage. I'm hoping to go in with Don Dachtler[141] (the schoolteacher) for 10 acres of

---

141. Don Dachtler. Schoolteacher on San Juan Ridge and graduate in philosophy from UC Davis.

prime central meadow—for horse and cow grazing, later. Total asking price is $50,000 we can still bargain. How much down not set.

Doing some good work on *Mountains and Rivers*. Tanning a beautiful little ringtail pelt—found it killed by car on Highway 49. Very rare creature now. I hope this finds you well; we are having clear, freezing, lovely fall days. Masa's two sisters, Reiko and Setsuko, are with us. The downward course of empire shows no change—but I think a lot of China these days. Chinese knew/know how to handle both power and quiet.

Hum!

Gary

124. ALLEN GINSBERG [SAN FRANCISCO]
       TO GARY SNYDER [NEVADA CITY, CA]

February 26, 1972

Dear Gary:

Gave musical at Zen Center this last week with four musicians (flute, cello, bass, and guitar) and did try improvising "Big Wheel Blues" (Blues = *Dukkha*?)[142] went on for 20–25 minutes covering the list I copied from your books including Wood Fish—began with Four Noble Truths and exfoliated outward including 8 Path 12 Chain 5 Klephas 5 Choudhas 6 Fields of Consciousness 6 Paramitas 5 Commandments 4 Vows and complicated EKO's. Some verses were apt, some awkward, but always interesting because everyone including myself was curious what rhyme next. Baker Roshi says they'll transcribe it for *Wind Bell* maybe. Three-line blues form used there probably not as economical as a quatrain'd be.

Enclosed check I sent Ginny Baker for land tax pay. I'll be back from Australia by April 1 or 2 if there's anything wrong with this form of check. So send me a postcard if you want different way of tax pay.

Leave tomorrow for Hawaii, Fiji a week and Australia—in case of non-existent emergency instructions: c/o Louis van Eyssen, Adelaide, Australia. March 5–30.

Wrote new "Don't Smoke Don't Smoke oh please oh please dope dope don't smoke don't smoke" quatrains, funny gravel-voiced lyric for A-major bottleneck guitar.

---

142. *Dukkha*. Suffering.

Love to Masa and all the swamis—*Om shalom*
Allen
[PS] Greensfelder phoned and offered to loan or advance me money for
the land purchase.

125. GARY SNYDER [NEVADA CITY, CA]
     TO ALLEN GINSBERG [C/O CITY LIGHTS, SAN FRANCISCO]

4.III.72 [March 4, 1972]
Dear Allen,
If you are thinking of building something next (the following) summer,
and would like to talk with our chief carpenter, contact Bruce Boyd. He
would like to talk design, scheduling, and financing with you soon as
possible. He wouldn't be dirt cheap—I'm not sure how much—but as a
boss and organizer, worth it. Just planted 4 fruit trees 2 apples, 2 cherries.
And leave, tomorrow, for the South.
    March 6–12 Redlands, CA
    March 13–17 Pennsylvania and Kansas
    March 19–29 Pomona, Mohave Desert, Death Valley (driving with
Masa and kids)
    April 1—onward here at Kitkitdizze
    late June—to Japan
    mid-August—back here.
    Chang's book on Avatamsaka helps me comprehend organic evolu-
tion, "a rimless net rolling forward on the energy of the natural karma
of all sentient beings."
    Also (from the Samantabhadra's Vows section of the sutra) "Why
should we cherish all sentient beings? Because sentient beings are the
roots of the tree of Bodhi. The bodhisattvas and Buddhas are the flowers
and fruits, compassion is the water for the roots."
    Hum
    Gary

126. ALLEN GINSBERG [ADELAIDE, AUSTRALIA]
     TO GARY SNYDER [NEVADA CITY, CA]

March 16, 1972

Dear Gary:
Itinerary April 1–7 San Francisco. April 7—maybe Alaska. April 12–25
reading tour. April 25—New York City.
   Your note reached me down under. When I get back I'll estimate $ and
plan with Bruce. Probably plan something modest, and expandable.
   Made contact with aboriginal songmen through university here, and
by including them in my poetry readings here have learned a little about
their chanting forms ("Into the whirlwind, one after one, the boys running") (*Wallpangka Tjarpama Ngana Ngalili*) with carved "song sticks"
like foot-long batons keeping time—repeat verse chanted eight or ten
times, then on to another of how many thousand? linked verses?
   Aborigine position here even more dreadful clear than U.S. Indians—
all their songs are histories of the landscape going back to creation of rocks
and hills when spirits of ancestors broke thru the flat plains to create forms
in "eternal dreaming time." Aborigine song men, big fat old baby eyed
happy giggly old friends, down in Adelaide a couple weeks, paint bodies and dance like kangaroos with cracks of big bottoms shown forth as
makeshift bathing suits are thumbed down for comfort dancing. Doing a
benefit reading/chanting with them tonight in poor section of town where
dislocated drunk aborigines hang around—Port Adelaide Town Hall.
   Voznesensky really in soul—maybe we someday read together N.Y.
Moscow or Paris. Leaving meet Voznesensky, read in Melbourne and
Sydney and then hope with Voznesensky and Ferlinghetti to go to Ayers
Rock Central Australia petroglyphs on this giant pink sun lit mountain
one single rock 5 miles long 1,000 feet high—central heart sacred place
in middle of desert in middle of giant continent isle. It is some kinda
prehistoric science fiction.
   Land here $50 an acre rich farmland near ocean with water, giant roll-
ing fields with eucalypt like Tamalpais grassy breasts—vast meadows,
climate and feel like California Mill Valley. If there weren't such tough
white karma I'd sell m'lot and emigrate and rusticate by the southern
oceanside.

Sitting an hour a day, before hotel telephone begins ringing local TV and newspaper longhairs. Taped some aborigine song on my new tiny Sony.

Love
Allen

127. ALLEN GINSBERG [NEW YORK] TO GARY SNYDER [NEVADA CITY, CA]

April 27, 1972

Hello May Day—Gary, Joel, Bruce:
Returned home yesterday not had chance to read and answer mail.

Gary, see you in Denver or Boulder May 5, 6. I'll stay on with Trungpa a week maybe.

Bruce, thanks for letter and drawing. I'll write on return from Boulder—must take accounts then and make decisions. All my money still tied up in recording and no contract signed yet.

Allen
[PS] I learned some aboriginal music and have song sticks.

128. GARY SNYDER [UPPSALA, SWEDEN] TO ALLEN GINSBERG [NEW YORK]

[June 19, 1972]

Dear Allen,
The conference was full of groups and people who came to argue over the spoils, not to quit spoiling. But David Padwa—Jack Loeffler—[Michael] McClure—Sterling Bunnell—and Indians—Darryl Wilson—Fred Coyote—David Monongye—others, we all came to some senses of agreement, and what can yet be done. Where will you be in October? Can you join a three- or four-day work-meeting to talk of what can be done, a small number of us?

I'm at Reidar Ekner's house in the country outside Uppsala. He's a poet, translator, professor, sends you his regards, 43—wiry—built his own house—buxom juicy young woman living with him—writes ancient poem of world soils and winds. Now I fly via Paris and Moscow to Japan.

Gary

129. ALLEN GINSBERG [CHERRY VALLEY, NY]
TO GARY SNYDER [NEVADA CITY, CA]

July 22, 1972

Dear Gary:

Thanks for report from Sweden. I left Boulder late May with Tsultrim [Allione] nun and drove north thru Wind River reservation Wyoming to Grand Tetons, thence thru Yellowstone U.S. flagged Old Faithful—thin earth crust weird infernal gasses and limestone beards dripping off rock. Then north to Bozeman, improvised 15-minute dharma-chakra[143] (Blues form) (Samsara = Blues). Then bypassing Butte, to Missoula, saw your Round River group and met Bob Curry, we all picnicked together up in their Bitterroot Mountain Camp—beautiful place Bitterroot Valley if you ever go back there. Then drove north to Glacier Park and approached holy Chief Mountain (fasting history) on Canada border. Then back to Butte and spent nite there in company of young Cassady disciple now working in Anaconda Pit who took me on 3 A.M. joyride down in copper pit in 100-ton stolen dump truck. "This load courtesy phantom driver" he radioed in at dawn, and we ran from the truck-parking lot and sped away in his car as sun rose over desolate landscape. Butte a study in terminal industrial mining cancer, wrote huge poem like our 1945 [*sic?* 1965?] Northwest trip one or two paragraphs a day. Then to Denver, stopping at Tetons for acid trip 10,000 feet up empty clouds silently shadowing snow fields—like sitting yogi in snow upper left hand mountain of a tanka[144]—saying *ah!* sub-vocally. *A ah sha sa ma ha!*—still at that. Then to Boulder, reread *On [the] Road* and finished *Visions of Cody*. Then Santa Fe a week with Nanao and Baghavan Das and Ram Dass and Tsultrim and Trungpa Chögyam visiting all in one house one day, singing and snapping photos. Then to N.Y. and Florida Miami Beach convention. Mixed with "Senior Citizens," had a "generation marriage party," and sat on convention floor for McGovern nomination.

All quiet in Miami except for Dostoyevskian snit-hassles between vicious zippies with young strength and tired yippies wanting to write books—instant karma. Now back at Cherry Valley, out of money, so couldn't go in on land purchase and had to bow out, sorry I kept your neighbors hung up so long.

---

143. Dharma-chakra. Buddhist wheel of teaching.
144. Tanka. Buddhist scroll painting usually hung near a shrine.

Stay here, hospital hernia operation August 3–8, then perhaps go say "*Ah*" Miami Beach keep peace Republican convention time. Working on many texts especially Poesy '66–'72 so will lay low here till fall. I have some reading dates already set up October, some with my father. If I am delivered West Coast I'll stop in.

I feel more pessimistic worse about my own role flying around exhausting gas.

Love

Allen

130. ALLEN GINSBERG [NEW YORK]
      TO GARY SNYDER [NEVADA CITY, CA]

September 11, 1972

Dear Gary:

Dave McReynolds of *Liberation* magazine asked me to write up one paragraph urging youth vote to McGovern, as not only the hack Democratic politicians, but also the political/anarcho left seems to be paralyzed and apathetic in the election activity. [. . .]

Nanao is here, we sit together an hour each morning. I've been doing McGovern benefits all over N.Y. colleges so he's been coming along and chanting Prajnaparamita. Decided to stay in city and work on the election insteada going upstate with him.

Finishing proofs of *The Fall of America*, poems 1965–1971 unpublished. Out in December for Xmas. I am now broke and in debt sorta happily after years of prosperity. I got ruined (absolutely ruined) by the Dylan record.[145] I'll go out and give a few readings in Kansas and Texas. But I feel lousier and lousier flying planes around in the middle of Nixon's smog prosperity to read poetry. Really maybe this spring do some cross-country walking insteada university readings.

I'll be flying to Boulder read a few schools November for Karma Dzong Meditation Center.

---

145. Ginsberg had paid for the studio recording of some of his own songs himself. Dylan played guitar on a few of the songs, but would not allow Allen to use his name and as a result no commercial recording company would handle it.

Nanao stuck in New York City with me, but the advantage is he's seeing the city actively, Brooklyn Bridge, museums, Con Ed smokestacks and all. I have a nice little meditation room fixed up in my apartment. So he's in there.

Peter and his girl Denise working out of local reform Democratic McGovern HQ. I have my head full of Vietnam nightmare electronic war statistics. I started really reading pamphlets and books—it's totally neo-nazi science fiction remote control police state crap, absolutely disgusting and I can't stand the idea of being comfortable in U.S. anymore, to the extent that comfort is externally socially nourished.

Love to you
Allen

131. ALLEN GINSBERG [BIRMINGHAM, AL]
     TO GARY SNYDER [NEVADA CITY, CA]

September 30, 1972

Dear Gary:
I am still burning oil, to Birmingham (and Tampa Fla) benefit Black Farm Project in Selma, and McGovern benefit in Park. Back in New York see Nanao October 4, and several McGovern benefits NYU, Columbia, etc. colleges in New York for vote to end automated electronic battlefield already "neo-nazi" (indifferent to mass murder pain) in quality. Alas Nixon sleepwalk victory hypnosis! Sitting regularly solid an hour a day! You helping McGovern??? I will. Left paralyzed! I won't fly out on tour this spring, a bus is a plus, a plane gives me pain.

Love
Allen

22.X.72 [October 22, 1972]

Dear Allen,

Just back from Utah dumb debate—nobody knew anything—and used delaying and diverting tactics so I couldn't make a clear statement of the situation—Energy, Politics in the '70s and '80s. Protein Politics in the '90s—I fear.

Read: John Holdren and Philip Herrea, *Energy [: A Crisis in Power]* (Sierra Club paperback) for objective and sensible assessment of the problems.

Howard T. Odum *Environment, Power and Society* (Wiley) for incredible theoretical comprehension—adamantine vocabulary—insights and facts.

I'm about to launch some sort of non-profit organization to handle various community projects—educational and cooperative—first off, for the building of the new school district school organized a group (my old house workers) "The Cherokee Labor Brigade" trying to get legal contractors' status now—sure would like to talk to you for advice. You come this way this winter? Join us for quiet winter days reading and meditation?

Zach Stewart and co. have done heavy duty labor getting the new school plans of a sane order—and under the motto "Serve the People" will start construction next spring if all goes well.

I'd do McGovern stumping if I was closer to town I guess. Starting November 1 I can combine readings at college with political pitch.

. . . but what I'm learning is how politics works. From yonder debate I realized I'm not ready to be aggressive enough at the right times. Is that what you have to do? Be on the lookout for "dirty tricks"?

How's Nanao taking New York City I wonder?

The Great Basin: Rain on the sagebrush / Home from Utah / misty full moon.

Picked and ate boletus mushroom (made me sick; nobody else—maybe I'm mushroom-sensitive).

I THINK: Four more years of Nixon let him be at the top while across the land we quietly move in on local government—"Grass Roots" if not too far fetched.

G.

133. GARY SNYDER [VIRGINIA]
     TO ALLEN GINSBERG AND NANAO SAKAKI [NEW YORK]

[November 14, 1972]

Allen, Nanao,
I stayed at Peter (Cohen) Coyote's farm. He said Nanao or both of you
would be very welcome—close to New York. Nanao would like it. Turkey
Ridge Farm, Mt. Bethel, Penn. Bus from New York City to Portland,
Penn. Seventeen people—good work. And now, westward and home.
    Gary

134. ALLEN GINSBERG [WASHINGTON, DC]
     TO GARY SNYDER [NEVADA CITY, CA]

November 25, 1972

Dear Gary:
Here in D.C. spooking the C.I.A. again, parties, reading at Smithsonian,
with Nanao. Rennie Davis, friend of pacifist [Dave] Dellinger, went thru
30-day water fast in Miami this year, is here sitting meditation with me
and Nanao. He has my pillows (*zafu*).[146] I gave him Kitkitdizze address,
he may show up there, please welcome him and show him camping place
if you're at hand. He may help build cabin. Really a learned politics activist all decade, now with purification (fast) experience a graceful soul. We
all been sitting and chanting Prajnaparamita all over Washington D.C.
Peter Orlovsky here too.
    Love
    Allen

135. GARY SNYDER [NEVADA CITY, CA] TO ALLEN GINSBERG [NEW YORK]

[December 11, 1972]

Dear Allen,
Here's your tax bill! Rennie Davis is welcome, but as you can see this
is no season for camping. When will you join us for zazen, walks, and
magick?

---

146. *Zafu.* Pillows used for sitting on during meditation practice.

EDITOR'S NOTE: *The above note was written on the bottom of a general letter about property taxes that Snyder sent to the members of the Bald Mountain Association. In part that letter reads as follows.*

Dear Bald Mountain Associates:

[. . .] For those of you not living here, you may be interested to know that in this recent cold spell the temperature has gone down as low as 8° F. and for five days has not gone above freezing all day. Snow is 13" right now. The sky is blue, the sun bright, and the woods criss-crossed with deer and black-tailed-hare tracks. The last section of road coming up the hill is not possible without 4-wheel drive. With 4-wheel drive plus chains we can break trail in this snow on roads where no car has gone yet. The ice on the pond is five inches thick. The cats stay out all night and suffer no harm: they have their winter coats. It feels good.

Yr Obd't Srvnt

Gary

136. ALLEN GINSBERG [CHERRY VALLEY, NY]
     TO GARY SNYDER [NEVADA CITY, CA]

December 29, 1972

Dear Gary:

Enclosed check for COP Inc. taxes on land. I have been up on farm here a week and half alone, snow all round a foot thick—everybody else gone to chase their lives so I'm left to guard the snow wastes for a couple months. Except for trip to New York read with Chögyam Trungpa at Columbia two weeks from now, I don't have reason to leave here for over 12 hours till late February, so I will try to stay put, alone as much as possible. First time in years nobody round. Peter's Denise has organized solid jazzy all-girl rock band, and Peter's enjoying New York City.

I saw Dudjom Rinpoche and renewed refuges and vows with formal ceremony with "His Holiness" and Sonam [Kazi] and Tsede [Kayi]—they kept him pretty much under wraps so I didn't get a chance to exchange any words with him except "Kalimpong" he said remembering previous meeting 1963—prompted by Tsede Kayi.

Rennie Davis really thoughtful efficient great maha anti-war bodhisattva now into first meditation (with me and Nanao, I gave Rennie my sitting pillow set—*zafus*). I told him to use my land as he can—it might profit you to put him up if its cold outside as he knows more history than almost anyone we've often met. U.S. history the last 10 years—anyway I hope you can help him in his *sadhana*. As he has been a leader of national counterculture politics community he would profit both from Buddhist view and We'pa communal grass roots—also he can work.

I invited him to build cabin if he liked the woods' looks. Well, you'll see him and size him up. I don't know when he'll show up.

Finished writing preface for Edward Marshall's selected poems, never published—and Kerouac's [*Visions of*] *Cody* is out, if one hasn't been sent you I'll send one, let me know. I wrote lyric preface to that too. Just received gargantuan big-little book, *Fall of America* poems 65–71 from City Lights also—and Bixby Canyon poem from Gotham Book Mart [*Bixby Canyon Ocean Path Word Breeze*] did you receive? Lotsa books coming out.

Saw *Caterpillar* your "Indian Notes"—terrific now that trip is really documented cubist! Peter also has a bunch of notes, I'll get after him to publish that! Lots of details in your papers that I had forgot—the name of hatha yogi at Shivananda Ashram, etc.

Nanao on phone says Philip Whalen be made sensei[147] sometime January or February? I figure on going by train hopefully Chicago—L.A. in May and then spend some time West Coast May–June.

Sitting still an hour a day, writing little poems, and re-beginning Milarepa and Chang book with more technical understanding.

Peter Orlovsky now cotton clad like Mila in serious white cold snows in New York City and here—he goes around hours outside impervious to cold in tee-shirt with war bomb statistics silk-screened on front and back.

Ed Hermit [Urich] says we should all write to our senators and especially congressmen before Congress starts requesting legislative action to curb bombing end war. They do count letters—if they get a lot of letters, it counts.

Maybe We'pa could do it as a small project—one swift letter each, or one letter, short paragraph, signed by all We'pa folk as local voters—if all We'pa acted, it would probably outweigh all other mail on subject which our Congressman receives—worth the hour's effort.

---

147. Sensei. In Buddhism, this denotes an ordained teacher below the rank of roshi.

I definitely want to go to Hanoi now. Imagine Joan Baez there under-going witness that holocaust!

Love to you, Masa, Gen, Kai,

Allen

137. GARY SNYDER [NEVADA CITY, CA]
      TO ALLEN GINSBERG [CHERRY VALLEY, NY]

                                          8.I.(73) [January 8, 1973]
Dear Allen,

The snow doth fall and we bound in and out in our 4-wheel drive Jeep truck thru all weathers. Beast-tracks cross-cross . . .

Sure, whenever Rennie Davis shows up we'll fix him with whatever he needs.

Dick and Ginny Baker were here for two days. They were given a dismantled little temple in Japan—Ginny's parents' money sending it via freighter and truck to this land, along with three Japanese carpen-ters—will be erected in June, probably on the oak knoll—same time, Cherokee Brigade will be setting up camp on We'pa land just north, to build the grade-school anew—and other builders underway—anything Davis does will have to be on his own in that local energies are all focused on the school project this season.

Yesterday whetted my knife and totally sliced and divided the body of a young male deer, shot by a novice fellow up the ridge who didn't know the cutting-up procedure—a real *chöd* meditation out in the cold, seeing myself cutting up myself and offering it away—cold fingers.

There is an air letter already addressed to go. Hisao wants the reference to your visit with E.P. [Ezra Pound]—he's writing something on Pound for Japan. I don't have any *Evergreen Review*s here anymore.

Thanks for tax check.

And will write on bombing—T. [Thomas] Parkinson put together sharp-stated opposition to bombing—for *New York Times*—I got signed onto that too. And am enjoying evening readings of the old Chinese Zen masters lives, again. Zen, special or unique aspect, emphasis on human-being teaching, and teaching via actual anecdotes of little *Nirvanakayas* in action—rather than big speculative sutra or archetypal ceremony . . . "After Niu-t'ou heard the teaching of Zen he gave up

sitting all day in his cave and carried 300 bushels of rice to feed people
thru a famine."

Love,

Gary

138. GARY SNYDER [NEVADA CITY, CA]
      TO ALLEN GINSBERG [CHERRY VALLEY, NY]

                                    Valentine's [February 14, 1973]

Dear Allen,

I heard you fell, slipped, on ice and broke your leg? True? And if so, will
you soon be well, and where are you resting? Writing on rainy days—wet
woods (am putting information together for the next study group meeting, this Saturday).

I didn't get to Philip's ordination because I got flu and boil on my
leg—and it got too troublesome. Now I'm OK. I hear from Don Allen
that [Robert] Duncan came!

Nanao was here for several days and we spoke much of his Suwa-no-se
work. Your letter to Yamaha is delightful—As he (I) say, the "Suwa-no-se"
type issue will be with us the rest of this century. We might as well figure
out a non-paranoid way to work at it effectively and enlightenedly.

Masa and I plan to make this main house more and more into a *zendo*,
library, and central kitchen. We'll build a little sleeping house to have for
ourselves. If you want to build up here you could do it really simply—i.e.
no kitchen, no running water, no bath etc. required because the main
house will be available to you. Did I say, pond was backhoe'd for us this
fall—half size of yours—nice for summer gardens.

April I go to Montana and spend three weeks with the Round River
people.

Speaking of patriarchs (your *Ocean Breeze* [*Bixby Canyon Ocean
Path Word Breeze*]. Thank you! Remember hearing it around the fire
one night—full of botanical haiku flowing and multitude of precise true
images). Just finished reading Chang Ching-Yuan's volume of translations from *The Transmission of the Lamp* (original teachings of Ch'an).
What a high period! 620–980 AD / such spirit of inquiry! Such detachment! C. M. Ch'en (yogi) is in California now.

Gary

139. ALLEN GINSBERG [SCOTLAND] TO GARY SNYDER [NEVADA CITY, CA]

August 14, 1973

Dear Gary:

Went with [Scott Eden] walking—climbing young poet to Iona Abbey where Christianity and Book of Kells was created for all England. Eden (25 [years old]) has maps and guide books of trails and read John Muir and has all your books too. Iona peaceful magic isle.

Love

Allen Ginsberg

140. ALLEN GINSBERG [CHERRY VALLEY, NY]
      TO GARY SNYDER [NEVADA CITY, CA]

September 1, 1973. Back from England two weeks.

Dear Gary:

Noisy beets boiling in the pressure cooker
Gas mantle mirrored white gold in the window
Answering letters September first midnight.

Chögyam Trungpa asked me, Ram Dass, and Baghavan Das participate in Buddha dharma-chakra effort Boston October 26–28. If you feel like cross-country plane trip to joining we have poetry reading they'll pay fare, etc. I've written Phil too, same invitation. We three could do reading—just an idea note,

Allen

141. GARY SNYDER [NEVADA CITY, CA]
      TO ALLEN GINSBERG [CHERRY VALLEY, NY]

7.IX.40073 [September 7, 1973]

Dear Allen,

Welcome back to Turtle Island with its charming chakras.

Dream Poem
he didn't go so much to the south
as to the west

following the hills
beating the bad,
greeting the good.

I can't go east until after Hallowe'en. Had a fine, robust, summer and learned more about love! from Masa, who is incredible.

Gary

142. GARY SNYDER [NEVADA CITY, CA]
      TO ALLEN GINSBERG [CHERRY VALLEY, NY]

[September 20, 1973]

Dear Allen,
No chance of going east in October. Tho go I must in November—read at YMHA day before Thanksgiving—where will you be then? Farm? Now's a good time to start moving on your cabin.

First clouds, wind-puffs
bring faint rain
hope smell—
Squirrel in the chickencoop
gobbling grain.

Gary

143. ALLEN GINSBERG [CRYSTAL SPRINGS INN, TETON VILLAGE, WY]
      TO GARY SNYDER AND OTHERS [NEVADA CITY, CA]

September 23, 1973

Dear Dick, Ginny, Gary, Werthimer, and Kriyananda:
I'm in semi-retreat sitting 10 hours a day with Chögyam Trungpa's group, so am answering in this form in hope that my letter can be submitted to all Bald Mountain Associates on October 3. Please allow Gary to make use of my proxy vote. I will be still sitting or in Buddhist seminar all fall.

Several items of business: I expect to transfer land title from Committee on Poetry Inc. to my own name, purchasing the land from COP Inc., as it will have easier use this way. I think trustees originally preferred to have the land in personal name rather than corporate. COP Inc. trustees now agree.

Secondly, I plan to build a shelter/hermitage on the land, below the meadow on spot known to most of trustees, where meadow meets wooded hill bordering on We'pa land—perched on downslope amid rocks and trees hid from meadow. Philip Whalen, Bruce Boyd, and myself have conferred on the construction so that it be appropriate to site. When plan is completed for next summer a copy will be circulated for approval of Bald Mountain Associates.

Thank you

Allen Ginsberg

144. ALLEN GINSBERG [TETON VILLAGE, WY]
TO GARY SNYDER [NEVADA CITY, CA]

[*ca.* September 23, 1973]

Dear Gary—Dear Masa:

Which chakra *muladhara*?[148] or what. Not seen movie [*Last Tango in Paris*], but they say Marlon Brando finally disclosed *muladhara* delights to astonished public. I'm sitting steady, finally got my breath down to somewhere an inch above pubic hair, free aeration that opens up a lot of space and ease and some bliss in sitting. We start 6:30 A.M. break 7:10–8:50 eat, sit till noon, 2½ hours off and sit 2:30–4:30, tea, 5 sit to 7 supper, 8–9 and done for day dark to dark easy schedule except my poor broken right leg is hard to keep in healthy circulation, but I'm making it all right. Should have done sushi years ago.

Love

Allen

[PS] Baghavan Das my roommate here. Chögyam not yet arrived, we've sat a week.

Mountain fog slow as breath
drifting over pine trees.

Peter with 20 h.p. tractor raised huge garden. We may get $900 45 h.p. tractor next.

---

148. *Muladhara* chakra. The center of energy located in the body between the genitals and the anus.

I expect to come to S.F. next spring with Peter and build house (poetry hermitage) at Kitkitdizze. Lucien Carr's son, Simon, is sitting at Bush Street Soto Center and knows Whalen! Generations pass flesh grass—upspringing!

145. ALLEN GINSBERG [TETON VILLAGE, WY]
    TO GARY SNYDER [NEVADA CITY, CA]

September 28, 1973

Dear Gary:

Our missives crossed in mail. Yes, I'm planning to come to California next spring with Peter and be there most all summer and early fall and build house. Will gather money now and am in touch with Phil and Bruce Boyd.

I'll be on short November 7–17 reading tour I don't know where and then return to Jackson Hole here till December 7 to conclude study and sitting—today finished 12th day of *sesshin*.

Love
Allen

146. ALLEN GINSBERG [TETON VILLAGE, WY]
    TO GARY SNYDER [NEVADA CITY, CA]

October 13, 1973

Dear Gary:

[. . .] When plans are finalized for building with Shady Creek, etc. and [Bruce] Boyd, I'll circulate a formal letter with plan asking permission. I've been in touch with Bruce.

Philip is much involved with training and sounds like he don't want (yet) too much responsibility for building (or occupying) the proposed house I'll construct / have constructed. He's not sure of his long future, etc. In any case I've been in touch with Boyd on some questions and ideas, and Philip has already given Bruce Boyd his own fantasies too. How was the meeting—anything important?

OK, I'll be in touch. Sat two weeks straight ten hours a day and now on another four-day ten-hour-day *nyinthun (sesshin)*. Then I leave here for twelve days and return for another twenty days sitting by December 7. Reading Abhidarma and Nagarjuna and getting Shandas and Dhaltus straight. Last nite Hakuin's commentary on Prajnaparamita, fell asleep over it—hot poesy! Catching up slowly on technicalities. Gotta go be timekeeper bell ringer this afternoon.

OK

Allen

[PS] I wrote Boyd I could afford about $8,000. Phil says no work till ground hardens—is that May?? Peter and I planning to be out in California late spring. May?

147. GARY SNYDER [NEVADA CITY, CA]
       TO ALLEN GINSBERG [TETON VILLAGE, WY]

16.X [October 16, 1973]

Dear Allen,

Here are papers of our recent Bald Mountain Association meeting—signed copies of your letter regarding site—and the map of Ananda retreat layout and number of homes, tents, etc.

Glorious weather. Drying chestnuts, apples, chickens running in the sun.

I go all November, East—Southwest in February it looks like. At the place you selected for your cabin in the big bedrock in front, buried under leaves, we found the hollows of Indian-made bedrock mortars!

Good *dhyana.*

Love,

Gary

148. ALLEN GINSBERG [TETON VILLAGE, WY]
       TO GARY SNYDER [NEVADA CITY, CA]

[December 10, 1973]

Dear Gary:

You back yet? Received house plans and air maps from Bruce Boyd, Shady Creek, looks fine, advantage of Jap mud walls—did anyone there really learn how? Sent him money for site survey, asked him his architect fee. When should I come west with Peter to work? Is early May alright? Should I get other workers or are there enough Shady Creekers there? Amassing money meanwhile.

All this sitting here finally managed to cut my dependency on imagining or projecting Blake Light Yogachara[149] visionary apparition on the poor white-barked aspen outside the window. Little fish of thought/ memory ate big fish—other day in sitting reverie seemed that the little fish evaporated right after swallowing big fish. Meanwhile Chögyam Trungpa's group planning a Naropa Institute sort of summer Buddhist style studies connected with Colorado University at Boulder—asked me advice on poetics course. I suggested (ideally) spiritual poetics five-week course July 17–August 15 myself one week, Phil Whalen next, yourself Gary if you're free to travel, Mike McClure, Diane Di Prima, and Anne Waldman. They'll pay roundtrip fare board lodging at apartment and $200 fee. This to let you know they'll write inviting you.

Chögyam been giving fantastic series of lectures beginning with *vipassana* thru Mahayana 10 *bhumis* now entering *vajrayana* and explaining mapping Tibetan tantras—got as far as *anuttara* in four-hour lecture and freaked out when someone tired asked if we couldn't continue tomorrow—was ready to expound on fourth yoga "Non meditation"—really beautiful weeks of exposition, exquisite teaching. I kept total notes. Only a few days left here *sesshins* till December 3 and then two more final lectures on *maha ati—samayas—mandals*—etc. You know all this Tibetan material? Apparently it's never been directly taught in West before, actual transmission.

We're doing basically *shamatha* (*samatha*) sitting—attending breath out front of nostril disappearing. Well OK.

Love

Allen

[PS] Back in New York next week. Reading Santedeva and Nagayana and Guenther, etc. Peter was here three days and sat ten hours too! Three hours in one sitting! Miracles! Ah Alan Watts.[150] We have his photo on altar while sitting.

---

149. Yogachara. School of Mahayana Buddhism.
150. Alan Watts had recently died, on November 16, 1973.

149. ALLEN GINSBERG [NEW YORK] TO GARY SNYDER [NEVADA CITY, CA]

[December 27, 1973]

Dear Gary:

[. . .] Have been exchanging letters with Bruce Boyd and Phil re plans
for small house. If you have chance, check it out with Boyd . . . or Erickson. I sent Boyd $200 to look over land, and asked him his fee, and said I
could send several thousand in January for advance purchase of materials
if useful.

I'll probably hole up for a month at Cherry Valley and sit as much as
I can daily. Then be in and out, traveling, or in city or goofing or reading
till May, and come west then with Peter to build. Phone me when you
have time. Can call collect—I'll be at farm January 4–January 28.

OK

Allen

Teton View
Mountain snow fields
seen thru transparent wings of a fly
on windowpane.

150. GARY SNYDER [NEVADA CITY, CA]
      TO ALLEN GINSBERG [CHERRY VALLEY, NY]

14.I.40074 [January 14, 1974]

Dear Allen,

I'd like to call you, but it seems I'm never near a telephone. A letter for
the nonce. (I'm doing a work-*sesshin* these days on Pleistocene man—
reindeer—early China—Japan—Kyoto / Ainu frontier Hokkaido—
civilization / wilderness—[elegant Buddhism: raggedy old barbarians]
liquid-metal fast breeder reactor . . . writing . . . my "book.")

David Padwa was here for Christmas and described in detail his *sadhana* under Dudjom Rimpoche.

Yes, dear friend, you are going to get a little house built this summer.
Did I tell you we found a Maidu bedrock mortar in the rock of your front
porch? When will you be out here?

Gary

Gary Snyder in his cottage garden in Berkeley, California, 1955.

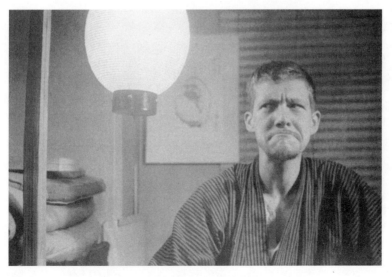

Gary Snyder in his cottage in Berkeley, California, 1955.

Allen Ginsberg on a train en route to the Japan Sea, Summer 1963.
© Allen Ginsberg.

Joanne Kyger and Gary Snyder in Kyoto, Japan, Summer 1963.
Photo by Allen Ginsberg.

Gary Snyder near the Sea of Japan, Summer 1963.
Photo by Allen Ginsberg.

Gary Snyder in Kyoto, Japan, Summer 1963. Photo by Allen Ginsberg.

Unknown man, Allen Ginsberg, and Horizawa Somon (Tendai priest) in Japan, 1963.

Gary Snyder "pissing in the no-wind." Glacier Peak Wilderness. Photo by Allen Ginsberg.

Gary Snyder, Peter Orlovsky, and Allen Ginsberg in Kausani, India,
March 1962. Photo by Joanne Kyger.

Allen Ginsberg with
Martine Algiers in Glacier Peak
Wilderness area, Washington,
Summer 1965.

Gary Snyder, Joanne Kyger, and Peter Orlovsky in Kausani, India,
March 1962. Photo by Allen Ginsberg.

Gary Snyder and Allen Ginsberg at Glacier Peak Wilderness area,
Washington, Summer 1965. Photo by Martine Algiers.

Allen Ginsberg, Maretta Greer, and Gary Snyder at the "Human Be-In" at Golden Gate Park, San Francisco, January 14, 1967. Photo by Paul Kagan.

Allen Ginsberg and Gary Snyder at the "Human Be-In" at Golden Gate Park, San Francisco, January 14, 1967. Photo by Lisa Law.

Allen Ginsberg, Maretta Greer, and Gary Snyder at the "Human Be-In" at Golden Gate Park, San Francisco, January 14, 1967. Photo by Leo Holub.

Gary Snyder and Paul Goodman at Gotham Book Mart,
New York City, 1971. Photo by Bill Yoscary.

"City Lights in North Dakota," March 1974. Photo by Laura McClure.
back row: Gregory Corso, Miriam Patchen, Kenneth Rexroth, Allen
Ginsberg, Lawrence Ferlinghetti.
front row: Joanna McClure, unknown, Shig Murao, Jane McClure,
Gary Snyder, Peter Orlovsky.

Allen Ginsberg and Gary Snyder
on a West Coast reading tour,
May 1973.

Gregory Corso, Kyle Roderick, Gary Snyder, Allen Ginsberg, Gelek
Rinpoche, and unidentified Tibetan monks in robes in Boulder,
Colorado, July, 1994.

Nanao Sakaki and Gary Snyder at Bedrock Mortar/Kitkitdizze, California, May 30, 1988. Photo by Allen Ginsberg.

Gary Snyder, Allen Ginsberg, and Nanao Sakaki in Berkeley, June 24, 1974. Photo by Kazunobu Yanagi.

Allen Ginsberg, Philip Whalen, and Gary Snyder in Davis, California, January 1996. Photo by David Robertson.

Gary Snyder in Allen Ginsberg's kitchen, March 1991. Photo by Allen Ginsberg.

[January 28, 1974]

Dear Gary:

I'll be out in San Francisco early May—up in mountains mid-May. Spoke to Bruce Boyd, he sounds more cheerful about plans, and sent him $200 for site survey. I have $2,000 of own money free now if he or Erickson or anyone needs it to order or purchase materials. Boyd said to wait till May for that, but I wonder. Anyway the money's ready anytime.

April I'll be doing a few "shows" maybe West Coast Bellingham and elsewhere with Baghavan Das to raise him some money and also raise some more house money.

If I sell the land to myself from Committee on Poetry, what should I charge? So as not to flout the law (tax) and same time not trespass Bald Mountain rules. Any idea?

The COP money you had sent is safe and waiting, no rush either way. Peter can handle any transaction (sign and send checks) while I'm away.

I've been sitting last two weeks in attic 6–8 hours a day—set up *zafu* by window overlooking western hilltops covered with snow and breathed. Couldn't maintain solid 8-hour day as I hoped but was interested to see attempt to integrate sitting at home all day—and mail answering and probably not conducive to real *sesshin* mentality whatever state that is. The attic is a great quiet (insulated from house-strife and clanking) place—amazingly silent and high up there on rugs—got pillows from Zen Center in Sharon Springs 12 miles away. Odd how late I'm discovering sitting. My main life problem seems to be the fucking karmic mail every day—new problems, proofs, contracts, appeals, and screw ups.

Enclosed an application form for COP to pass on to whomever you think wants to apply.

Did Naropa Institute write you? Never mind answering till there's a letter reason.

Peter bottling dried basil plants he hung in attic all fall. Tomorrow go to N.Y. Dylan concert (Boy he sent us four tix!!) and then read in Maine and do non-violence workshop benefit in Atlanta, GA, then home farm sit two more weeks homemade *sesshin*. Been in touch with David Dellinger a lot.

Has Bruce Boyd showed you his house plans? You're building a sitting hall this summer? I'll be at Kitkitdizze all summer except one or two weeks late July early August to teach at Boulder Naropa and see Chögyam. Peter will come west too.

Oh! Burroughs returning to U.S. He'll be big professor at CCNY February–May, two hours a week sharing some special chair with [Kurt] Vonnegut.

[PS] Parkinson mentions poetry confab Berkeley summer '75.

EDITOR'S NOTE: *Gary Snyder sent the following letter to five friends: Kenneth Rexroth, Lawrence Ferlinghetti, Allen Ginsberg, Michael McClure, and John Little. On Allen's letter he included a short note.*

151. GARY SNYDER [NEVADA CITY, CA]
       TO ALLEN GINSBERG [CHERRY VALLEY, NY]

31.I.40074 [January 31, 1974]

Comrades,

I write you to speak of a problem that has come up at literary conferences in the past, and is about to arise at our coming gathering in March at the University of North Dakota. It appears that there may be some inequity in the fee structure. I don't blame Mr. Little of North Dakota for this—he's doubtless trying to do what he thinks right, and perhaps meeting the demands of agents. In the case of a special gathering of this sort, however, where we are all in a powerful sense peers, I think the money should be distributed evenly.

I don't know what the actual case is beyond this: John Little just mentioned to me in a letter that the budget had run low and Michael McClure could only be offered $500. (I was to get $1,000.) I have written Mr. Little saying that in my opinion the whole fee system should be equalized, giving Michael an even share. If Mr. Little can't do that, I'd insist that at least my fee be equally divided with Michael so we'd get the same.

If you agree with the thrust of my thought please write Mr. Little a card.

fraternity, *égalité*

Dear Allen,

Am I doing correctly? I hope so, just looked at some drawings of your proposed house—pretty keen—had a comment to make ("more closets"). Doing a five-day *sesshin* this week, seven people sitting.

xxx

Gary

153. GARY SNYDER [NEVADA CITY, CA]
    TO ALLEN GINSBERG [CHERRY VALLEY, NY]

12.II.74 [February 12, 1974]

Dear Allen,

I am planning to fell three or four medium-size ponderosa [pine] in the swale southwest of house to let in more light for vegetable garden. If I hear nothing from you I'll take it that you have no further questions about it.

Yours very sincerely,

Gary

154. ALLEN GINSBERG [NEW YORK] TO GARY SNYDER [NEVADA CITY, CA]

February 15, 1974

Gary:

Yes, quite right about North Dakota fees. My agent negotiated fees without full awareness of context (which context got enriched by late inclusion of Mike [McClure], Gregory [Corso], and Peter [Orlovsky]). I spoke to John Little and things have been evened out a lot. Tho fee owing to COP will be same with inclusion of Peter which was Little's solution. If it's still unsatisfactory COP can give grants to even it out more but I think it is being balanced. I generally ask agent to get $1,000 a day anyway since bulk of my fees via COP get siphoned out to other poets anyway; but I didn't pay particular attention to North Dakota $ scene since I didn't take time, not knowing problems would rise. Anyhoo— you're right and it's good thing you reminded us all. See you in a month.

Allen

[PS] Ferlinghetti split his fee with Gregory. I'll be in North Dakota the full week 18th–23rd.

Met Gary Lawless in Maine who wrote later saying he and girl think of coming to Kitkitdizze this summer? I told him check with Erickson and you.

EDITOR'S NOTE: *Gary Snyder addressed a letter to Bruce Boyd and Allen Ginsberg about the building of Ginsberg's house and attached a personal note to Allen at the bottom of his copy.*

155. GARY SNYDER AND BRUCE BOYD [NEVADA CITY, CA]
      TO ALLEN GINSBERG [CHERRY VALLEY, NY]

February 18, 1974

Dear Friends,

Concerning the building of Allen's house this summer. I have been speaking with Bob Erickson and some thoughts come to mind. It's already February and time is growing short. I think it would be wise if both of you could clarify and come to some agreement on construction procedures for this summer. I see several possible ways of working:

1. Allen's house built entirely by Shady Creek Construction Company;

2. built by Shady Creek but with help from volunteer labor, friends of Allen's; camping in the meadow;

3. built by non–Shady Creek local carpenters following Bruce's plans and perhaps with occasional advice from Shady Creek;

4. built by local carpenters plus volunteer workers;

5. any combination of the above.

The reason I bring this up is because people are already laying plans for their summer work and although it's not possible to make definite commitments of potential workers yet, we should be preparing to do so as soon as possible.

From April on, actual work could begin. From the end of May volunteer workers could camp without fear of rain.

Allen, of course, is welcome to make Kitkitdizze his headquarters and dwelling during the building period; but if there will be volunteer workers, Allen should set up separate kitchen facilities in the meadow.

Now is the time to cut poles. If the house plans call for poles, there are men here who could be hired to select and cut the necessary lengths fairly soon. Other possibilities of gathering materials come to mind. I write to stimulate thought and generate suggestions. There may be other ways of working that I haven't thought of. In any case, I'd like to help in any way I can. So please let me know what to think.

Regards,
Gary

Allen,
Sorry I've been a poky correspondent but now trying to make up.

1. If you sell the land to yourself our agreement says you can only raise the price 5% per year, I think. I should think that COP would sell it to Allen at original price of $250 per acre, though. Dick Werthimer is talking of selling his share to Yvonne of Zen Center for the original 250 price. Did I tell you we did a little mid-winter *sesshin*? Now spring is starting—planted three fruit trees yesterday. (Will be doing readings mid-March to mid-April) . . .

Hum
Gary

156. ALLEN GINSBERG [NEW YORK] TO GARY SNYDER [NEVADA CITY, CA]

8 March 1974

Dear Gary:
Spoke to Bruce Boyd, Bob Erickson, and Jonathan Keehn on phone few nites ago. Will send Bruce $1,000 this week to begin whatever purchases necessary. See you in a week anyway in North Dakota. Apparently Bruce was still unsure the actual site. I thought with site survey he'd already gone over that—and knew the exact spot we'd selected. If you see him please see that he's directed to spot. That may be reason for his hesitancy. Yes, all Shady Creek construction work, as I'd OK'd before. Peter and I will be there all summer probably mid-May on, so any preparatory work should be done from now on. Railroad ties or poles, or prostration-fit floor (which I may do, and explained needs to Bob, Bruce, etc.). I'll see you in Grand Forks for more talk plan.

Love
Allen

157. GARY SNYDER [NEVADA CITY, CA]
      TO ALLEN GINSBERG [CHERRY VALLEY, NY]

10.III.74 [March 10, 1974]

Dear Allen,

Ray Dasmann, wildlife ecologist who lives and works in Switzerland for
the IUCN (International Union for the Conservation of Nature) was
up here last weekend with Peter Berg. Dasmann has been mapping out
"biotic" regions of the earth—first step toward re-aligning our senses
of place from political to natural boundaries. We spoke of becoming
each by each *ad-hoc* "shadow governments" for these true regions, make
decisions, do studies, far ahead. Peter is publishing *Planet Drum* as part
of this—next issue will be focused on North Pacific rim. Yesterday had
monthly ridge-wide study group meeting and discussed (33 people) how
to make some local choices, for example, doing our own deer census.
Also heard from Ananda people about their own rather large future
plans.

Bruce and Jeff were here, went down and looked again at site—your
site—"Bedrock Mortar" right there. Fine place. We're all—you, us, going
to have a good time together this summer! If you don't have too large a
crew camping with you we can do it all out of my kitchen area perhaps.

[...] Also, you never sent COP forms as mentioned in previous
letter. I want Berg to apply to COP in hopes of continuing work on
Planet Drum publishing etc.—a new type of magazine there.

Am doing finishing touches on New Directions book of poems for
fall.

See you in North Dakota.

Gary

158. ALLEN GINSBERG [SAN FRANCISCO]
      TO GARY SNYDER [NEVADA CITY, CA]

15 May 1974

Dear Gary:

Not yet seen copy of your invite to ceremonies "declaring Lew Welch
empty." I'll probably drive up with Phil Whalen and Larry Ferlinghetti
on 22 May. All my readings/travels since January—37 readings—are done,

no dates made ahead. Bruce Boyd says many difficulties now are arising re budget and time (his and others) and pay to foreman of work crew. Had lunch with him today. We'll discuss all that next week while I'm up there. My fall trip to Europe is cancelled so I'm completely free. If immediate work is off (Bruce actually wants to wait till next year) (!) this month I may sit a month in Shobo-an. But I'm ready for anything, including nothing. See you soon.

Love
Allen

159. ALLEN GINSBERG [SAN FRANCISCO]
      TO GARY SNYDER [NEVADA CITY, CA]

Midnight—18 May 1974

Dear Gary:

I'll probably drive up with Phil and Larry Ferlinghetti 22 May. Seeing Huey Newton tomorrow with Baker Roshi. Sunday will meet with Jonathan, Bruce Boyd, Erickson, and others. Bruce says he will be too busy with school to do my hut proper this year, and that Jonathan may want too much money to be foreman, and that a logistics/planning/buying foreman is needed to translate his architect plan to workable 3-D manifestation. Well, I'll meet and talk this weekend. Peter's arrival delayed till Shady Creek mind is made up. I'm game to go on and build a shack anyhow. Not going to Europe September so plenty time. See you next week.

Someone asked me three weeks ago "What Welch ceremony?" and I said "Ceremony to declare Lew Welch empty."

Love
Allen

EDITOR'S NOTE: *Ginsberg and Orlovsky did spend time that summer building Bedrock Mortar on their property. Allen spent a good deal of time teaching at the newly organized Naropa Institute in Boulder, but Peter worked with the carpenters in the community and finished the main part of the structure before the winter. Allen enjoyed working with his hands while he was there, and relied on others for building expertise.*

7 October 1974

Dear Gary:

Here are manuscripts of poems this summer for *Kyoi Kuksu*.[151] I don't have Dale Pendell's address with me. There's one longer poem and a few gauzy fragments. Probably should refine them more but they're readable as is. Can you give them to Dale?

Also enclosed a letter (xerox) I got from Dave Dellinger—who of all people in the political movement seemed most sincere and just to me—and effective. He's discussed this with me before, tho I hadn't suggested your name (or Ram Dass) directly ever—it's his idea—and if you think you have occasional material it might be worth encouraging him. It'll be the same genre as *Liberation* and *WIN* but (he hopes) more national scale.

Done typing, arranged what I could for Leary in relative secrecy, and ready for dharma reading tonight. Spent last nite with Anne Waldman high strung from N.Y. (bread 90¢ a loaf and pneumatic subway drills for new Second Avenue line out her windows and a quarter block away)—encouraged her to visit you, but she may not have time brief visit. I'll be here till about the 15th. Supper tonight with Phil and Mike and DiPrima and Anne and Dave Meltzer and Grant Fisher at Pot Sticker on Waverly, then we go to auditorium and have some champagne with Chögyam who said he'd try to come—he's exhausted I suspect. OK.

Love

Allen

[PS] I'll be back [in San Francisco] as said November 21 for Lone Mountain College and DeYoung—maybe a day earlier. I'll let you know plans.

Thursday October 10, 1974

Dear Gary:

Poetry reading was fine, Phil went to supper with us and m.c.'d. Joanne [Kyger] was really down home, superior to any easy style I've ever seen—

---

151. *Kyoi Kuksu*. A periodical edited by poet and alchemist Dale Pendell.

first time I saw her poetry working—and [Robert] Duncan had a velvet suit, Chögyam came early with bottles of Karmapa[152] long life pills for all and champagne. So mostly all OK and quiet full early audience.

No new development on Leary mystery just silence again. I'll be here till the 16th or 17th now—at City Lights (I'll write Jonathan and Tanya and Bob when I leave). Saw Bruce and Jeff today and chatted. Seen lots of Mike and Phil this week. Tomorrow we'll have a poet's audience with Karmapa.

So I'll be in N.Y. all winter. Been seeing dentist here $600 worth, *oy govolt!* Getting my teeth fixed up for the next couple of generations.

Rain yet??

Love

Allen

162. GARY SNYDER [NEVADA CITY, CA]
      TO ALLEN GINSBERG [NEW YORK]

12.X.74 [October 12, 1974]

After all those rainy rumblings it never sprinkled more than three drops and now it's clear and fairly warm again. I wrote Dellinger and said yes. Ray Dasmann (chief ecologist for the IUCN—headquarters Switzerland) was up for two days and bought 22 A [acres] of land adjoining Steve Beckwitt's new place down on Purdon Road. He's very friendly (works with Peter Berg and Bob Curry).

Front end of the jeep went out—Rod's working on it—another $150—to fix. Alas.

Bob and Margaret seem at ease at your place. Who gave Herb Caen[153] all that information I wonder? Had a nice letter from Philip. And a card from Denise [Levertov].

Gary

---

152. Karmapa. The title of the spiritual head of the Karma Kagyü school of Tibetan Buddhism.

153. Herb Caen. San Francisco newspaper gossip columnist.

November 5, 1974

Dear Gary:

Since leaving and arriving in N.Y. I've been more immersed in trying to unravel Leary scene—too much to detail here, but in sum it does look like he's turning on his lawyers and others, and his lady Joanna is crazy or something. Long jail seems to have changed him—haven't had direct contact, only with his "control agent" in L.A. all very Burroughsian.

Twas Ferlinghetti answering Herb Caen phone call gave that information about our mansions in heaven.

I'll go out and get more money for the land this and next month, I already spent my fortune on teeth and tractors. I'll send appropriate checks out to Werthimer and Yvonne Rand soon as I score for money, probably take till December now.

Don't know if CIA funds Trungpa, doubt it (I mean it hadn't occurred to me). I'll be in Boulder next summer trying to organize poetics teaching. There'll be three-week poetry invitation to a dozen or so poets to visit in July, and maybe Phil teach all summer if he wants to visit and vary his scene. I know you're not likely to be free—or desire Boulder trip—but you know, you're wanted, if you found a way, to teach or read there. I'll try to get Corso, John Wieners, Burroughs, Duncan, Creeley, McClure, Philip Whalen, Kenneth Koch, John Ashbery, and several others together—that combination S.F. and N.Y. and Burroughs hasn't ever ripened yet and the Boulder Naropa group is willing to host and do logistics.

I sit every day in bedroom, eyes out on apartment space age buildings and balconies and Manhattan sky an hour. So many letters and phone calls it's bewildering but still interesting—like swimming in rough surf—wrote some poems tho—and got mugged half block from my house on Tenth Street. Grabbed by neck and downed to pavement and slowly (chanting *om ah hum*) dragged into burnt-out street level store behind closed metal door, watch and wallet stole, "Shut up or we'll kill you" by three teenagers. What a weird time slow down—many neighbors (half block from my house and I don't even know them!) on stoop (teenagers) watching (lost $70 and credit cards). The other nite, on way to Ramsay Clark tiny poetry rally, Senate race politics.

Note from Bob Erickson I'll answer.

Black Crown ceremony had sort of pretty *Dharma-Sangha* majesty, tho foreign in costume. Better than pretty. Spent last evening with Dave Dellinger discussing and retrospectively reviewing our own dubious public situations and hypocrisies. I suppose my support of Chögyam may end that way. If Leary scene can be interpreted as a bummer which it isn't actually—it's too strange to be totally unpleasant.

Love
Allen

164. ALLEN GINSBERG [NEW YORK] TO GARY SNYDER [NEVADA CITY, CA]

Tuesday 24 December 1974, Xmas Eve Afternoon
Dear Gary:
Writing poems, sitting an hour morns in New York City, hanging round the streets, and trying to get the land $ together. Received invitation for round table with McClure and yourself, I answered OK, but consult McClure.

Finished planning Naropa poetics summer, got OK from Burroughs, Corso, Ted Berrigan and Ed Sanders and Phil Whalen and Diane di Prima to teach at least a week each. I'll be there all summer to supervise and teach with Anne Waldman. There'll be a slush fund for visiting poets or passers thru to teach or read and get put up and paid a little. If you and Masa are still coming thru early August to Wind River please try come early and give reading or lecture. I'd suggested to Naropa they write you inviting you to lay out U.S. Buddhist / Ecology / Anarchist Work / Poetry view to introduce such ideas forcefully into the scene there.

Sidney Goldfarb phoned and said also he invited Burroughs, Duncan, and yourself and me to Boulder for Colorado University in late May. Bill and I may come early and then stay on for Naropa. I haven't received invite yet.

How's water system? How's your Japan Roads book [*North Sea Road*]? I'm having Xmas eve supper with Burroughs tonight—one charming place I went is Marquette, Michigan—way way up on Lake Superior shores 400 miles north of Detroit—a sort of culturally "isolated" iron mining area with great bars and lively country-headed people refugees from Detroit, Hemingway Big Two-Hearted River country—and bought a fine $1 good wool English cloth Marquette tailored brown suit, so I'm wearing suits and ties (on weekends).

Peter and Denise say hello, miss your compost pile tickle your feet Kai in the sky and "Does he want copies of Happy Traum cassette banjo instruction cassettes?" Peter doing lotsa chin-ups in N.Y. apartment.

xxx

Allen

[PS] Spending all January getting my mouth operated on and sitting total *sesshin* eight hours a day.

165. GARY SNYDER [NEVADA CITY, CA]
     TO ALLEN GINSBERG [CHERRY VALLEY, NY]

31.XII.40074 [December 31, 1974]

Greetings from the end of the year. And thanks for tax check. Yes, rec'd invitation to panel with Odum here too and very pleased with that possibility. I wrote them suggesting Dan Ellsberg as possible addition to panel and also wrote Dan explaining why I thought he should be interested in this; saying if interested he should contact them directly. I cannot say how he'd feel but I can see it as step #1 in preparing him to run for president of Eco-party (third party) ticket in 1980.

Hmmm, Dick Baker just turned up—we'll all go over to We'pa tonight for New Year's Eve party and music-dance.

Water system not quite hooked up yet, Jonathan worked on it today.

Phil Plaza, Peter Bluecloud, and I spent a day walking around near here counting deer turds and looking at the condition of the browse. Quite a number of deer this year.

Day before Christmas, Mike Getz, Barbara, and I rode on three horses from their place up eastward on the ridge singing wassail songs—visited thirteen households—ended up they stayed the night here, and Masa rode one horse back down to their place, with them, Christmas morning. First time for her ever on a horse.

Mike got kicked in the forearm two days ago by his jumpy horse Misty—broke the arm bones two places and dislocated the elbow. Always say don't stand near the rear of a horse.

Dick is on good terms with new California governor Jerry Brown. Maybe a gathering two weekends from now with Oregon energetics people, McCall of Oregon, McClure (and Ellsberg) and some others, myself, with Brown, at Green Gulch. Possible that California may adopt an Odum-type energy program! (That is, no energy developments that don't demonstrably yield net energy.)

([Edward] Teller has come out and said that fusion is a dream.)

Cold now; pond frozen for 10 days; a little snow on the ground. Your house is super-cozy.

Have a good January of *sadhana*.

Love,

Gary

166. ALLEN GINSBERG [NEW YORK]
     TO GARY SNYDER [NEVADA CITY, CA]

Jan 19, 1974 [*sic:* 1975]

Dear Gary:

Fine build 10' x 11' hut, sounds ideal. Thanks for note that water flows. I'm still involved extricating myself from Leary karma, preparing *habeas corpus* papers to get him before a judge. What a lot of work! Peter and I went to Washington D.C. and had our teeth capped and I had gums cut and bone scraped and two teeth pulled forever, watched in hand mirror while painless skeleton was scraped and blood flowed and nitrous oxide also flowed. Love to Masa Gen and Kai. Nanao writes come to Japan but I can't—supposed to be meditating tantra here—beginning prostrations finally. But N.Y. is so full of business! My mail a mess! Aho!

Love

Allen

167. GARY SNYDER [NEVADA CITY, CA]
     TO ALLEN GINSBERG [NEW YORK]

10.III.75 [March 10, 1975]

Dear Allen,

I still remember your warm introducing me at St. Mark's [Poetry Project] in your elegant and trusty salt and pepper suit. Met William LeFleur (Dept. Religion, Princeton) who is doing Saigyo translations (Japanese wandering poet-monk hitherto untranslated into decent English).

10,000-year-old pottery dated in Japan makes Japanese pottery oldest in world now.

And; maybe, living creatures create and regulate ozone layer—as one whole organism-permitting life of cells on earth out of the water "The Goddess" a more-than-viable notion. Maya / *prajna*.

Two gates built: $120 each.

upper gate split 3 ways = $40 each.

back gate split 2 ways = $60 each (you and me only users)

Fire extinguisher + $20 for your house—I bought because it needs it. You owe me $120. I hope you don't mind me unilaterally buying fire extinguisher for you (dry chemical under pressure) but it seemed very worthwhile. See you in April in Florida.

Love

Gary

168. ALLEN GINSBERG [NEW YORK]
    TO GARY SNYDER [NEVADA CITY, CA]

May 3, 1975

Dear Gary:

Drove to Tallahassee airport to pick up [Buckminster] Fuller. His speech similar to Odum's except opposite conclusion. That with rational design structures dome shell instead of [square] wood and brick pile, there was enuf material to house expanded population; that by spread of electric energy population would go down, etc., electric from wind and waves, etc. I gave him Odum's net energy essay reprint, he said he was not familiar with Odum's detailed work just by reports from students, etc. "If earth were 15 inch diameter stainless steel ball, and you breathed on it, the gauzy film of breath would be equivalent to depth of ocean on earth."

I'll come down to San Francisco May 20, teach seminar poetics at Padma Jong in Mendocino County, 23–25 of May and try to be at Kitkitdizze May 26–27 and fly Sacramento to Boulder May 28 late in day. Tight squeeze. Still sick with flu, I'll be in hospital for exam this weekend. Vietnam War over!

Amazing,

Allen

169. ALLEN GINSBERG [NEW YORK] TO GARY SNYDER [NEVADA CITY, CA]

May 20, 1975

Dear Gary:

Sick in hospital last two weeks, can't come to West Coast, please tell Jonathan and Bob work on anything convenient. I'll write them when feeling better. Had to cancel all travels in May, lying dizzy in hospital. I'll be in Boulder hopefully May 29th and settle there quietly for summer. Congratulations Pulitzer Prize, sweet *New York Times* write-up—said we sometimes chanted together.

Love

Allen

[PS] He's going to be in hospital till end of this week. It may have been bad side effects from antibiotic that doctor said to double up on to get rid of flu. Take care, love to all, Peter Orlovsky

EDITOR'S NOTE: *In the next letter, Ginsberg is responding to something Snyder had written to him about foreign publishers. That letter appears to be missing.*

170. ALLEN GINSBERG [NEW YORK] TO GARY SNYDER [NEVADA CITY, CA]

N.Y. Hospital
May 24, [1975]

Dear Gary:

I don't remember correspondence with these fellows. Maybe Nanda Pivano could advise you on this practicality. I thought you already had work or publisher in Italy? You might get a publisher with large distribution—thru Linder Agency (which is agent for City Lights and New Directions in Italy). Is Franco [Beltrametti] there to advise? If nothing else is happening, sure why not these kids? But you do need someone with mature taste checking out their translations, and their business praxis. The main thing, however, is the translator. Maybe forward this letter to Nanda for advice.

I have been in N.Y. Hospital for two weeks, after a stupid prostate biopsy. Subsequently poisoned by the antibiotic (Keflex) they vein-fed me. My real (original) trouble turned out to be herpes simplex (virus inflammation of head nerves) which has led to Bell's palsy temporary paralysis of right side of my face. Once diagnosis got straightened out (day before yesterday) and proper (I hope) cortisone pills prescribed for both ills (total body skin rash antibiotic allergy) and herpes/face paralysis, I have been feeling lively again and sitting up reading and meditation and eating well. I should be out of here in a few more days. West Coast and Logan (alas) Utah trips cancelled. I'll just about make Naropa class June 9. So I'm OK, but gotta take it easier.

Saw Buckminster Fuller I think I wrote you. He emphasized that atomics was burning up the planet.

With half a smile, as ever

Allen

171. ALLEN GINSBERG [1621 9TH ST., BOULDER, CO]
      TO GARY SNYDER [NEVADA CITY, CA]

June [*sic:* July] 11, 1975

Dear Gary:

Forgive me for not writing, long slow lethargy after hospital and lotsa work and people here I just let mail pile up and sent messages with Phil.

To the point: Enclosed your $50 check returned, I'll charge rent on the place normally but between us it's a family matter and there doesn't seem to be need for so formal a rent arrangement, especially for Masa's parents. Besides which the amount of attention and work you've put into the house and general overseeing you do balances out any rent, etc., if reasons are necessary. Gimme a kiss instead.

Anne Waldman and Michael Brownstein plan to spend part or all of September there—Michael has a poetry reading October 9 in Bay Area—so they'll be there till at latest October 5, probably leave a week earlier.

I haven't written to Jonathan or Bob Erickson about general state of construction, tho both've written me, inquiring a bit. Haven't been writing letters—but received note from Bill Crosby saying he needs shelter for next winter and offering work-exchange, which sounds fine, if he can accommodate to early October move-in. Says he can put in firewood during summer and build woodshed, which'll be great improvement. I'm going to take a month solitary retreat this fall maybe September, but I think I'll do it on some Chögyam land to get experience how they organize it traditionally and then can use cabin later for any similar solitudes with some quasi-formal experience. I'll be in San Francisco maybe in December—Anne mentioned that Michael McClure mused on setting up a Six Gallery memorial reading then.

How does Bill Crosby sound as tenant? Had you any other idears? I'd write him directly but want to check with you first. If it's OK let him know if not write or phone me collect here.

Naropa Kerouac School of Poetics been lovelier and livelier even than imagined. Burroughs was here a month, he and Trungpa circling each other warily and finally meeting drunk last nite of his stay long talk, taped. "Well if Mr. Burroughs wants to take a typewriter with him into month retreat, maybe we make special dispensation." "Well if the Trungpa says no typewriter, maybe I won't take a typewriter." Gregory Corso here outrageous shithead borrowing money from students calling Trungpa a "dumb asshole" in midst of all *sangha* assembled speech, SHUT UP! *vajra* voice from Trungpa's chair—and then they had tea the next day, and we all taught a poetry class together—final exam all the students wrote poems about how they all loved Gregory and everyone taking Gregory as some kind of human koan. What to do with him? He's been in basically good shape for him—with French girlfriend no dope but Darvon. Up in the mountain W. S. Merwin—sitting and coming to classes on Vajrayana and having intelligent suppers with Gregory and Anne and Joanne and Peter Warshall. My parents here for two weeks in my big apartment. Ed Sanders and wife and babe here now. Philip been here, and Ted Berrigan and New York poets Anne brought in Dick Gallup—local poets Jack Collum—extended meeting, and we're all housed in eight-apartment ghetto one big house with Lama Karma Tinley and Francesco Freemantle Sanskritist just published new translation of Book of Dead. Merwin and John Ashbery read next all-school reading—been having big readings every Wednesday. Bill and Gregory to start, then me and Phil, then Diane di Prima and Berrigan and Anne Waldman, then Sanders and Brownstein. Peter due out here to teach bucolic poesy in a month.

Will you be passing thru? Session runs July 21–August 23, then maybe I'll take off for retreat or a week's *sesshin* to begin with—dunno. If you're still planning Utah trip let me know—plenty room here for stopover. Warshall taught all the poetry classes too with slides on animal aesthetics. Gregory taught my class the first week I was sick. Merwin, Anne, Gregory, and I each read Shelley's [*Ode to the*] *West Wind* our own interpretations in one class—three or four older poets listening in each class. I started with "Seafarer" and read thru Shelley and Marvell and Smart when I discovered half my class never read nothing but Snyder and Kerouac and *Howl* in high school and college—half the class had never read *West Wind*, so I went back in time and taught weird selected survey course "Scepter and Crown must tumble down," etc. Winding up tonight with William Carlos Williams and Kerouac end session—my father taught Keats my last class.

So—Ed Sanders may drop by before September. He's in four-wheel drive land rover headed west to Bolinas.

Joanne acts crazy when she's drunk—Chögyam told her sit more. She seemed relieved.

I'm recovering tho still my stamina is low. Going to homeopathic doctor. Finished book of songs [*First Blues*] and sent it to printer Full Court Press care of St. Mark's Project—illustrated with lead sheets music for half the songs.

OK—love to Masa. I hear your little retreat cabin's great beauty and done already.

Love

Allen

PS If Bill Crosby is OK, tell him, if not phone me discuss other idea. Taking week off to go to Santa Fe see [David] Padwa, Lama, etc. with my father and mother, back July 21.

172. ALLEN GINSBERG [BOULDER, CO]
         TO GARY SNYDER [NEVADA CITY, CA]

August 2, 1975

Dear Gary:

Yes, OK Bruce and Holly stay in Mortar shack October–May. Usual $50 rent-work fine—advantage of Crosby was he offered woodshed and I wonder if Bruce will have time to do it, even next summer. I guess he can probably organize its doing. Jonathan may still have some $ building money leftover in bank. If you see Bruce, ask him call me (or I'll call him in San Francisco) and rest mind.

I'll go retreat sit after here couple weeks and then to N.Y. Having homeopathy and acupuncture for tired face.

Allen

173. ALLEN GINSBERG [NEW YORK] TO GARY SNYDER [NEVADA CITY, CA]

October 24, 1975

Dear Gary:

OK, do what you think best about "Stone Mortar" cottage (as Philip Whalen more prosaically wrote, once). I don't know if Bill Crosby still needs a place? Either way rented or unrented's all right. I may be able to use it for retreat for a month sometime this year, or not. Dylan (Bob) called and asked me to join his troupe for a month's traveling road show— small colleges maybe—thru November. I'd scheduled a month retreat at Tail of Tiger but I said "absolutely yes" to Dylan anyway. Form's empti-ness anyhoo. So I guess I'll be gone all November with a troupe of musi-cians making movies and maybe get a chance to sing onstage.

OK

Love

[PS] Been writing haikus. New York apartment is great.

174. ALLEN GINSBERG [NEW YORK] TO GARY SNYDER [NEVADA CITY, CA]

December 10, 1975

Dear Gary:

Just returned home from Dylan Rolling Thunder tour, learned how to sing better, learned some show biz, and tried to infiltrate some dharma into the community scene—wrote a few poems for tour xerox newsletter which'll be published in December 30 *Rolling Stone.* I gave Sarah Dylan your *Earth House Hold,* as she was interested in Mamma Goddess (read-ing Robert Graves). Dylan says he wants to produce my songs on records; and *First Blues* is out (book) I'll send you. Enclosed tax check. Phil said:

"Stone Mortar" in a letter some time back. Anybody using it? How's your Kingdom?

Love

Allen

[PS] Dylan and I made blues movie on Kerouac's grave.

175. ALLEN GINSBERG [NEW YORK] TO GARY SNYDER [NEVADA CITY, CA]

January 19, 1976

Dear Gary:

Glad someone's in house. I haven't been there much because this period, last few seasons, I've been occupied with illness, Naropa, editing, more illness, settling and moving in new apartment (437 E. 12th St. New York City Apt 23 same phone), etc. Of course I wasn't bugged at the building of the Stone Mortar née Bedrock Mortar house—it's a "tiny wooden palace" as far as I could describe it, the building problems like kitchen floor are minimal and'll be dealt with one year or another. If Skinner can move the gas refrigerator nearer the house, have it repaired, or junk it when the ground is solid, that'll be alright. Seems to be a white elephant, according to my own experience and Anne Waldman's. I just hope it isn't laying too much of a trip on you to keep the house under your protection. Is/was the Ashley stove useful in actual cold? Bob gave me to understand it was superfluous, the house is so tight. Gas stove's a great idea. If Skinner can do something about the refrigerator, in the right season, if he's still there, I'll be grateful—sooner or later I'll get that unkinked.

[Lewis] MacAdams is scheduled to interview me for *Rolling Stone* sooner or later also. Give 'em everything Heaven and Hell. Did you see my poems in *Stone* with photo Dylan on Kerouac's grave? (January 15 issue.) Have you also received *First Blues* book yet? I'll be recording it in March. I may be on West Coast April or May before going to Boulder for summer. I'm up to 9,700 prostrations but I keep getting sick—started last year this time, was in hospital all May, started in September and sat a week 8–12 hours a day with my nephew Alan [Brooks], and then had ladybug sized kidney stone and had to cancel two week solitary cabin—now have toe operation get rid of corn-bearing bone spur, and a hernia to get operated on. God knows when I'll finish, probably at Kitkitdizze in 1999.

Going to Brussels—Paris for a week and half, see Gregory in Paris (free trip from theater there in Brussels). Then to read at Corcoran Gallery, Washington D.C., with Burroughs February 9, see D.C. society and CIA, etc., again. Then late February early March record what I can of *First Blues* at Columbia with various musicians I've worked with—Arthur Russell on cello and 19-year-old Botticelli-faced idiot savant musician from Rolling Thunder Tour, David Mansfield, who plays steel pedal piano and violin and piano and guitar and mandolin, and Jon Sholle who's worked with me on three previous music albums, Blake, etc. Then Trungpa in N.Y. a month till late March so I'll hang around. Then Naropa two weeks—and then after April 11 maybe West Coast for couple weeks. You're teaching somewhere in spring three months, I forgot?

Let me know what metalbestos costs. I took part last summer at an anti-plutonium rally at Rocky Flats outside of Denver, but came away realizing I didn't really know the facts in extenso and wonder if anyone does. Wrote a big huge letter poem to Nanao called "If Plutonium" which amused him—don't remember what I said.

Trungpa keeps hammering away at what he speaks of as "Ginsberg Resentment" as a bad karma political style—it keeps me awake at nites.

Working with Gordon Ball on *Journals 1953–61* a lot of it typed, he's editing for Grove Press a volume of selections. I have a secretary Richard Elovich who lives with Burroughs' secretary Jim Grauerholz, so we got a machine going all together, some kind of writing machine filing machine—beginning to get my files in order, gathered from Cherry Valley and Paterson in New York City new apartment. Peter plunking banjo, Denise electric guitar hours and hours a day. Peter working on poem book, he needs a secretary too for 20 years of scribbled journals.

Love to Masa and Jonathan, Bob E., and Kai and Gen—and anyone and Jerry Brown too. Peter's sitting often almost regularly more regular than me lately in fact. Anne Waldman and Michael B [Brownstein] are in Boulder—hope you get there somehow next summer passing thru.

OK

PS I taught William Carlos Williams—Reznikoff—Marsden Hartley—Pound—Bunting—Lawrence mostly W.C.W. [William Carlos Williams] at Boulder last year and ended reading you, Philip Whalen and Philip Lamantia and Jack [Kerouac]. In selecting your work I went thru last book looking for examples of hard-line riprap solidity and noticed you were getting as bad as me into psychopolitical generalization which

violated "no ideas but in things" rule. The one particular poem notice-
ably "faulty" was first two lines of "Front Lines"—first two lines and lines
16, 17—edge of cancer, pulse of the rot, etc.—seem off key compared with
solidity of rest of poem. Particularly the image of cancer set against where
we must draw the line is, like, mixed metaphor so to speak—the precision
of rest of the poem too good to be spoiled by the over-wrought cancer
beginning. I used "Steak" p. 10, "The Bath," " Front Lines," "Call of the
Wild," "Ethnology," "Two Fauns" and "What Happened Here Before"
as examples of basic solidity. But the cancer line in "Front Lines" in the
context of a solid month of William Carlos Williams seemed crazed.
The class cast a cold pitiless Sophoclean-light eye on it. I guess teaching
perverts the mind.

Terrific curricula you have for the school district!

Love

Allen

176. ALLEN GINSBERG [NEW YORK] TO GARY SNYDER [NEVADA CITY, CA]

January 23, 1976

Dear Gary:

Wrote you last week. Ron Sukenick of University of Colorado in Boulder
will be writing you inviting you (and McClure) to literary conference in
Boulder sometime between June 21 and July 4 this year, and Anne Waldman will be writing you re Naropa for same period, so maybe between
the two they'll be enuf work money and people to make it interesting.
I'm leaving for two weeks Brussels/Paris mañana. Maybe you could teach
both places same week if you're able to come.

OK

Allen

177. ALLEN GINSBERG [NEW YORK] TO GARY SNYDER [NEVADA CITY, CA]

[ca. April 13, 1976]

Dear Gary:

Back in New York after couple weeks Boulder teaching. How's Cincinnati instructions? You had ambitious program—found students to study,

and read the books? I've been doing a basic course Reznikoff—W. C. Williams for *vipassana* focus, with side looks to Pound, Bunting, Marsden Hartley's poems, Lawrence, and others for observation of details—using that as basic platform to explore emptiness (Mahayana) and craziness (Vajrayana) poesy styles. Not much of a system, more a progression, i.e. Grounding students in minute particulars before teaching Kerouac or Céline.

Where's a book of L. Woodworth Reese, you ever had one?—looking for American details.

Going to L.A. this Sunday for a local Buddhist festival at UCLA—meet Ken Kesey and visit Leary in San Diego Federal Jail—working on his case again with PEN Club and Amnesty International to get him out. He says Gov. Brown visited him in jail, before he was released from California authority last year.

Is Brown ripe enuf to run for Prexy?

I'm mostly at my father's side during tumor wasting illness—in Paterson a week at a time.[154] Also been recording songs for John Hammond Sr. for Columbia.

Love to Masa,
Allen

178. ALLEN GINSBERG [NEW YORK] TO GARY SNYDER [NEVADA CITY, CA]

July 18, 1976

Dear Gary:
    "Bookkeeping in the moonlight
        frogs count
        my checks"
          —1974
Allen

---

154. Ginsberg's father, Louis Ginsberg, was dying of cancer and Allen tried to spend as much time with him as he could.

September 15, 1976

Dear Gary:

Thanks for your newsy lightningbolt epistle. To house business, any arrangement you make with May and Goshi is obviously ok since I am not there on hand in place to have differing mind. One distant obsession I do have though, is having the west side porch finished, not too big a job, if May and Goshi run out of work on my house as you guess. The porch girders are in place, I think I once ordered and put under the house enough wood for joists (not sure). So need to buy flooring for porch.

I saw Jonathan in Boulder with Tanya on way to Egypt, also saw Skinner briefly and we talked a little about house; I sent him check for $100 a few weeks ago to cover whatever costs were leftover from woodshed; in addition to what money was left in bank with Jno.

Propane stove fine, has anyone found that useful? I talked with Skinner about moving outdoor kitchen once and for all to spot near Bedrock Mortar where we set up extra water tap (near carpentry shelves in trees). IF outdoor cooking's finished for the season, that's for next spring. The propane icebox still isn't working, is it? Do Goshi and Skinner have any way of trucking it out to be fixed, or dumped if it's unfixable? Last but not least if you run into an organ-fixing genius, the bellows of that organ needs work. Needs an experienced hand, I finally found someone in N.Y. to fix up one in my apt.

I've been getting more into keyboard and'll get a piano in the city one day or month soon. Finished full-scale blues record with John Hammond Sr. produced for Columbia records—a few spots of genius, the rest melodic but probably heavy-labored vocally, good accompaniments.

Cherry Valley in good shape, big garden this year by tenants, caretaker gang includes farm boy Graham who grew up on adjacent cow farm now sold off by his family; Peter has tractor and's piled up vast compost heaps. I've been absent for more than a year so came back and found all sorts of manuscript and book treasures and long forgotten mail.

Next week Burroughs and I are going to Germany—Berlin, I've never been there—spend two weeks and give reading and check out translations and publishers since I'll be there; then a week in Paris stay with

Gregory in Trocadero area, he has baby Orpheo Max Corso, see to proofs of four books being put together there, then home a few days then join Peter in Northern Wisconsin at Naropa/Vajradhatu Seminary (same I went to three months fall 1973)—my practice been desultory so will use time for lots of sitting and prostrations. Prostrations got me stuck at 10,000—some kind of Jewish unwillingness to enter and strain the body is Chögyam's guess. Anyway plenty of time there to work it out. Also will teach some poetry there. After December when I get out, plans are open, probably give as many readings as I can get, maybe tour with musicians, I've been broke and slightly in debt paying so much attention to summer Naropa, helping support it $$ in fact; beautiful scene poetically in summer, beginning to shape up now in fact as some kind of continuity socially and poetically, we're experimenting still with what results from so much concentration of people and time. I got a lot of work done—10 years' typing—with my apprentice course over last two summers—can use that for big projects; and I tend to organize my poetry thoughts for teaching and read more—like *Paradise Lost* and Wordsworth—to check up my rusty opinions. The main problem is having genius young poets to teach so that there's a real transmission. That kind of genius is slowly appearing there, it'll take years to develop something real. This year, I mean, I've become conscious of half a dozen poets 20–30 years old who seem to have a sense of reality and some Orphic spark—mostly people I know from letters—one "Antler" in Milwaukee works in can company especially, long poem *Factory* that Ferlinghetti has. I mean an organized generational transmission of info and character—but I'm beginning to think it's possible. Next year course I'll teach "Literary History of Beat Generation"—might as well do that once for all. In 1975 I taught W. C. Williams, taped it, and now the 25 hours of tape of that sequence are being broadcast over N.Y. Pacifica WBAI every Thursday noon—exposition of W.C.W. [William Carlos Williams] *Collected Earlier and Later Poems*. Phil and I taught a sort of crazy quilt course together, unplanned from week to week, anything we were preoccupied with. Let me know if you'll have time to pass thru and dig the scene next summer. I'll also be there two weeks in March.

Working on various books, poems 1972–76 for City Lights called *Mind Breaths* and book of 1950–60s journals Gordon Ball's editing. But my mind is scattered mostly, maybe permanently.

Put out what money you think proper; I'll have money after December to pay you back. Make what house arrangements you find best. My own worry is porch, outdoor kitchen, icebox, organ.

Love

Allen

[PS] Burroughs' son Bill, 29, had liver transplant operation in Denver a few weeks ago, still survives, no one knows. Burroughs Senior stayed with him thru this week, will go to Berlin and then return to Boulder and stay there till his son's a little stronger, the illness brought them together a little . . . So meanwhile Bill Sr. will teach a fall course at Naropa. Trungpa came to hospital so they got together there as well as public reading with me and Anne Waldman. I'm sick of gurus and Buddhism and sitting and lineages and Naropas, but there seems to be no other way, it's tough.

Apartment in New York pretty well fixed up, maybe I'll take on additional next door space, I'm getting too crowded in with books and now I want to get a piano for Xmas and more tape equipment, as music seems more and more pleasurable, and possible to do well, write songs and record. You still got a cassette player?

Love to Masa Kai Gen We'pa Skinner Toshi and Mai, tell Will I got his poem thanks.

How's [Gov.] Brown and your Arts Council? Interesting conversation with Duncan about philosophy of subsidies, he said he thought Brown was hysteric, i.e. ideologue, i.e. theoretic ideas, moralist. Does Brown believe in God? [Jimmy] Carter's God's a little zany. Trungpa's teaching of nontheism seems to have penetrated my skull finally. It does seem strange that for 20 years I've been yapping about God. Why didn't you tell me to shut up?

180. ALLEN GINSBERG [LAND O' LAKES, WI]
        TO GARY SNYDER [NEVADA CITY, CA]

November 1, 1976

Dear Gary:

Peter and I been here since a month, seminary weeks of sitting alternated with study of *sunyata*, Bodhudta, Atisa's "Drive All Blames Into One" (one's self)—terrific. Peter's really stream-winner! with a hundred other idiots here. I'm teaching Reznikoff / W.C.W. [William Carlos Williams] as *shamatha-vipassana* style "Poetic Grounds" so to speak. Be here till December 4, then New York City. Head now full of dharma, last month full of Berlin and Paris. Finishing *Mind Breaths* poems 72–76 for City Lites. All your wood chopt for winter? Thin Ice is *sunyata* classification glimpse so to speak?

Love
Allen

181. ALLEN GINSBERG [LAND O' LAKES, WI]
TO GARY SNYDER [NEVADA CITY, CA]

November 26, 1976

Dear Gary:
My card and your letter crossed in the mail. I'll write when I get out of here. Thanks for accounts. Lovely woodshed news. Studying co-emergent wisdom Tibetan style here. OK to take Goshi rent out in your work. But I still would like to arrange gas refrigerator situation, which he might do sooner or later if it's possible. Either fix it if it's not working, or get rid of it and look for a new one by the time land gets hard enuf to transport it and air hot enuf to need it. Also still interested in side porch. I can send money for materials for either. I'll be in Bay Area and hope to visit after mid-April probably—be reading touring then West Coast.

Love
Allen

182. ALLEN GINSBERG [NEW YORK] TO GARY SNYDER [NEVADA CITY, CA]

December 14, 1976

Dear Gary:
Glad the Servel's[155] in the shed hooked up. I was worried that it was sitting eyesore in the Ponderosa Circle. Yes, get hose and lamps. We have propane lamp fixtures at Cherry Valley.

I'll be two weeks in Boulder March 28–April 8, teaching Naropa mind to page poetic forms something like that, and read at Ft. Collins with

---

155. The propane gas refrigerator.

Duncan April 7. Then I thought to go to San Francisco if I can find readings out there mid–late April, so probably May Day be perfect time for me to show up at Kitkitdizze, maybe a few days before. I'll be away from New York so you're welcome to use my room, Peter and Denise may or may not be at the apartment, my room will be empty, with desk in it. So I'll be there May Day '77.

I'm broke (did I say so last letter?) so I've got to go out do readings, all last year Rolling Thunder Daddy Death and Sitting Dharma kept me poor, so my April May movements be regulated around readings but certainly'll be open around May Day, just right! [. . .]

Karmapa Lama in town, interesting activity round him, he lectured to tantra cabal tonight Peter and I went, we were all sitting silent 10 minutes, he went "PHAT" real loud all of a sudden. Last nite left reception for him with Oda Roshi who took me and a couple others for sake and sushi at Saito restaurant here and we got drunk and gossiped. He asked about you, said he sorry never met face to face. He sees Muyra Roshi here twice a year. See Karmapa in San Francisco if you have time—heir to Milarepa!

Love

Allen

[PS] All sorts Japanese journalists coming round lately. Anything beside Suwa-no-se news I should tell them?

183.   GARY SNYDER [NEVADA CITY, CA]
       TO ALLEN GINSBERG [NEW YORK]

                                      25.XII.76 [December 25, 1976]

Dear Allen,

A moment of quiet as Kai and Gen are down to your house, playing with Gen Kogure. Masa in India. Me just finishing three days of mail, and looking at latest *C.Q.* [*CoEvolution Quarterly*]—Peter Warshall's "watershed" editing.

Three bucks: one 4 point; one 2 + 1 point; one forker (= 2+2) at the pond. Lots of flickers.

I'll be in New York for the Chinese poetry conference April 17–24. Rexroth has already lined up the [James] Laughlin apartment. What actually about me staying at your apartment that week? Maybe with Masa? If ok, book us for it. Also, I don't think I know its actual address, etc. Peter and Denise there? Then.

So, we'll see you around May Day. News for Japanese journalists. I guess I told you typhoon #17 (mid-September) ruined the gardens (two meters water fell in three days)—landslides crushed houses—four or five killed including a week-old baby and Ueji, the tough old deep-diver from Okinawa, in his 80s. They will be a long time recovering. Yamaha's installations not so hard-hit on Suwa-no-se Island.

And, the rise of ethnic pride amongst the Ainu. Also Nanao translated all of *Turtle Island* into Japanese and turns out to be a very superior translator of poetry—it might be an influence (via his fresh ways of using Japanese)—on future poetry there. I gave all Japanese rights to *Turtle Island* to *Buzoku*, so if it sells it might well help re-build the ashram. [. . .]

Love

Gary

184. ALLEN GINSBERG [NEW YORK]
  TO GARY SNYDER [NEVADA CITY, CA]

December 27, 1976, Merry New Year

Dear Gary:

All sorts of Japanese magazine ladies and gents coming by suddenly, I refer them further to Nanao—one lady brought gift box of Ogura Hyakunin Isshu (100 poems at Ogura Mt.) on tiny bright colored cards.

Maybe I'll be out in April late, certainly May Day. Reading at St. Mark's with Robert Lowell February 23—strange karma he's out of hospital.

Hope this check don't bounce. I've been unnaturally broke—not reading much occupied with father's bedside last year, Rolling Thunder, Naropa summer and fall seminary—nice to be dollarless relatively for a while.

Love

Allen

185. ALLEN GINSBERG [NEW YORK]
    TO GARY SNYDER [NEVADA CITY, CA]

January 4, 1977

Dear Gary:

Our notes have crossed in mail? I don't alas get *C.Q.* here. My apartment will be open with plenty room when you're in New York as I'll be in San Francisco. So we'll rendezvous in Kitkitdizze by April end for May Day. So when you and Masa get to N.Y. or before, phone the apartment or send card so that Peter or Denise will meet you. My place is all fixed up and expanded.

Some Jap company is publishing most of *Allen Verbatim*, as of a while back. You're blessed to have Nanao translate *Turtle Island*; I have awful feeling Yu Suwa's old translation of my poetry's only deranging Japanese minds that read it. Your *Buzoku* royalty grant makes sense. I'm tangled with 10 different manuscripts translated in French and German and Spanish I'm trying to correlate and supervise. Leaving for several weeks anonymous immersion in furnished room in Baltimore with kid poet friend and try read *Paradise Lost* and *Jerusalem* aloud!

Love
Allen

186. GARY SNYDER [NEVADA CITY, CA]
    TO ALLEN GINSBERG [NEW YORK]

[*ca*. January 6, 1977]

Dear Allen,

Goshi paid December rent with $12 worth of work (putting shingles on outhouse) and $48 cash. You have $108 credit now—to use for materials, etc.

Snowed a little. Good quiet days. Baker was here over New Years.

Love,
Gary

187. ALLEN GINSBERG [NEW YORK] TO GARY SNYDER [NEVADA CITY, CA]

June 27, [1977]

Dear Gary:

Excellent news ramada completed. Enclosed check for $250 to cover expenses, thanks for putting it out. Any chance of completing or starting the side porch if I send lumber or carpenter money?

Hilarious paranoias here. Ed Sanders *Investigative Poetics* course is investigating the Bly-Merwin-Trungpa-Naropa complex.[156] Seems Bly questioned here in Boulder at his reading whether Merwin wasn't personally raped in 1975. That's maybe what was on Bly's mind. Anyway Sanders is checking out in skeptic groove every direction, a terrific local shot.

I read "Bard Contest" [i.e. "Contest of Bards"] here with 10-piece orchestra recruited from my poetics class, gala symphony nite and Peter read ¾ hour and sang and Gregory introduced sober in white suits. He gets along well with dharma heir, Ösel Tenzing. Lotsa horrific soap opera round Gregory and babe and his nutty mother—all ironing out smooth.

Maezumi Roshi of Los Angeles here, he's fine, I been sitting watching.

Love to you—Joanne Kyger taught first day here.

All going well, broke as the school is. Sorry Peter and I missed May Day late. We did both however turn in manuscripts to Ferlinghetti. Peter's first book [*Clean Asshole Poems and Smiling Vegetable Songs*].

Love to Masa and all,

Allen

188. GARY SNYDER [NEVADA CITY, CA] TO ALLEN GINSBERG [NEW YORK]

7.VII.77 [July 7, 1977]

Allen,

Thanks for the check; it brings you up to a minus $27 balance—all's fine—but you should send another 2 or 3 bills for lumber to do deck.

---

156. The affair, which became known as "The Naropa Poetry Wars," began when Trungpa ordered an unwilling W. S. Merwin to be stripped and brought to a party by force.

Hey!! the refrigerator works. Goshi kept fooling with the adjustments until it suddenly started full-scale freezing. Very nice.

Enclosed, the book-list I gave out in Cincinnati; finally found it. Will be doing an emphasis on oral literature up in Washington next week with Philip—Some Ainu oral epics translation—by Don Philippi—still unpublished.

J. Brown is looking for land to buy near us—he was here over the 4th weekend. He'll be making an offer on a piece this week.

We all got in the Willys pickup and drove clear out to Allegheny and got picked up by a gold-miner in a bar and taken down into his mine-shaft, all dark and muddy. (This land-search is to be kept quiet, so that people won't raise their prices.)

Been reading Dogen [Zenji], *Shobogenzo* in the [Kosen] Nishiyama—[John] Stevens translation. Francis H. Cook (who has a book fresh out on Hua-yen [Avatamsaka] philosophy) says it's not a perfect translation by far, but anyway, Dogen's a genius and almost-poet. Cook is a professor of Buddhism at Riverside, and a student of Maezumi Roshi.

Good summer, no fires so far.

Love to you, and to Peter, and Joanne if she's there; and to Anne W.

G.

189. ALLEN GINSBERG [NEW YORK] TO GARY SNYDER [NEVADA CITY, CA]

September 15, 1977

Dear Gary:

Peter and I returned from Naropa this week, after spending 10 days in prostration-retreat at Libre Commune in southern Colorado Huerfano Valley. Every time I go on such retreat I vow to cut off all excess baggage and come back to N.Y. and find it bigger than ever—papers, apartments, interviews with *NY Times*. You would enjoy Libre—that's where Nanao lived in cave—vast view of Sangre DeChristo range from opposite wall of Orphan Valley. The social group there reminded me of the coop individuality of San Juan Ridge and Kesey's Springfield gang of families—matured from '60s idealism (Peter Rabbit of Libre and others, Dean Fleming painter formerly a founder of Six Gallery) started Drop City, learned caution from that, and went up to Libre in '68. Several other

communal landowner groups—Red Rockers and Anonymous Artists of
America, are scattered within eagle's eye view of each other—as well as
reformed peyote-Christer "Ben Eagle" formerly founder of N.Y.'s evil
Motherfuckers group with 300 acres where he holds peyote meets with
traveling Indians. Sheriff's friendly, they grow tall grass and have vegetable
gardens, rock bands, exquisite carpentry, panoramic isolation 9,000 feet
up, and competence and curiosity. They'd like you to visit. Peter and I
and Gregory went down to do a benefit in a large dome for their local
clinic, and they arranged cabins for retreat for us—have horses—one farm
has blacksmith group and horse-team vast gardens and Chinese medicine massage students—three hours south of Boulder by car.

I'll be in New York this fall and winter, some trips to Coast and Okla-
homa for readings intermittent. Book of *Journals Early '50s Early '60s*
came out from Grove, did you receive a copy? Working on proofs of
Mind Breaths till 6 A.M. last nite, including my punk epic (I left in "lilac,
honeysuckle, rose")—all typed and cleaned up. Also did a little book
of stray poems for Charlie Plymell's Cherry Valley editions [*Poems All
Over the Place*], assembled index and manuscripts for two books, *Collected Interviews* and *Assembled Prose* (for City Lights and Grove) and
have proofs of a hundred-page academic book of literary essays and
interviews for Don Allen, working on that this week. Wrote intro and
am editing my texts for Shambhala Press volume, *Annals of Jack Kerouac
School of Disembodied Poetics at Naropa Institute Teachings 1974–77* by
Duncan, Dorn, Rothenberg, Burroughs, Clark Coolidge, Ted Berrigan,
Corso, Walden, Whalen, Miguel Algarin (on street poetics), McClure,
Brownstein, etc. etc. Real discourses on method and minds. So I've been
working with furious frenzy.

Apartment in New York lovely, plants on windowsill and millions of
papers and files and meat in the icebox.

I haven't sent money for the porch lumber at Bedrock Mortar because
I was broke. Is it too late to truck in the lumber? I have some gold at
hand.

Students in Apprentice Class at Naropa did encyclopedic work for me
typing and indexing all these books. Ed Sanders "Investigative Poetics"
course organized a sensational comical book, *The Party*, an investiga-
tion 200 pages time tracking the Trungpa-Merwin Vajrayana Seminary,
and left a copy in the Naropa Library for interested scholars. General

conclusion was that Merwin was acting panicky and somewhat snobbish in wrong situation he himself helped set up, Trungpa was crazy
with alcohol or wisdom, one or another, but working hard, and that Bly
was bumbling and gossipy. At least that was my conclusion and seems
general, for this "can of worms."

Which brings me to subject of this letter. Can you visit and check
out the scene and teach, even if briefly, next summer? The assemblage
will be solid: Sanders coming back to teach Greek prosody and rhythm,
Duncan, John Wieners, McClure, myself, Burroughs, Corso (who held
five-week once-a-week workshop students thought was the most live
teaching there—Gilgamesh, Bacchae, Céline, the Great Year, etc.), Anne
Waldman and Michael Brownstein and Dick Gallup all teaching longer
courses 2½ weeks to all summer. Kenneth Koch, Ken Kesey, and LeRoi
Jones will visit, with probably John Ashbery. Some plan afoot to invite
Bly to speak or read, too. Kate Millett to teach Chaucer, Audre Lorde,
and a few others, Donald Sutherland who lives in Boulder. We'll apply
for a grant with Bill Matthews of Colorado University to bring Basil Bunting over for the summer, his daughter lives in Boulder. Brakhage will
have film series-lecture (he did one presentation this summer). So that's
what we have planned. Orlovsky be the heavy in the poetry workshop
run by student next summer. Can you come for a class or a few classes,
and a reading? We'll try to get other gigs for you nearby to make up the
money which is scarce. But there's fare round trip, apartments, and a
few hundred dollars and vast strange company. The students this year
included a whole generation of interesting poets—Antler from Milwau-
kee, Bobby Meyers from Pittsburgh, Andy Clausen from Oakland—who
took Gregory C. and Max back with him to Oakland with Andy's wife
and three kids. Gregory been in touch with Peter Coyote for Maestro
Program, hope that works.

Naropa's becoming more secular, intentionally, Buddhist based but
less Tibetan sectarian, with time year maturity, an inevitable development, at least that's the plan—that's why I wish you'd come and bring your
nature. Can bring family. If you could do 2½ weeks visiting poetics that
be great but if you can at least drop in and read and look around I'd appreciate your advice to see how it's going. This year was the first it seemed
to me where there was a gang of poet students strong as the faculty—
i.e. half a dozen original minded younger poets, another generation

evidenced. Paul Shippee and I and a few others are working to get [E. F.] Schumacher there next summer too, to set up dialogue between Hinayana economics and Vajrayana approach. Burroughs, Leary, Trungpa, yourself, and others seem to have in common a "pessimistic" view of population, I just realize in common—Burroughs' latest book *Cities of the Red Light* is about a plague wiping out all but honest junkies; Leary wants to leave planet like a broken eggshell; you're ready for Neolithic 1/10 present population; Trungpa's got his Vajrayana mandala readying for the Kali Yuga,[157] it just sunk into my brain the similarity of estimate, or "realism" you might say. I was always a liberal optimist, whatever that means, with a happy go lucky irresponsible vagueness about what's gonna happen. But it did, this summer, amaze me to realize that various folks I respected did have this slow crisis view of the planet. Schumacher, in a way, is planning for a less catastrophic future. I suppose that's what I mean by Hinayana boy scout work vs. Vajrayana *sauve-qui-peut*. Just an odd thought of the last two weeks.

Write me a note. If I can and should, I'll send a few bills for the porch project. I'll be in California maybe at Davis in November, or earlier on a project to interview Dylan for his movie. Thanks for sending your reading list, I put copy in Naropa Library with Philip's and Bill's and others.

Let me know if you can come visit Boulder (and maybe side trip to Libre—they'll come and get you and bring you back) next summer or what your other travel plans are.

Love, as ever

Allen

190. GARY SNYDER [NEVADA CITY, CA] TO ALLEN GINSBERG [NEW YORK]

[after October 1, 1977]

Allen,

This land will be the site of a village temple-and-*zendo*, finally rolling.

Gary

---

157. Kali Yuga. The final of four Hindu stages in the development of the world.

October 3, 1977

Dear Allen,

Thank you for so much letter! Lots of news there—starting at the top, [...] in spite of all of your very attractive blandishments, I can't go to Naropa, I am learning not to make promises ahead so that I can get my work done. I did go last summer to Port Townsend, mostly for the money, and even that was too frantic for my summertime taste. Large groups of literary people (or even Buddhist-minded people) seems suspiciously like an excessive energy hit.

About money for porch lumber, the money will work any time you send it; and the roads are certainly not muddy yet; so we could go ahead and work on it. You now have a minus credit of $67.23; that's partly because I bought another propane tank for your place, for an extra, and something left over from the purchase of the fire pump. Your ramada is exquisite. Goshi has also built a fine heavy-duty outside kitchen work table which is in the ramada. I think, if you can, you ought to send about $200 for lumber (actually that's not enough. Need more like $350 to cover everything) and see how that goes.

Hey—just because the world's coming to an end, doesn't mean that my position is like a "Vajrayana *sauve-qui-peut*." And the Hinayana (what I mean is, Hinayana does nothing except as when the Marxist *bhik-khus* [like in Ceylon] start rolling. The most active Mahayana group politically is Nichiren—the Soka Gakkai—I get their newspaper—pretty interesting sometimes) doesn't do boy scout work much on that either. It's Mahayana that we, I trust, are all inspired by; and as I said at the end of "Four Changes," there is nothing really to be done—so that's why we do it. That, and a lingering sense of (as Jeffers would say) the beauty of things, which makes one think that keeping a small planet in shape is part of our practice; Oda Sessô Roshi called it "the garden"—and as you know in Zen we meditate and we sweep the garden. Yeah. Burroughs has been harping on the theme of coming crisis for a long time. I guess something will happen; but then things might surprise us and go on just as they are.

I'm having a fine time working six days a week twelve hours a day at Ditch Hut doing the actual writing on the prose book about Asia—I do about five pages a week actual writing. It's like digging in bedrock. But it's very exciting: I have just re-translated a Neolithic love song from *The Book of Odes*; and Masa spent all last night working in the huge Chinese dictionary for me trying to identify three plants mentioned there. I am at work on the origins of Chinese patriarchy and hierarchy. And, what organization and intelligence, and how early! And, what a marvelous thinker and writer Chuang-tzu was. But you will see these things soon enough (when my book's done).[158]

Give my love to Peter and Denise; my stay in your apartment was just perfect, and I appreciate that visit immensely.

Philip was great in Port Townsend, too, he always got up to do zazen.

Faithfully,

Gary

[PS] Here's minutes from the first meeting of the suddenly organized local community to buy jointly a five-acre park and build a hall etc. on it. Be a good place to hold a *sesshin* if we ever get it together for the building.

Going camping up high with family tomorrow—one cold fling—been reading Dogen.[159] He's something.

[This is a reference to a copy of the October 1, 1977, minutes for the Land Trust Association of Fire Access Road.]

192. ALLEN GINSBERG [NEW YORK] TO GARY SNYDER [NEVADA CITY, CA]

November 11, 1977

Dear Gary:

All my running around, fuckit I'm broke, so can't send porch lumber dollars. Enclosed check to cover my debit $67.23.

Left a month ago for Tulsa, Minneapolis, dropt acid there and did couple hours prostrations and *samatha* (nose outbreath) (mindfulness) and then got up and driven thru skyscraper landscape in funny Volks bus to Walker Art Gallery—the patrons looked as funny as the modern portrait pops—then onto airplane to San Francisco, went to meet Dr. [Albert] Hoffman, [Timothy] Leary, [Richard] Alpert, [Ralph]

---

158. The book was never done.
159. Dogen Zenji. A 13th-century Japanese Zen Buddhist teacher.

Metzner,[160] and the doctors who invented DMT and STP (turns out my cousin [Oscar Janiger] of Los Angeles invented DMT . . . he sez). I decided "LSD is ok because it teaches you not to cling to anything including LSD." Had long talks with Dr. Hoffman, said he last dropped acid with Ernest Juenger poet in 1970. Asked what he learnt in all he said, there are many realities, I asked why no more take, he said, I had the experience, no need go back repeat. Seemed most just, right words.

Ah, let's see—yes, thence to Hawaii, East West Convergence Conference with K. Oe, Ramanujan, *Abhidharma*-professor-playwrite Saraschandra from Sri Lanka (we performed blues with harmonium, student lute, and he on violin-like *esraj*,[161] which has microtonal blues wail echo of human voice) and Koreans, Iranians, Wole Soyinka, etc. Some scholars you knew—V. H. Vigliemo. I gave East-West discourse-convergence talk comparing or converging experience of Himalayan-American Vajrayana practice with LSD, a subject so specialized I don't know who would ever understand it or understand the humor of such a presentation— thence off to Kuai saw *King Kong* [movie] scenery (this inaccessible sea-valley used for King Kong helicopter background shots)—midst nature be mushroomed (local) the movies interposed their maya. Then to L.A., working daily with Dylan on exposition of text of his movie. Called your hotel room too late after you checked out, didn't connect with [Fred] Coyote till much later. I think its good to give Gregory grant for several reasons, based on close watch on him at Naropa and his social effect, and checking out his scene in San Francisco. Students found him the most live or inspiring teacher—they were most awake and alert in his class, and *sanghic* community found him workable enough to want him back all next summer as regular lecturer, difficult as he is. In San Francisco he's written a number of interesting texts—prefaces, newspaper pieces— which in decade's time will seem very sharp. His effect on local community is actually "enriching," in short run and long run. In long view he's an asset to the community around him, in an odd way both direct and indirect—it's an old story of artists. I'm talking in shorthand, I know the extensive reasoning based on social praxis that might discourage

---

160. Hoffman, Leary, Alpert, and Metzner were all noted authorities on the effects of drug use.
161. *Esraj*. An Indian stringed instrument.

$$ sympathy for him as beyond the pale of communal workability, but in this case I don't think life works that way, there's enough element of Coyote in his social person that makes him valuable local genius as well as sonofabitch as Coyote also was, remember that element of irreducible orneriness in Coyote, human stupidity. Anyway I sent formal letter to Peter (the other) Coyote as member of National Institute Arts and Letters re-recommending consideration of Gregory. Reasoning (1) despite appearances he's creating actively, (2) despite appearances he's socially useful, (3) his situation is old one, Van Gogh, Crane, etc. i.e. really difficult, oft half mad, but still spirit of genius is there working, producing artifacts which enrich others later in gross and fine ways both. It's odd. Didn't Bear or others get so mad at Coyote they wanted to kill him? For good reason? There's some puzzle like that here.

Back in N.Y., Voznesensky's here, we read together on Staten Island Ferry, and went to Max's[162] for punk rock led by Denise [Feliu] in purple lipstick and white fur jacket showing her bumpy bellybutton. Love to Masa. I'll send land trust fire money soon.

Allen

193. GARY SNYDER [NEVADA CITY, CA] TO ALLEN GINSBERG [NEW YORK]

December 6, 1977

Dear Allen,

Here's your tax bill for the year; Goshi has been putting in a lot of time this fall doing timber stand management (to apply on his rent), limbing, and clearing around your place; we have really reduced fire danger and it looks really good. The screen of manzanita on the side toward the meadow has been kept however, because I remembered your desire to have a sense of privacy that direction. Weather has been dry, so we still have a good chance to get lumber and start work on the deck. Right now is Rohatsu Sesshin—11 people sitting every night and morning—all of them practically veterans now, carrying the stick with true *manjusri*-dignity. In the chilly barn, lit by kerosene lights, with Tara at the altar. Have been reading [Kosen] Nishiyama—[John] Stevens' translation of

---

162. Max's Kansas City was a popular nightclub on Park Avenue South.

Dogen lately; he invented a new prose style. (Dogen did "Non-dualism prose" I'd call it.) Also, Francis Cook's new book on Hua-yen philosophy.[163] Pretty soon Bert Hybart will come and enlarge the pond, the bees are taking a nap, it's still a warm winter, all's well here.

Love,
Gary

194. ALLEN GINSBERG [NEW YORK] TO GARY SNYDER [NEVADA CITY, CA]

December 12, 1977

Dear Gary:

In one half-year spasm of literary orgasm I got *Journals Early '50s Early '60s* out with Gordon Ball, Cassady correspondence with Barry Gifford [*As Ever*], and *Mind Breaths* poesy 72–77 with Larry [Ferlinghetti], as well as concluding a volume of Naropa discourses by all hands [*Talking Poetics*]. Let me know which of first three haven't floated thru your window.

Enclosed $147 for rent and $153 toward porch lumber. I'll send more as more $ comes in. And am still planning on contribution to *zendo*/community hall. I've hardly read anything this year since Blake. I think I'll try to lay off editing my monumentalia for a while. I have the Yohoi volume of Dogen. Peter now this year has bees and we've already et some of their honey, a modest culling.

Went to party at Mrs. Kress' penthouse across from Metropolitan Museum of Art—Drummond Hadley had his wedding here—what a classic N.Y. palace! Marble bathroom and bedroom floors, Franz Hals on walls, or Velasquez, I forgot, Steinway pianos! It was a poesy party with [John] Ashbery, [Kenneth] Koch, and I'm happy to report that at 72 Stanley Kunitz wrote some sharp excellent short poems! We all read for charity that nite. Uptown charity. Where's Drum?

Well, love see you in time. Denise [Feliu] in England with drummer named Rat Scabies.

Allen

---

163. *Hua-yen Buddhism: The Jewel Net of Indra.* Penn State University Press, 1977.

195. GARY SNYDER [NEVADA CITY, CA] TO ALLEN GINSBERG [NEW YORK]

December 28, 1977

Dear Allen,

Received your checks, thanks a lot. Rain has really come in the last two weeks; we're up to normal rainfall now—with 18 inches so far this year. The pond is within two inches of being full and overflowing. Which means that we can't get lumber in now to build your deck until spring—so the money will be kept til then. Chuck Dockham says he'll work with Goshi to make sure it's well done. What a relief to have water now running through rivulets and cracks and filling up holes in the clay and making the ground mushy. Your three water tanks sustained your house with the Kogure family in it through the whole two years of drought. I don't think I pumped more than three hours total well water into it during that time; which means that you could keep a small garden going plus catch your domestic water off of those tanks in any normal year.

Don Allen is going to publish my old B.A. thesis "Dimensions of a Myth." Nathaniel Tarn has already written a funny little preface to it, comparing it with what it might have been if I had written it after the work of Levi-Strauss was better known. Anyway, it has taken me back to reviewing anthropology and myth and oral literature studies the last few weeks, thinking of what it was I was trying to learn when I did that work. Actually, the study of how we get conditioned, and how we condition that which conditions us, myth; I guess that led me on to Buddhism as way around myth? Or truer myth? But with Zen, really, myth of no need for a myth. It goes on from there, too.

All this anthropology study ties into work I've been doing also on Japan and the Ainu—did I tell you I've gotten to know Donald Philippi pretty well, amazing early Japanese literature scholar turned Ainu oral literature scholar, was twelve years in Tokyo, graduated from Shinto Priests University, now living in San Francisco? Friend of Irving Rosenthal, for a while he was in the Angels of Light. He does a northeast Pacific hunting peoples newsletter, called *Maratto*, under the pseudonym Slava Ranko. So, this week I'm writing an introduction to Donald's forthcoming book of translations of Ainu oral epics—really just a note to be published by University of Tokyo Press. Ainu have a really beautiful symmetrical hunters' world viewpoint. World folklore and mythology seems like mankind's natural collection of koans.

I'm also undertaking, without explaining to you exactly why, a minor repair on your outhouse—when you see it again, it will be all shiny and sanitary on the part you sit on. This will cost you a little; it's worth it.

Had Christmas in Grass Valley with my mother, who lives there now, and my sister; the first time the three of us have been together for Christmas in over 30 years. It was really mellow, and nice enough that we'll probably do it again.

Love,

Gary

[PS] Tell Peter that next fall I'm going to plant a whole hillside (well about a half acre) of fruit trees, if the soil looks right.

What is this punk rock craze?

Still raining.

Maezumi Roshi said "chant the *Dai hi shu* like rain falling all over the world."

196. ALLEN GINSBERG [NEW YORK] TO GARY SNYDER [NEVADA CITY, CA]

January 7, 1978

Dear Gary:

On reverse is a little ole poem to punk rockers ["Punk Rock Yr My Big Crybaby"]. It's certainly some kind of '70s style/movement, slight shift in thinking. I interpret it variously (1) Revolt against elitist commercial star system Jagger-Warhol fashion degeneracy using some of their ideas like pop clothes (pants made of plastic garbage bags instead of expensive Dior degenerate clothes @ $1,000, pants made of plastic garbage bags held together by safety pins). (2) Frank statement of hopelessness of "world situation" not dissimilar to your own realization earth can only support 1/10 present population: "No future for you / No future for me." Actually while everyone official is trying to patch the whole monstrous ecologic mess together, they just say from teen vantage point, "Ugh! Nowhere to go, I'm horrid, you're horrid, fuck us all!" Kind of refreshing public message compared to most public messages. From Buddhist point of view it might be interpreted as recognition of First Noble Truth of total suffering; as opposed to Utopian assumption that everything's basically all right and trouble's only temporary. (3) Just a new wave of intelligent vigorous kids inventing their own black comedy in a seriously post-atomic world irrevocably poisoned by plutonian cesium, etc.

I'll send more money for porch for next spring soon. How much was common assessment for *zendo*? Peter planted a lot of fruit trees, this fall. He finally got a copy of Schumacher's tree bible, *Tree Crops: A Permanent Agriculture* by J. Russell Smith Devin.

Fine about toilet seat. Peter and I going off in hour for tantra group weekend, setting prostrations, tape lectures by Trungpa, community meet, and 2½ day *sesshin*.

Love

Allen

[PS] Happy New Year to your mother.

Punk, just basically a new conscious generational change, precipitation of urban indecision thru '70s. Old fairies appreciate it.

---

197. GARY SNYDER [NEVADA CITY, CA] TO ALLEN GINSBERG [NEW YORK]

January 10, 1978

Dear Allen,

California drought done now, eight inches of rain the last 10 days, the pond overflowing for the first time in 2½ years. Green squishy ground everywhere. A little deer seemed all drenched by it and came and stood in the garage under shelter shivering; next morning it was dead. This-year buck fawn. Goshi and I skinned it and checked it out, it appears to have died of pneumonia. So now we are butchering it and preparing to divide it up. In a normal year, I understand, only 60% of the fawns will survive a winter. The first year is critical.

A little accounting: your last check for $153 gave you a credit of $146.72 (subtracting something that you owed me). The heavy rains have made it impossible to bring in lumber for the time. However, I have spent $44.15 having your mandala framed and mounted, and put out $41.20 for a forest service type stainless steel fly proof toilet seat (and stool) to go in your benjo. The toilet seat that was installed there by Bob E., though aesthetical, not practical; and I decided to switch my toilet and yours at the same time to fly proof and sanitary washable seat and stool. I'm sure you will approve when you see it. Goshi will switch toilet seats today. So my total expense is $85.35 which leaves you a credit of $61.37. That is not quite enough probably to get all of the lumber necessary for your deck, so you should try to send a little more further on, so we can do it right.

Do you remember Non who was here with us the summer you were building your house? She came by New Year's Eve with her old man and a friend of her old man living in a converted Baptist church bus that still had Longview, Washington, written on the side. They have been living in tipis in various parts of the Southwest the last few years, going through cold winters in tipis, and she has two little babies now. The first was born in a hogan, the second in a tipi. They are all very glowing brown-skinned bright-eyed healthy American Indian looking people now. Non does all kinds of elegant crafts for sale, and her man, who calls himself Bird, makes silver and lapis lazuli jewelry. It was good timing, because we had a big Japanese style New Year's Day feast the next day. Non sends her greetings to you.

I read that nobody went to the Sex Pistols in Nashville because they all went to Elvis Presley's birthday memorial.

Gary

198. ALLEN GINSBERG [BOULDER, CO]
    TO GARY SNYDER [NEVADA CITY, CA]

January 20, 1978 [*sic:* 1979]

Dear Gary:

Me and Peter here till March 15–20 in Boulder at 1439 Mapleton Avenue we have a little brick house facing southern sunlight, afternoon brightness in living room, plus dining room and two bedrooms and kitchen. It's short walk from Pearl and Broadway the center mall, I teach Blake's prophetic books Monday and Thursday eves around the block at Casey Jr. High School. Lafcadio here visiting, jumpy and innocent as ever. I'll be in New York City for one-week visit February 16–24. Get National Arts Club gold medal 22 February read at Allentown Muhlenberg College the day before. What're your travel plans? If you're anywhere near here, please stop over a few days and check out the scene (as otherwise described in *Harpers* article well written and thoughtful by Peter Marin).

Spent weekend in brief *sesshin* with Peter and 80 others sitting 9 A.M.–9 P.M. with three hours out to eat lunch and supper, and some talk about gentleness, tasting the heart, etc. Did Ferl send you Peter's book?

Love

Allen

[PS] I have no phone (at last)—had headaches all fall, stress, said doctors.

Burroughs here till end of January, and Anne Waldman till March and Michael Brownstein and Dick Gallup. Enclosed summer schedule from new catalog. Saw Zen Center school poster looks solid too.

199. ALLEN GINSBERG [NEW YORK] TO GARY SNYDER [NEVADA CITY, CA]

January 23, 1978

Dear Gary:

Punk is here to go!

Love

Allen

PS Saw Dylan movie tonight with Denise, it's fine and dandy. And long. [Basil] Bunting is broke by the way. I'll invite him (Basil B.) to Naropa and get grant for that. Enclosed letter from Bunting. Anything can be done in California?

200. GARY SNYDER [NEVADA CITY, CA] TO ALLEN GINSBERG [NEW YORK]

May 3, 1978

Dear Allen,

Seventy inches of rain this year. Practically wiped out the effects of the drought as far as we can see. Getting grass tall, or fruit trees planted. This is to bring you up-to-date on your house. May and Goshi moved out in early April and he finished out his time partially in work and partially in paying cash for rent for several months so that you now have a plus balance of $283.37 in your account. With that money it should be possible to do at least half of the building of a deck sometime this summer. The house is sitting all clean and empty. Another proposition has come up—several families near here including Masa are investigating the possibilities of receiving special funding under a new California law for a small local alternative school for one year only. If the school board looks favorably on their request, they are wondering if you would be interested in renting your house for all '78–spring '79 to the school board for use during the day only by a maximum of 12 students. The house would be insured for fire and damage, and liability insurance would be taken out. The teachers would be running the classes on a basic curriculum and good manners model, so that there would be no fear of careless danger and damage to the house, and anything that would be broken by accident would be repaired or replaced. Rate of rent would be established later, quite likely higher than what you were getting from Goshi since rents do keep going up. Anyhow, if you have an interest in this, let me know. Or objections. May and Goshi seem to be doing ok, and that would give them until September to decide whether or not they thought they should move back up here at the last minute.

Franco Beltrametti, Harry Hoogstraten, and Jim Koller were all here last weekend at the far end of their swing around the country giving poetry readings at various places. They gave a poetry reading at the big old house out across the large meadow and had a crowd of close to a hundred local people on a Sunday afternoon. Jim has a batch of fine poems with some combination of magical shamanistic turn and Chinese silence. I've started running from time to time—Jim does too, so he and I ran three miles together Monday morning early and saw a red-tailed hawk take off from a snag. It's true, running is like an analog of sitting, like floating sitting, quite lovely balance to the still kind of meditation. So we're all healthy, and wish the same to you.

Love,

Gary! Gary!

[PS] When you come here again?

201. ALLEN GINSBERG [NEW YORK] TO GARY SNYDER [NEVADA CITY, CA]

May 23, 1978

Dear Gary:

Been in and out New York. Three days at Creative Music Studio, Woodstock, teaching syllables and quantities of vowels and organizing a lousy performance of Blake's "Tyger" and other works. Had a good time and learned some more music. "Tyger" is coming along, I had the idea of trochaic heartbeat for it, finally got it down in tune.

I want to come out to Kitkitdizze for a month's retreat August 25–September 25 or some such month, after Naropa ends summer session August 20 or so. I don't know how that fits with the school renting idea not sure when school begins. I could shorten my retreat or shift to barn if necessary. Anyway I need a solitary month somehow and might as well try out Kitkitdizze, Bedrock Mortar, etc.

I'll leave for Naropa summer June 6. Phone me if need be for advisement if my plan's inconvenient. Ferlinghetti will be camping at my place or near some weekend this summer. If anyone needs work, please ask them to start on the deck, I finally have enough money to do it up-enclosed another $150—ask whoever does it to send me an estimate what more is needed $.

Otherwise the house is OK for school use. If retreat there really balls up the school deal, I can do it in southern Colorado Huerfano Valley, they've offered a cabin on mountain where I spent 10 solitary days last year. Retreat means prostration retreat cook food, leave notes if I run short of this or that, and see no one if possible for a month. What a gas! Socialize days before and after. (Or I could move up to Shobo-an if need be once school starts.)

I've been writing a lot, and escalated my activities so much beyond reason that my life is a total mess worse than ever—letters, projects ineptly completed, etc. Naropa, music, FBI-CIA investigations for PEN, studying Blake, miscellaneous filing systems—meditation wobbly—yet I seem to keep writing poems in a chain. I've probably got to do something to straighten it out.

Peter's upstate following Schumacher/J. Russell Smith plow—putting in trees, nuts and fruit.

Love

Allen

[PS] Organizing sitting—May 27 U.N. Mobilization for Survival.

EDITOR'S NOTE: *The school idea did not work out. The school board couldn't afford to do it, so Allen's cabin was free after all.*

202. GARY SNYDER [NEVADA CITY, CA] TO ALLEN GINSBERG [NEW YORK]

7.VI [June 7, 1978]

Dear Allen,

We may be gone all or part of August. Someone will be watching the place. Masa will be gone all July, but I'll be here. If gone in August will be to film petroglyphs in the SW—whole family along—no side-trip to Boulder, time too tight for that. Jonathan is going to do the deck some-time in July. 95° here today!

Gary

203. ALLEN GINSBERG [BOULDER, CO] TO GARY SNYDER [NEVADA CITY, CA]

June 19, 1978

Dear Gary:

Here's a new poem, "Plutonian Ode." I sent Larry Ferlinghetti a copy, and will send one to McClure. I sent a bunch of poems weeks ago to Larry for your *Journal for the Protection of All Beings* and *CoEvolution* issue and xerox J. Russell Smith *Tree Crops* argument his first 30 pages recommended by Schumacher and analysis of Rockefeller group's major investment in nuclear fuels—a mass of stuff to choose from, hope you and Mike get a chance to check it all out. Also I suggested to Larry, Peter's recycling poem "NYC Get Your Shit Together."

Been up all nights writing odes, sitting on Rocky Flats RR tracks, arrested, reading poem in court, etc.

Love

Allen

204. ALLEN GINSBERG [BOULDER, CO] TO GARY SNYDER [NEVADA CITY, CA]

August 22, 1979 [*sic:* 1978]

Dear Gary and Masa:

It's 7 A.M., been up all nite packing away the summer to leave this noon for Vancouver, thence to Bay Area around August 29, and spend time finishing book proofs with Don Allen. Then probably around September 7 or 10 we come up to Kitkitdizze. I have reading date at Las Vegas Col-lege, maybe depart Sacramento for that September 21 reading (leave day before?). Reading September 15 all fine for Grass Valley. I'll try to get up to Sierras, maybe with musician Steven Taylor, early as I can. Peter here, coming too. OK can talk then re *zendo*. I taught first five nights of "Vala or the Four Zoas" of Blake.

Love

Allen

205. ALLEN GINSBERG [SAN FRANCISCO]
     TO GARY SNYDER [NEVADA CITY, CA]

Saturday September 1, 1979 [*sic:* 1978]

Dear Gary and Masa:

Staying here at Shig's in San Francisco working with Don Allen on proofs may take a few more days, then will try to get up to Kitkitdizze as soon as we get a ride up. Have a pile of manuscripts to bring along—dead paper karma—and quiet mornings sitting to anticipate. I'll see Philip Whalen and Mike McClure probably before I leave. Peter here too, and my guitarist from N.Y. Steven Taylor and his girl. I may bring Steven up for the reading is it September 14 Friday (not September 15) according to posters? I have to fly to Las Vegas for reading September 21 so will leave probably a day or so earlier. Peter's typing up his student grades, I'm reading proofs.

Love
Allen

206. GARY SNYDER [NEVADA CITY, CA] TO ALLEN GINSBERG [NEW YORK]

3.XII.78 [December 3, 1978]

Allen,

Right now in Rohatsu Sesshin. Eighteen people sitting in the barn. Frosty cold, new crescent moon—good for little Buddhas.

G.

207. ALLEN GINSBERG [NEW YORK] TO GARY SNYDER [NEVADA CITY, CA]

December 27, 1978

Dear Gary:

Thinking of Land Trust and my own estate and Peter's fate and clean arrangements and consulting tax lawyers light bulb lit in my head re status of Bedrock Mortar. I would like to put it back into Committee on Poetry, Inc. This would make it easier to perpetuate as poet's hermitage. Taxes and upkeep are minimal so there'd be no problem keeping it up as it stands legally even if I weren't there to pay the bill, and it is probably beyond ken of my brother's heirs if it were in my private estate. Inhabitants or users could maintain upkeep $$ as directed by COP Inc. trustees Peter Orlovsky President and later yourself as trustee if I pass on to my reward. Please submit this for approval by Bald Mountain Association when convenient.

My further convenience is served by that fact that we can easily exchange Bedrock Mortar for the upstate N.Y. COP Inc. farm, which would then pass principally into Peter's hands, whereas it would be an unmaintainable tangle if it were COP Inc. property. He wouldn't be able to inherit it—unless I paid cash for it now. It's been appraised twice this year at roughly $19,000. Bedrock Mortar is worth more.

Lawyers advise me this arrangement is legal, unshady, and an excellent solution for what might be inconvenient tangle of management and inheritance of the two properties. If this prospect seems agreeable to you, my brother will contact Werthimer (with whom he's done business before over same land) to manage the technicalities, which seem to be minimal.

I think some sort of appraisal will have to be worked out, whatever sum is set as legally correct by Bald Mountain and real estate practice will be fine. If it's over $19,000 that'll be fine, COP Inc. will owe me money. Probably deed transfer will have to be registered at county courthouse.

Let me know if you can think of any problems, especially in regard to appraisal or re-registering deed—these can probably be worked out between Eugene Brooks (lawyer for COP Inc.) and Werthimer.

By this arrangement, New York land will happily be delivered to Peter as his own in time, unencumbered by COP Inc. ownership. It'll still be usable here for used poets in any case under his proprietorship, and I'll no longer be dependent on New York City apartment if I want to cut down expenses and labor, in future. Terrific! And Bedrock Mortar will be more secure for latter days. We'll still be able to visit and pass time and improvements can be made with tax-free monies from COP Inc.

I'll leave for Boulder/Naropa to teach Blake "Vala" January 5 to March 16, then trip a little, then teach John Ashbery's Brooklyn College class April–May 24, then take off with Peter for various poetry festivals Genoa, Paris, Cambridge, Brussels for a month and return a few weeks late for Naropa June 20 probably summer session.

Jonestown Guyana[164] interesting sent shudder through all populations

---

164. Jonestown had been the site of a mass suicide of more than 900 people that year orchestrated by Rev. Jim Jones.

unconsciously hooked on authority including my own *vajrayana*—"I got the fear!" as Burroughs character screamed 20 years ago. Bill B. said "It explodes all authority hypnosis everywhere" meaning also the queen, the governments, presidents, the boss at office, the bossy lover. Interesting how it seemed to penetrate whole populace like koan, lighting up all subliminal authority fixes. Patton leading his soldiers to egoic deaths, Nixon's favorite movie, shewed in N.Y. same week Jones headlines and TV pix.

Hanging around with Andrei Voznesensky, tripped to Boston with him, Harvard Faculty Club, Hunter College, and UN reading his English texts. He announced at UN in front of Mrs. Troyanovsky, Ambassador's wife, that me, Peter, and musician were to tour Russia next October, she said "What a marvelous idea," everyone applauded and he later said in the limousine, "That's how things get done in Russia, announce it as if officially and nobody doubts it until later and by then they'd be embarrassed to change plans." Some mysterious "authority" (him) announced it, and it may be sort of a fait accompli. We'll see.

Writing little poems, new book *Poems All Over the Place* out from Cherry Valley (Plymell) as well as Bremser (Ray) poems 1958–70, years overdue, they'll do Huncke's long-delayed *Day the Sun Turned Red* [*sic: Crimson*] sketches 200 pages next. Peter's *Clean Poems* arrived in N.Y., big party at Gotham Book Mart with Voznesensky, Ashbery, and 100 quarts of home made Orlovsky apple juice for celebration. We sent you invite card for fun?

Gregory I hear is in fine shape at last sober. I'll try going on road with him sooner or later. Peter eating raw foods, plenty energy. December issue—*New Age* journal [Peter] Chowka U.S. food exposition current issue excellent to read, summarized a lot of info. Nanao was here, we went to parties.

2:40 A.M. up late making checks paying bills, tomorrow we go sit for portrait (second in 15 years) by Raphael Soyer 79-year-old Russian ashcan school painter. Lots of activity here, Burroughs' Nova Convention weekend celebration big theater Waldman, John Cage, Patti Smith, Frank Zappa (reading talking asshole sketch from *Naked Lunch*) lotsa poets and French scholars and semiotics professors and punk rock bands down the street. New Years Day be giant St. Mark's benefit same theater—50 poets—7:30 P.M. to 2 A.M., two to five minutes each, I'll read at Whitney Museum W. C. Williams exhibition series January 2 and take off for Shambhala Kingdom in Boulder as said before, with Peter and

Lafcadio coming along for old times' sake. Bill Burroughs saw Cassady movie set [*Heartbeat*], said it might be OK, actor [Nick] Nolte uncannily like Neal he said, gave him a turn when they lunched together in S.F. Denise playing CBGB's punk club more, got band together eight months now steady.

Love to Masa, Gen, Kai, and Nanao if he's there. And You.

As ever,

Allen

[PS] I'd proposed you and Bill Burroughs for American Academy and Institute of Arts and Letters, second and final ballot your names been eliminated by preliminary vote, and Hollander, Kinnell, Irving Howe, Robert Hayden, and Brodsky and other modest talents there. Aargh, seems cabal of university poets Wilbur, Nemerov, Moss, Merrill, Wm Jay Smith, Hecht, Snodgrass, William Meredith, etc. rule and increase by inertia. I freak out at meetings and they yawn and mock. Awful mortmain.

208. GARY SNYDER [NEVADA CITY, CA] TO ALLEN GINSBERG [NEW YORK]

14:II [February 14, 1979]

Dear Allen,

[...] Just back from Alaska—at the northernmost point—Point Barrow—2,000 Eskimos living. All white, and 40° below. Masa danced, I did poems. They are starting a little university there—to be run by the Eskimos. They need donations of books—if Naropa or anyone you know has extras etc. they could send them (50 students) to: Rachel Craig, Inupiat University. No roads etc. only plane contact with outside, 500 miles to Fairbanks.

I might be able to stop by Boulder next three weeks, not sure yet. Am off to Tennessee and Kansas February 19th–March 2. I forwarded your invitation and address to Nanao, who should be at [David] Padwa's by now.

Will write again about your ideas on land-transmission. Baker and I have been talking about that too—good you're working on it; I think we all ought to organize some process.

Best

Gary

209. GARY SNYDER [NEVADA CITY, CA]
TO ALLEN GINSBERG [BOULDER, CO]

17.II [February 17, 1979]

Dear Allen,

Furtherance. Peter B.C. [Bluecloud] is clear with you for two months rent now—i.e. up to December 16. He'll come up with the rest later I think—he's broke right now, and except for gutters not much more to do for you—so will go to work for me in March—carpentry—and get some cash.

You got the mining stuff? We've a big fight on our hands with St. Joe Mineral who wants to strip-mine the diggings. If you're going to be out here, Nevada County, in April, May, or June, let me know. Maybe you and I (and Peter) could do a big reading in Nevada City—benefit—help raise something toward $5,000 for lawyer.

May would maybe be best. What chance? Later OK too—early fall—if you have plans to visit.

Masa and I just back from Alaska song-and-dance. WOW what space—civilization little islands surrounded by vast slow nature process cold moss-and-spruce—windy worlds. Feels very correct. Very *dharmic*. -40° at Barrow—wonderful middle age Eskimo lady Mormon who supports the old ways—my hostess. Masa did S. Indian bird-dance in Sari, on the edge of the Arctic Ocean (indoors of course).

Aitken Roshi did a *sesshin* in October here with us all—18 *sanzen* students—an excellent teacher. I hope to continue with him. Having done *mu* some time ago, he put me on one I'd never heard of—a "checking koan." "What is the source of *mu?*"[165] I'm still at it. Maybe go to Hawaii in June, do a little sitting at his place. Chilly winter this year.

Love,
Gaered

---

165. A well-known koan, about a monk who asked his master, "Does a dog really have buddha-nature or not?" to which the master answered, "*Mu.*"

March 20, 1979

Dear Gary:

Packing up to leave Boulder till summer. Peter and I weekend off to New Orleans then N.Y. till March 25. A couple weeks ago we read with Creeley and Nanao in Albuquerque (anti nuclear waste dumping) and Nanao came up to Boulder with us, so had interesting time discussing evolution of our flowery power views. He's translating *Plutonian Ode* and has been mixing with students reading with us in small poetry soirees in town.

Lots of excitement and screaming me, Ed Dorn, and Tom Clark over Boulder local magazine publishing Sanders' report and long funny interview with me which I didn't get to edit so I got mad for a week, having got caught with my pants down insulting Merwin, Burroughs, Trungpa, Corso, all at once. I wrote Merwin and apologized at great idiotic length. I hope he has a better sense of humor than I did. Even Sanders got mad, since I said he'd been "into" Black Magic and [Alastair] Crowley, meaning observing such matters; but he thought the gentle reader would mistake my loose language to Ed and Tom as meaning he endorsed Crowley and practiced the Black Magiks.

I'll be in New York two months, I think I wrote, subbing for Ashbery at Brooklyn College creative writing course. Broke after three months here teaching in return for rent, but keeping up New York apartment is a drain. I decided I'll cut down on my New York expense, keep a small apartment and come back here next year and teach winter spring and summer, get the poetics school a little more solidly boned, and teach English "Basic Poetics," try to (Seafarer—Kerouac). Finished Blake's Lambeth (Prophetic) books to Urizen 1795 and found out what they meant, going over texts with students—a more communal group of students now, tho less meditative than party going and arguing.

Anyhoo, I'll be in Europe May 25–June 20 and then back to Boulder for summer, then out to Vancouver. Peter will be your replacement on that Warren Tallman reading. If I get back in time to S.F. I'll take your Turtle Island course at Santa Cruz or Green Gulch wherever it is. Anyway I should be in Bay Area and visit, late August or September, to Kitkitdizze. If Peter Blue Cloud's in residence we'll sleep in your barn or camp out, I guess Peter'll still be there.

We could do that St. Joe Mineral benefit sometime early September maybe, in fact for sure. I'll be on Coast (Vancouver) anyway. Be great to read in Nevada City. Peter Orlovsky there too.

Didja find the source of *mu*? This year first time I've been getting some much clearer sense of one hand clapping as just straightforward action solitary without excuse, rationalization, etc. Not that I've been working on it as koan but it seemed recently as an appropriate expression for some situations I've found myself in, and no one to explain to.

Interesting you're working with Aitken Roshi.

If the idea of transferring title of [Bedrock] Mortar house jells, let me know how much or what money needed for an appraisal so it's done correctly.

I'm under no pressure for money so whatever Bluecloud does is OK. Gutters or something sooner or later.

Studies with Trungpa continue to unfold tho my practice is not steady enough to take full advantage. Still, I set pretty regularly daily, but probably should get more centered into long range active practice more serious and lengthy retreats and Peter's caught up to me 30,000 prostrations, still long way to go. Prostrations series is sort of *dharmapala* barrier, amazingly total as involvement and a sort of purificatory run thru reminder of conditions of being in a body.

Got a gold medal for "Distinction in the Arts" from National Arts Club. Lovely nite, Mailer, Burroughs, and Ashbery all made sweet speeches, and I apparently put my foot in my mouth by reading dirty poems to the club in black tie (me too) not realizing they actually hadn't quite read my poetry but only their literary committee had. The lady president was shocked. So I sent her an apology for offending her inadvertently. I was really amazed anybody even listened to what I was reading. I discovered a week later they misspelled my distinction on the medal.

Peter's huffing and puffing packing bags.

I wish you'd pass thru here sooner or later and check it out. Nanao had a pleasant sake-saturated brief meeting with Trungpa and his dharma heir after a giant community meeting.

OK. Love to Masa and Gen and Kai and the Ridge folk.

Allen

April 3, 1979

Dear Allen,

Thank you for much information and good promise to come here in September. We will set up a September probably weekend date at the Veteran's Hall in Grass Valley for our joint benefit reading—you and me together, with maybe Don Scott playing some songs and some other musicians? Should be good. Is there any date in September that would be impossible for you; otherwise we'll just try to get it somewhere around the middle? That is to say, the first weekend after Labor Day. Have read all the elaborate Naropa journalism being generated; it is bemusing. I love Ed Dorn's comment on "the structure of Tibetan policing methods." At this considerable distance from it all, I have quixotic feelings namely that I never had any trouble taking off my clothes in front of anybody; I seldom waited to be told. And secondly, a kind of old Zen gut level feeling that if a roshi wants to do something with a student physically, he would do it himself with his own hands, rather than have somebody else do it for him. I do hope all of this simmers down and everyone can proceed on their profound, inconceivable, dharma liberation studies. Peter Bluecloud will be leaving your house probably at the end of May, and Scott McLean and his wife will be in it until around the first of September I suspect. I do rather think that your house will be vacant and available for you all of September; if you wish to set a date up from which time it should be available just say so and we'll see to it that it is. It looks beautiful. Green grass coming up around here and my much larger pond very inspiring. You will hear in another letter, in a few weeks, about our plans to build a *zendo*! With donated labor from local practicers, and donated money from whomever we can get to contribute. I leave in two days for three more weeks of poetry readings; how do you manage Europe? It seems too scary and complicated to me.

Love,

Gary Snyder

212. GARY SNYDER [NEVADA CITY, CA]
    TO ALLEN GINSBERG [NEW YORK]

May 23, 1979

Dear Allen,

Nice talking to you on the phone the other day. I've been really on the move this spring—finally a chance to get caught up on news and information. One interesting contact I made recently was with Murray Bookchin—Peter Berg organized a little conference in San Francisco around the reinhabitation theme, decentralism, bio-regionalism. Murray came out for that and he and I were on the same panel. I have never met anyone who seemed to have done the homework on revolutionary political history in the Occident so well—plus basic anthropology, and he's now in the process of developing an anarchist critique on Marxism. Also, formulating the principles of revolutionary ecology, and linking it to third- and fourth-world interests. He has a monthly or so newsletter which goes around.

What I really wanted to tell you about though is the evolving community practice here, that has led to the point of us wanting to build a *zendo*. Not only me but a number of my neighbors have become students of Aitken Roshi, and he will be coming at least annually from now on, as long as his health holds out, to lead *sesshin* with us. We had a full barn *zendo* house of sittings all this last year, and have about out-grown the barn. Many questions arise with the new project. One question is location: I want to ask if you would have any objection if the *zendo* were possibly built toward my end of the meadow and into the trees, right near where the new orchard is. This is one possibility. If such is done, it would require a proper granting to the *zazenkai* association, of "share" in the land-association; by some device, probably me simply subtracting a couple of my shares and giving them to the *zazenkai*. Or, if you and Dick were interested, you, Dick, and me each subtracting a one-third acre share from our own shares, adding that up, and giving a one-acre share to the *zazenkai's zendo*. I think that this would be basically legal. Another possibility is that it will be on another piece of land altogether. We'pa, or Michael Attie's. All of this brings me even closer to the point of wanting to refine our land-holding procedures and guaranteeing ways of orderly transmission. Another thought I've had is that in the long run I might want to make all or virtually all of my share of the land into long-range Buddhist practice trust country temple?—or school?—and that even, possibly, Dick might want to go along with that. But I also have to think of my sons, and future world events which may give them little place for survival except right here; so that they should be guaranteed a corner to have their families and grow their food on. Which leads me to one suggestion or proposition for your consideration: (Your suggestions about Committee On Poetry and your brother in regard to your land are well-taken. This is not a rejection of them, but a suggestion of another alternative that can also be considered.) That is, would it be at all interesting to you to arrange it so that eventually—after your life is over, or whenever you decide that you no longer want or need the interest in it, that your share of the Bald Mountain land be bought out by me (including the house) and I would put that over to my boys? We could make such an arrangement so that you would be paid within a few years, but have full use of it as long as you wish, coming over to our side as I said at some much later date. This becomes a concrete possibility for me now, because I am arranging with [Jack] Shoemaker to sell most of my archives to UC Davis, and will have—if I so structure it—adequate capital in hand to do such and advance reimbursement with you. I would, of course, want you in no way to take this as a sign that I think you're done with this place—I truly hope you'll be spending much time here (and it would be good for you). I'm thinking really about the situation farther down the road.

I don't know if I mentioned Aitken Roshi's book *A Zen Wave*. It's a series of *teishos* he did on Basho's haiku—it's excellent both from the Zen side and from the side of illuminating haiku. His lineage is the *sanbo kyodan*—which means association of the three treasures, the lineage started by Harada Roshi about a century ago on the Japan seacoast north of Kyoto—a small country temple. Maezumi Roshi of Los Angeles and Kapleau at Rochester are in the same line. It is a synthesis of Rinzai and Soto teaching and practice; doing, as far as I can see, koans in the Rinzai style. It's nice to be doing koan again. He really is an excellent teacher, and one with whom I've had a correspondence and affinity for a long time simply because of his outspoken and righteous anti-war stand going back 20 or more years. He got started on Zen when he was interned in Japan during World War II in the same camp with R. H. Blythe, where he learned to do haiku study (he was captured as a civilian construction worker on Guam, at the very beginning of the war).

So, this seems like a relation which will be going on for a while, not only with me but with some of my neighbors. The *zendo* will be built for about 30 sitters, inexpensive and straightforward construction, all donated labor, and I am making the money myself. That is—donating some poetry-reading time and also writing around to dharma-supporters and asking them for a little cash donation.

Peter Bluecloud will be leaving your place in a few weeks, and Scott McLean moving in on June 7. Peter has had a hard time getting work this winter, and will owe you some back rent for a little while, but will eventually be able to pay it. He has kept the place very neat and clean both inside and out, and recently put up the gutters. Scott will be paying straight forward cash all summer, which will build up the cash reserves for future projects and maintenance of your place unless you want me to send the cash right out to you. As I said, it will be vacant I'm quite sure in October and if you wish, from the middle of September. Note: See PS at the end of this letter for further thoughts on poetry reading benefit date in Nevada County.

Last Saturday was the big spring May Day gathering, 200 or so people with real maypole dancing; raccoon, bear, and coyote skit by Peter Bluecloud; and much else. And the weekend before that, some of us went over to Chico to attend some educational workshops on the Ishi Wilderness proposal and then to go hiking into the Ishi Wilderness. It was cold and rainy the day we went in so we didn't stay long, but that is certainly one interesting wide rugged low-elevation wilderness area.

Everyone is well; flourishing; Kai has become speedy with his karate kicks and blows from a year's lessons, and Gen has been taking special lessons from Masa in how to skip. He is getting better. Have a good swing through Europe, and summertime at Naropa. Take care of yourself!

Love,

Gary

PS: Can we plan September 15 (Saturday) for benefit here (Nevada City) instead of 9? Turned out I had a commitment that weekend.

213. ALLEN GINSBERG [THE NETHERLANDS]
     TO GARY SNYDER [NEVADA CITY, CA]

June 14, 1979

Dear Gary and Masa:

After triumphant tour of the capitals of Europe—Genoa, Milan, Spoleto, Paris, Manchester, Cambridge, London, Amsterdam, Rotterdam—we're dragging our weary tongues o'er the sea to Newcastle to visit [Basil] Bunting and last reading there. Thence London and New York arriving Boulder June 20—and zap back to Rome June 29 for two days, they'll give three grand $ to Naropa if I do. Peter a *succis fou* in Italia and Parigi. We brought Steven Taylor to guitar and sing and all turned out funny and energetic like a folkie tour. Saw one Ato Lama in Cambridge who teaches the Six Doctrines, been sitting a little on the way. How are you? We'll be on West Coast after August 20. Brueghel's *Tower of Babel*'s in Rotterdam.

Love

Allen

214. ALLEN GINSBERG [BOULDER, CO]
     TO GARY SNYDER [NEVADA CITY, CA]

July 9, 1979

Dear Gary:

Nanao here, finishing Jap *Plutonian Ode* translation and I'm looking over his new English poems, we gave great July 4 reading with Ken Kesey full house Boulder Theater. Returned from Europe two weeks ago found your May 23 letter, then went back to Rome to read with Burroughs, Waldman, Corso, Orlovsky, Ted Berrigan, [John] Giorno, LeRoi Jones, Yevtushenko, Diane Di Prima, etc. on beach Ostia near Rome. Stopped an Italian riot invasion of stage with ah'ing and meditation five minutes, and third nite read before 20,000 people all of us, 4 hours 8 minutes each 23 poets wow! Beck/Malina of Living Theater've long depended on Bookchin. I sent for Newsletter for Naropa Library. Delighted to hear you're working with Aitken Roshi. I had tea with Myazumi Roshi his "Dharma Uncle" two weeks ago, I may go down to Los Angeles around September 20 do reading for his center. Would you like to come, visit him and read? Just sociable. Yes, great, build *zendo*, and hereby you have my OK to give ⅓ acre share to *zendo* for *zazenkai*. Peter out-living me will probably use our cabin and some land but we can work out something for your family as you wish. I'll be in Bay Area via Vancouver the end of August thru September 22—so will do retreat at our cabin and spend couple weeks there with Peter I hope in early September. Use Peter Bluecloud's back rent for *zendo* money or if he is hard up, I don't need his rent money. No don't send me Scott's cash; but I may want to inhabit cabin early September, not sure yet maybe September 7. OK. September 15 Nevada City reading.

Love
Allen
[PS] I'll write at greater length soon. Just back here.

215. ALLEN GINSBERG [BOULDER, CO]
TO GARY SNYDER [NEVADA CITY, CA]

July 10, 1979

Dear Gary:
So September 13 [*sic:* 15] fine. I'm not sure whether I have any other readings lined up in Bay Area. If not, I'll hope to spend first weeks of September in Bedrock Mortar. Is that inconvenient for Scott? I'll know more in a week. Nanao busy here. Kobun Chino Sensei coming for tea tomorrow. Peter back from Isle of Lesbos next week.

Love.
Allen.

216. GARY SNYDER [NEVADA CITY, CA] TO ALLEN GINSBERG [NEW YORK]

July 23, 1979

Dear Allen,
Got your two postcards—great successes in Europe! Don't worry about Scott; he will be returning to his teaching job in Indiana in the third week of August. So your house will be vacant and waiting for you. Ok, then, on reading for September 15; the hall is arranged and publicity will be starting in due time.

Had a marvelous 10 days in Hawaii—actually cooler weather than here; bursts of rain, squeaky lizards on the roof, ripe mangoes and avocados falling on the ground all the time. Sat through a weekend *sesshin* with the roshi on Maui, and then did the benefit in Honolulu for him ([W. S.] Merwin and I)—with wonderful tropical flower arrangements put up by some of the roshi's students. Reading was low-key, went well. Merwin's more recent poetry has some punch. He and Dana both seemed to be very dedicated *sanzen* students now. Aitken will be coming here the third week of October to lead the second *sesshin*. Other things—*zendo* location, land future's resolution, we can talk about when you get here. Am looking forward to it—maybe we can sit together in the mornings now. Hello to Peter. I guess Nanao will be here in a couple of days to join us on the mountain *sesshin*.

Love,

Gary

217. ALLEN GINSBERG [NEW YORK] TO GARY SNYDER [NEVADA CITY, CA]

October 10, 1979

Dear Gary:

Back in the moils of N.Y. I forgot to take back that transcript of my haiku. Blake-Kerouac-Trungpa class I left with you. You still got it? If you get a chance mail it to me. I was s'posed to edit a piece of it for *Zero* magazine.

Going to D.C. for Gay March this weekend then to England Germany Italy Holland end of October to Xmas.

Love

Allen

218. GARY SNYDER [NEVADA CITY, CA] TO ALLEN GINSBERG [NEW YORK]

October 16, 1979

Dear Allen,

How did you survive Las Vegas? It makes Reno seem like a staid little old lady. I forgot to tell you, when you were here, that Maurice Girodias (formerly Olympia Press) is now into bio-regional, ecosystem, international politicas. Here is a xerox of his text of "Declaration of Independence of All Human Minorities"—finally in English translation—and he has asked me to ask you to read it, and if you like it to drop him a note saying that it is ok to use your name under it in some big Paris newspaper.

Nanao left a few days ago and went on down to Berkeley, thinks to New Mexico till December or January he said. Then, I think he plans to come back and stay in your house during the coldest season. He was saying he is getting too old to go through that intense cold all the time anymore. I didn't go to meet with the Dalai Lama; too much going to do—still haven't got in the firewood, and tomorrow leaving for 10 days in Montana, Bozeman, and Missoula, talking to environmental and university groups, reading poems. As soon as I come back, Aitken Roshi will arrive and will then be into the *sesshin*. After that I really mean to finish up the better part of the study of China and nature: the section to do next is on "mother/fox"—attitudes towards women and magic and poetry and nature in China as they all mutually reflect on each other. Ok.

November 5—

Here's the manuscript! Sorry it took so long. Had a fine *sesshin* with Aitken.

Just back from Montana coal-strip-mine environment conference—glide in canoe across a still lake, geese fly up! It's all alive!

Love,

G

219. GARY SNYDER [NEVADA CITY, CA] TO ALLEN GINSBERG [NEW YORK]

December 19, 1979

Allen Ginsberg,

Antler's poems in *CoEvolution Quarterly* are marvelous. I sure goofed in failing to respond to his poetry—something went the wrong way for me when I first looked at them.

Hey, we have to fight the MX[166] now. Most (65%) of the system will be on land the Western Shoshone have been trying to get back, in Nevada.

Gary

---

166. The MX was a new U.S. missile project at the time.

220. ALLEN GINSBERG [NEW YORK] TO GARY SNYDER [NEVADA CITY, CA]

December 27, 1979

Dear Gary and Masa:

We took this philosopher's walk [reference to a picture postcard of Heidelberg, Germany] ambled and presumably pissed on by Hegel, Hölderlin, and other worthies, and smoked some hash provided by local vegetarian editor of *Kompost* ecologic mag, who explained that Bader-Meinhoff "Terrorist" scene originated 1968 student killed protesting against royal treatment of Shah visiting Germany, plus later police agent-provocateur supplies of guns like in U.S. Delighted!!!! you were able to have chance to re-read Antler who is a marvel. Please send a word to Larry Ferlinghetti, who does want to publish entire great *Factory* poems. Please? I'll read and respond to your letters in a week when I get back to Naropa for winter-spring-summer January–August stay. Germany poets want you to visit and Michael Kohler can set up a fine lucrative tour including Masa. We just got back three days ago. Corso reminiscent in extraordinary new work! Miracles!

Love,

Allen

[PS] Peter and I both got ten grand each $ NEA grants. We're rich! I found out about mine in Nevada, Las Vegas. Kali Yuga!

221. ALLEN GINSBERG [BOULDER, CO] TO GARY SNYDER [NEVADA CITY, CA]

April 28, 1980

Dear Gary:

Enclosed copy of *Nation* article if you haven't seen it, and copy of interview Clark/Dorn some time ago, sent me by Alan De Loach recently, to be published in *Little Caesar* L.A. punk/gay high class little magazine in summer. Clark seems to be against meditation.

I'm teaching lots, sitting couple hours a day, and writing lots. Enclosed recent poem written for March Anti-Draft rally ["Verses Written for Student Antidraft Registration Rally 1980"].

Saw Dan Ellsberg here an evening for Rocky Flats[167] demo. He came over we talked till 2:30 A.M. and had lunch next day. He sez threats of

---

167. Rocky Flats was the site of a nuclear trigger factory just outside of Boulder, CO.

limited war publicly made escalate the nuclear danger. Also says he wants to drop out and write awhile. Who's at the cabin now? I remember Bedrock Mortar's rented summer–September. If it's open still in May, perhaps Ellsberg could rusticate there? I wasn't sure, told him to write you. He needs a rest, and he meditates now.

Allen

222. ALLEN GINSBERG [LAKE LOUISE, CANADA]
       TO GARY SNYDER [NEVADA CITY, CA]

May 7, 1980

Dear Gary and Masa:

I drove that red car (you see on postcard photo opposite) up here to join Anne Waldman and 300 other practitioners for *Vajrayana* lectures at end of three-month seminary. Sure is complicated and beautiful, the "old dog" end lecture. Range of people here amazing.

Small lake, big mountains, I've walked around half lake but not been up climbing. Mist over Mt. Victoria, going in shrine room (Meditation whiskers dissolve into razor of breath).

Love

Allen Ginsberg

[PS] Peter is in New York planting trees (Cherry Valley).

223. GARY SNYDER [NEVADA CITY, CA]
       TO ALLEN GINSBERG [BOULDER, CO]

20 V [May 20, 1980]

Dear Allen,

Here's a little bundle of stuff. The "comments" on the by-laws was well-received at a meeting with Baker and Kriyananda on 13 May—and we will proceed to work out a legally acceptable language (Baker's lawyer) and then pass it around again for your official approval.

I may form—perhaps with Richard—a legal Buddhist organization here to help Ring of Bone Zendo[168] and carry out my own work—"Bald Mountain Temple" or somesuch—that's still in the future.

---

168. Snyder named the *zendo* "Ring of Bone" in honor of Lew Welch.

Lovely spring lots of fruit set on the fruit trees!
Lovely red car you have there. (In Canada.)
We pick up Aitken Roshi at Sacramento Airport today.
Gary

224. ALLEN GINSBERG [SEATTLE, WA]
     TO GARY SNYDER [NEVADA CITY, CA]

June 4, 1980, Seattle Airport
Dear Gary:
Spent three days at Evergreen State College, Olympia, took small plane
early this morn and flew around steamy cusp of Mt. St. Helens,[169] a light
silver ashy film over all the green hills approaching from north, rivers of
silver mud in green farm valleys distant. Now the top's still snowy on the
south side but the Fuji-like top's gone off, ⅔ of it is a thin crescent ridge
and the whole middle of north side's a black hole with clouds of steam
immobile hanging in air above the hole. Flew back to Seattle airport and
going back to New York City for a couple weeks—back in Boulder June
20. Received your letter and noted your comments on Bald Mt. papers.
Seems ok, I'll re-read papers in N.Y.
    OK
    Allen

225. GARY SNYDER [NEVADA CITY, CA]
     TO ALLEN GINSBERG [BOULDER, CO]

August 10, 1980
Dear Allen,
[. . .] Just back from the "Mountains and Rivers" *sesshin* of the Ring of
Bone *zendo*. This year ten of us went for eight days—six walking in the
high country of the John Muir Wilderness in the Central Eastern Sierra.
Sat every morn and eve. Climbed one 13,700' peak—Mt. Abbott won-
derful snowy rocky high country. Big thundershower one afternoon.
    Zendo received gifts of $11,000 toward a building (tax deductible). So

---

169. The volcano Mt. St. Helens erupted on May 18, 1980.

we're getting serious about styles and sizes. Aitken Roshi was here in May for a *sesshin* and drew up a fine ground plan and *zendo* layout.

Masa's been in Connecticut six weeks dancing with Balasaraswati—the boys and me here—gardening, fishing—doing some research and writing, too. Hot right now.

Scott and Pat McLean are renting your house until mid-fall, about. Your funds are building up! Going to Bob Erickson's now for dinner.

Faithfully

Gary

226. GARY SNYDER [NEVADA CITY, CA]
TO ALLEN GINSBERG [NEW YORK]

September 2, [1980]

Dear Allen,

Here's my book of interviews [*The Real Work: Interviews and Talks*]—my contribution to the genre. Poets interviews books all around us.

Philip Whalen has been here four days—leaves on the Greyhound for Zen Center this afternoon. We've had a fine time. (Peter Coyote was here three days too.) Philip enjoyed Naropa summer. How was Bisbee?—I couldn't go again; trying to keep time to work on China book—also apple harvest, we're getting lots of apples now. Making sauce, drying them.

I'll be in New York City October 2–6—where will you be then?

Faithfully

Gary

227. ALLEN GINSBERG [CHERRY VALLEY, NY]
TO GARY SNYDER [NEVADA CITY, CA]

September 15, 1980

Dear Gary:

Thanks for sending new book—I think I've read most of it and will scan it again, yes it's a new genre, edited conversations.

Bisbee was colorful and Peter raised a ripple of civic protest (sour-puss head of YWCA in one-woman anti-porn-poesy campaign) with the poetry-bread he cast on the waters. Peter Warshall and Dick Felger showed up so we made up a poetry-nature panel together, and visited mountain hummingbird sanctuary with Joanne Kyger and McClure and Bobbie Hawkins.

Then Peter and I went to Drum's [Drummond Hadley's] ranch, on the border (two wetbacks sitting Mex style under the wall the first morn). Drum is surprisingly conservative politically. But his poetry's really good—long melodious vernacular lines—and true work-life stories—like Robert Service and Olson and West Coast profundity. I wrote Larry Ferlinghetti and Don Allen that he has a really good book. Then we drove up along the Rio Grande up to Taos and gave a reading at town auditorium for Maggie Kress gallery—Peter, me, Drum, Hopi poet Michael Kabotie, Harold Littlebird, and—Nanao! Great night, solid men.

Despite stationery, I'm up at Cherry Valley with Peter and Lucien Carr and his wife 24-year-old black lady Sheila. He's going to AA [Alcoholics Anonymous] and also quit tobacco a year ago—sweet spirit now.

I proposed to Trungpa a Dharma Poetry Conference for summer 1981—suggesting it come half from Buddhist *dharmadhatu*, half from Naropa, and invite Burroughs, Whalen, yourself, John Cage, Miyazumi Roshi, Aitken Roshi, Anne Waldman, me, Diane Di Prima, and, if Aitken is willing, also invite Merwin. All for a week of workshop poetry, practice, and discourses. Could be done other than at summer time tho. Maybe Giorno too, Nanao? Merwin been visiting Dudjom Rinpoche in N.Y. and seeing Giorno last year.

I'll be reading in Texas and Kansas then return to New York City after reading in Williams College on October 2, so be back October 3 on Friday evening. I'll be in N.Y. till Saturday October 11, then with Peter take off for two months in Yugoslavia and the Balkans—maybe Hungary—then Germany, Switzerland, Vienna—and return after 60 days. Steven Taylor with guitar come along if it all goes as planned. Then I'm free till March—probably take a month's retreat before returning to Naropa in spring.

So—yes I'll be in city. Do you need place to stay? There's room at my apartment. Phone Peter at farm and he'll arrange key; or phone Bob Rosenthal who'll be secretarying there daily. Denise also is now next door same building. You may already have Laughlin's place arranged, tho. Anyway, there's room and I'll be back the day after you arrive, after three weeks absence.

Good thing you're leaving the 6th otherwise you'd get invited to maelstrom of party at Books and Co. Bookstore Madison Ave. for a new bibliography of everything I wrote, sang, interviewed, taped, published, 1969–77. Peter and Ted Berrigan read at St. Mark's on Wednesday the 8th October! So Peter be in town probably before you leave, down from the farm.

Farm's a bit run down, our absence so long at Naropa and care-less care-taker. Maybe Andy Clausen and family take over next spring.

Thanks for poem. Your own apple trees bearing?

Faithful and true,

Allen

PS I'm compiling all my writings on Kerouac for Dial Press' Joyce Johnson.

In New York be prepared for critique of your last visit (spoken and unspoken) that on last visit your poems were inconsiderate of urban nature, "fucking insulting" said St. Mark's Church Poetry functionary and once small press distributor-poet Ted Greenwald. Not that anybody will likely confront you, actually. Actually he had an interesting line—that high culture country living is still dependent on urban moneys—grants, lectures, planes, arts councils.

228. GARY SNYDER [NEVADA CITY, CA]
     TO ALLEN GINSBERG [NEW YORK]

[October 1980]

Dear Allen,

Thanks for news and schedules. Drum's ranch really great place! I love his singing-poems too. Allen, I'll be staying at J's [James Laughlin] apartment on Bank St. basically. Will get together with you after 3rd I hope. Great acorn crop this year! Also surprising number of first-year bucks with velvet spikes. All's well—kisses to Peter.

Gary

229. ALLEN GINSBERG [BELGRADE-BUDAPEST]
TO GARY SNYDER [NEVADA CITY, CA]

On train crossing border Belgrade to Budapest 7 P.M.

October 31, 1980

Dear Gary:

Black smog autumn leaves turning brown in Belgrade. We stayed with diplomat's son in nice central Belgrade apartment. He has all your books and wants to translate Buddhist-ecologic essays by you—Mirko Gaspari, he'll write you. Problems of royalty pay in dollars may inhibit New Directions deals, but private enterprise publishing there is legal and slightly underground. Not much censorship. Toothless ladies say to vote for Carter! Vojo Sindolic and David Albahari and Vladamir Bajac will write you probably re translating your poetry. From this spot the Turks stopped at outermost border of their empire for 500 years and looked out greedily at Europe across the Danube.

Love to Masa and Gen and Kai.

Allen

[PS] Back December 10.

230. ALLEN GINSBERG [MUNICH, WEST GERMANY]
TO GARY SNYDER [NEVADA CITY, CA]

November 16, 1980

Train Innsbruck to Munich 4 P.M.

Dear Gary:

Came from Vienna to Innsbruck thru Tyrol Valley (Alps) and stayed last few days in Innsbruck—I knew the name, had only vague inkling of the visionary mountain landscape. This town on Salt Trade Route cross Alps to Brenner Pass Italy, Switzerland, Germany. Ski resort valley walled in to "Inn" River glacial flow—old old town, ancient Imperial dignitaries bronze tombed statues. But the panoramic vastness is amazing, and the old civilization town settled down along the river within minutes' drive and cable car and ski lift to mountaintops is something you might really enjoy seeing. Can get readings here too to sponsor trip. We read in English to 250 folk.

Allen

231. GARY SNYDER [NEVADA CITY, CA]
    TO ALLEN GINSBERG [MUNICH, WEST GERMANY]

November 26, [1980]

Dear Allen,

Well there you are traipsing all over! Hello to Michael Koller. I had a nice autumn in New Hampshire and Wisconsin—learning new Eastern trees with the excellent Audubon guide to Eastern trees.

All's fine here—I'm paying the land taxes for you out of your rent earnings so no worry for you. Found a big, healthy spike buck dead on the road last night—Hwy 49—so skinned and cleaned it last night (hung it up from a beam in the *zendo* under Fudo's compassionate glare) and am butchering it today, much to share with neighbors. A translation of the *Zenrin-kushu*—students' pocket book of Zen poetry etc. quotes—is coming out. I'll send you one.

Yrz Faithfully

Gary

232. ALLEN GINSBERG [SWITZERLAND]
    TO GARY SNYDER [NEVADA CITY, CA]

December 9, 1980, 2 A.M.

Dear Gary:

We went up on railroad to Jungfrau on foggy day saw only our own white breath. Every new private house built in Suisse has government-subsidized $5,000 foot-thick-wall-door-window'd nuclear bombshelter!! The doors are precision balanced like bank vaults! Every country in Europe is a world of own, I get weird info everywhere. Like above! They got a tear gassed youth movement here demanding anarchy art house space from elders. Back in New York mid-December.

Love, Merry Xmas

Allen

233. GARY SNYDER [NEVADA CITY, CA] TO ALLEN GINSBERG [NEW YORK]

[December 10, 1980] Bodhi Day

Dear Allen,

We had a marvelous October *sesshin* with 20 people. Aitken Roshi and his attendant (Steve Nemirow) lived in Shobo-an; your house was kitchen and dining hall. Our tatami-room[170] served as *dokusan*-room,[171] and some of us slept in the house. The boys stayed with Jean Greensfelder, so we all lived in and sat and chanted and went to *sanzen* and heard a daily *teisho* and took turns cooking for five days and nights. Very inspiring. Everyone thanks you for the use of your house—which right now is empty, clean, and quiet.

I'm trying to write another chapter for my "Great Clod" book, this one on women, foxes, sex, magic, and wilderness in China. Will be doing a week in SE Alaska (Juneau, Sitka, Ketchikan) at the end of January. That really pleases me.

And Lawrence [Ferlinghetti] and I are going to do a benefit for Fay Stender (who is an old friend from Reed days), the lady lawyer who got shot last spring and permanently paralyzed. In April. A dry spell, so a perfect time to burn some brush piles which I will now go out and do.

Yours in the inconceivable hair-raising dharma (as Bob Thurman once said to me in a letter).

Gary

234. ALLEN GINSBERG [FRANKFURT, WEST GERMANY]
     TO GARY SNYDER [NEVADA CITY, CA]

Wuppertal-Frankfurt train,
December 13, 1980, Merry Xmas

Dear Gary:

Riding on train along east bank of grey Rhine River past craggy castles and nuclear cooling towers, black coal and log freight-boats and tugs on the water, smoggy midafternoon—churchspire and white building

---

170. Tatami-room. A room carpeted with woven straw mats.
171. *Dokusan*. The process of studying with a Zen master, the same as *sanzen*. This would be a private room for student-teacher meetings.

fronts on waterside, at a turn between gardened small hills, called Boppard.

Sit *sesshin* tonight with dharma group in Wiesbaden, and read in Frankfurt, then plane home day after tomorrow to N.Y. Received your Eastern trees—tax—spikebuck—Zen quotes note yesterday. We saw this "Mad Ludwig" castle [reference to picture on the postcard].

Love
Allen

235. GARY SNYDER [NEVADA CITY, CA]
TO ALLEN GINSBERG [NEW YORK] AND OTHERS

January 6, 1981

Friends:

Having studied the situation long, I would like to fall about 14 pine trees on the east and south of my place, carefully selected, to open out the forest, reduce fire hazard, and let more sunshine in. Since this is a somewhat larger project than usual, I thought I should let you know. I would be happy to walk thru it with anyone concerned—if I hear no response in two or three weeks though I'll assume it's ok.

Fraternally
Gary Snyder

PS If any boards are milled they will go to the *zendo* project.

236. ALLEN GINSBERG [NEW YORK] TO GARY SNYDER [NEVADA CITY, CA]

January 24, 1981, End of Great Cold Sit

Dear Gary:

Ok on cutting and cleaning pines east and south of your house.

Re [John] Lennon's death—the Lamb needs Protection, Fudo, that's for sure, *vajra* guards or something like non-violent roadies.

Amazing interesting re Phil Whalen moving on and teaching. I sent a summary or survey of Deukmejian[172] enforcement in California

---

172. Courken George Deukmejian. California attorney general and later governor of the state who led a high-profile campaign against marijuana use.

from yipster paper in N.Y. That's the only notice of it here East—an underground paper. Poor Beckwith. Joel Goodkind caught too? What's Jacques' consequent troubles? The question is, who put pressure on to crack down? How organized was it and where and why? I don't think it happens without meetings, conversations, agitators, and money appropriated in the inner or outer reaches of bureaucracy.

(to be continued)

February 17, 1981

Dear Gary:

I'm sorry I've let your letter go unanswered so long—pressure of many deadlines and little illness.

My apartment in N.Y. is not permanent and the building is up for sale, so I may have to leave the city within a few years. The cabin at Bedrock Mortar is the only house or place I actually own, of my own, and had meant it for retirement tho I may need it before that time.

I was glad to have Bedrock Mortar used and useful to anyone when I was not there. But the situation you describe, building zazen temple next to it and using it at scheduled times, with prospect of its being used exclusively for Zen Center in near future—five years or so—actually cuts me out of a place completely. That doesn't make sense.

Writing this letter in haste. I am overwhelmed by work and in not great health the last week—just to avoid further delay. I'll write more at length.

Allen

---

237. GARY SNYDER [NEVADA CITY, CA] TO ALLEN GINSBERG [NEW YORK]

26 II 81 [February 26, 1981]

Dear Allen,

Your letter came really as good news. I'm touched and pleased that you look on your house as future home and refuge, and in that light clearly understand your feelings about not having a *zendo* breathing down your neck. No problem. I can put it up at this end, by the lower orchard—and we'll have to get started soon!

Only questions left are how to render a patch of land—a Bald

Mountain share—on the lease? From my shares, to the Ring of Bone Zendo board, so that the actual building and its land will be secured as a future practice site. Dick Baker and I have been thinking.

Sorry you've been unwell. The trouble is just winter flu I hope. I just got back from a *sesshin* in Honolulu. Snowing around here; in haste and love,

Gary

238. MASA SNYDER [NEVADA CITY, CA]
TO ALLEN GINSBERG [NEW YORK]

March 13, 1981

Dear Allen,

It was nice to talk to you on phone. I'm really sorry that you were so upset even for two weeks. I want you to know that I was delighted to hear, on the contrary, that you still might come and live at Bedrock Mortar eventually. I had a feeling that you had given up that idea somehow.

I talked to the Pacific telephone engineer again and now it's very likely that they will bring the semi-trunk line into our fire road and that Bedrock Mortar being so close to the line, your cost will be much lower than anybody else in the area for sure. (They give us each the first 300 feet from the trunk-line free.)

Peter and Marilyn Coyote are with us this weekend. We are cutting firewood (Peter with his new chainsaw) for next winter as Gary will be out of the country in major part of summer and fall and no time to cut firewood before winter.

Barbara Getz and I are giving a lecture-demonstration on March 28. We plan to show in one long dance how the poetic text (Tamil) is translated into dance mudras and *abinayas* (gesture, language, expression) and give the background of Tamil culture and poetry tradition, a bit of Hindu mythology and cosmology etc. . . . how they are reflected in the dance. Gary will speak some part. This lecture-demo is a benefit for Cherokee Labor Brigade to raise the fund for restoring N. Columbia School House (not being used as school anymore), which will hopefully be a local cultural center. I'm reading Zimmer, A. K. Ramanujan, and George Hart again. Lots of fun.

Ring of Bone Zendo general meeting this afternoon (after firewood work) and pot luck dinner afterwards. I hope your health is better now. Hello to Peter.

Love,

Masa

[PS] Kai's voice has changed. Dark line around his mouth! He has grown almost three inches in a year.

239. ALLEN GINSBERG [NEW YORK]
TO GARY SNYDER [NEVADA CITY, CA]

March 17, 1981

Dear Gary and Masa:

Just back from mixing eight-track rock-n-roll record. I'll send copy of the new poem when Xeroxed. In haste—heading to Boulder Naropa for six months day after tomorrow.

Love

Allen

[PS] I called in to phone company and requested phone as per Masa's call.

240. GARY SNYDER [NEVADA CITY, CA]
TO ALLEN GINSBERG [BOULDER, CO]

May Day [May 1, 1981]

Dear Allen,

Do you remember KANASEKI Hisao from Japan?—urbane teacher of contemporary literature? He will be in the U.S. in August and hopes to briefly interview you for Japan. He's excellent—as translator, critic, and friend.

Hot days here, won't last though; too early.

Yrs,

Gary

241. GARY SNYDER [OKINAWA, JAPAN]
     TO ALLEN GINSBERG [BOULDER, CO]

5 VI [June 5, 1981]

Dear Allen,

Traveling *en famille* thru the southern islands meeting old friends from
Suwa-no-se days and also Masa's many Okinawan relatives (mostly farmers). Planted sweet potatoes yesterday—going fishing this afternoon. Kai
and Gen doing right well. Back to Kit Kit by 1 August, to leave again in
mid-September for Australia. *Zendo* will be constructed next June.

Gary

242. ALLEN GINSBERG [BOULDER, CO]
     TO GARY SNYDER [NEVADA CITY, CA]

July 18, 1981

Dear Gary:

Things fine here—tell Nanao if you see him OK I write something for his
book. So much happening!

25th Anniversary *On the Road* publication summer 1982 Naropa will
try to hold giant ceremonial celebration academic festival with Kerouac's
poet and prose friends Whalen yourself McClure others invited more
later. China trip when?

In haste

Allen

[PS] I'll be here till December except September trip to Europe, and
Dharma Arts Fest with Trungpa, Whalen, and Kyger reading September
24–27.

243. ALLEN GINSBERG [BOULDER, CO]
     TO GARY SNYDER [NEVADA CITY, CA]

[July 20, 1981]

Dear Cliff and To Whom It Concern:

(Gary or Nanao or House Watcher.) This will introduce Cliff Fyman
student at Naropa and my neighbor in N.Y. who has my permission to

stay in cabin if it's empty (Bedrock Mortar) or camp nearby and use my ramada—assuming the cabin's empty. Cliff can juggle, write poetry, and drive a cab.

Best wishes,
Allen Ginsberg

244. GARY SNYDER [NEVADA CITY, CA] TO ALLEN GINSBERG [NEW YORK]

6:VIII:81 [August 6, 1981]

Dear Allen,
Just back from Japan. I tried to call you in Boulder but a woman said it wasn't your number anymore; just to say hello. After five days I'm beginning to get over jet-lag; was waking up in the middle of the night.

John Brandi is going to publish a book of Nanao's poems. I did a little foreword. Many in Japan say hello to you, including those you've never met. Report on Japan later.

Right now catching up on mail and getting ready (already) to go to Australia with Nanao in September–October. [...]

Telephone plans progressing. May I sign permission for you as your proxy for underground telephone line right-of-way along fire trail on Bald Mt land?

I hope you are well and having a good summer. I just heard Rexroth had another severe stroke and is quite disabled.

Gary
PS Just read your letter. You write something for Nanao's book too, great!

245. ALLEN GINSBERG [BOULDER, CO]
        TO GARY SNYDER [NEVADA CITY, CA]

August 11, 1981

Dear Gary:
If you go to Adelaide, the Berendts (John and wife) anthropologists at the university are in contact with Pitjanjara tribe song men. They were helpful to me. To go to Yirkalla tribes or anywhere in N.W. Darwin Land, you need aboriginal bureau approval, it takes weeks, or did in '72.

Nanao! I haven't answered his letter yet, of course I will write appreciation of his poems, forward and backward. When is deadline?

Been drinking sake with Eido Roshi visiting here, and Bro. David Steindle-Rast—Trungpa sickee, too much sake and duodenal ulcer. Dalai Lama and Burroughs arrived 9 August, so plenty spectacles and conversation. Gregory sleeping on my couch, Peter here, we're looking for a house as I'll be here most of the year the next few years. Next summer Naropa folk suggested we hold a giant 25th anniversary *On the Road* celebration academic festival and invite all Jack's fellow prose-poets-publishers-family-friends-musician acquaintances. May do, making plans for funding.

Term ends in 10 days, gotta move house and piano and library, finished *Plutonian Ode: Poems 1977–80* and now xerox it and send to City Lights, write liner notes for two-record music/blues/rock-n-roll album John Hammond Sr. will issue this November, do my grades, read proofs of German booklet, and take off for Morelia, Mexico Poetry International. I'm scheduled also by USIS to read with W. S. Merwin in Mexico City August 25—then to Toronto *Kaddish* on stage, then N.Y. 10 days then Florence Italy then S.F. Dharma Arts Festival then back to Naropa and settle till December! Yes OK permission telephone line.

Allen

[PS] Love to Masa. Regards to George Balmer. Richard Muir is here.

246. ALLEN GINSBERG [BOULDER, CO]
    TO GARY SNYDER [NEVADA CITY, CA]

[mid-August 1981]

Dear Gary and Masa:

I think Gary's still in Australia. UCLA folk said they'd invite Gary to February meet with Red Chinese delegation of poets.

Did you get my invite to 1982 summer nine-day Kerouac celebration? Corso me Burroughs Creeley McClure so far OK'd. Co-sponsored by *New Age Journal*.

Cliff Fyman who stayed in my Bedrock cabin awhile back would like to spend January there. Is there any other *sesshin* use planned for it? I told Fyman to check with you.

Allen Ginsberg

247. GARY SNYDER [NEVADA CITY, CA]
    TO ALLEN GINSBERG [BOULDER, CO]

10 XI 81 [November 10, 1981]

Dear Allen,

Back from Japan, back from Australia—Moon and falling leaves here. Nanao's in your cabin a few days, then goes on to Taos. (We traveled 400 miles west of Alice Springs to camp in desert with Pintubi nomads.)

Zendo building takes place this summer. Also regularly scheduled *sesshin* last week of July. So I said on postcard "no" to Kerouac gathering—too much (and too many days long, that affair). Sorry. It's the worst possible timing for me.

Nanao wrote three more fine poems in Australia. He's really on!

Cliff [Fyman] hasn't written about using your Bedrock in January—if possible we'd like to be able to have people sleep over there January 22 and 23 (Friday–Saturday) as part of the Great Cold *sesshin*, two nights only. Otherwise the house is available.

Saw your picture in the *San Francisco Chronicle*—somebody saved it.

The heat is rising on nuclear war consciousness. Something beginning to move. Old networks re-activate I pray (with more wisdom than before).

Yrz.

Gary

248. GARY SNYDER [NEVADA CITY, CA]
    TO ALLEN GINSBERG [BOULDER, CO]

[December 31, 1981]

Dear Allen,

Rohatsu Sesshin fourth day—doing quiet work; chilly gray day. [. . .]

Cliff Fyman wrote and I said ok for January, allowing as he might have some guests on January 22–23. A weekend *sesshin*. Put some folks on his floor.

I'm still getting caught up, early rains filled the pond early, but slow down brush-pile burning. No increase, no decrease. Great mushroom year! Most get eaten by deer. Hope you're well. Will send you *zendo* work-schedule calendar soon.

Hello to Peter wherever you are.

Gary

[PS] Heard many recollections of you in Australia.

Allen, someone from Los Angeles (CSU Long Beach) mentioned in a letter that you had said I was to be at a meeting with Chinese poets in February in Los Angeles—I haven't heard of it??

249. ALLEN GINSBERG [MANAGUA, NICARAGUA] TO GARY SNYDER [NEVADA CITY, CA]

January 28, 1982

Dear Gary and Masa:

The southern countryside is cow green idyllic, huge freshwater lake fringed with isles with shacks and cottages and stone walled tiny castles and suburb houses. Like clean Floridas. Saw Margaret Randall,[173] heard much confusing about mosquito Indians, met opposition newspaper folk and commandantes and old Pound poets.

Allen

250. ALLEN GINSBERG [NEW YORK] TO GARY SNYDER [NEVADA CITY, CA]

Feb 17, 1982

Dear Gary:

Chinese conference cancelled. I'll be in L.A. anyway w/ my cousin Dr. Oscar Janiger from Monday February 22 till Friday 26 February, mostly free all week. Spoke to Dylan and invited him to Long Beach. I'm going there (to Long Beach) for Friday evening Levertov reading. Then I read morning and you're scheduled 3–5, so we'll see each other. I leave next day for Chicago, I'll be with Peter and Steven Taylor (guitarist). Weekend before that 19–21 February I'll be at Beyond Baroque in L.A., then Santa Barbara, then w/ Joan Halifax at Ojai. Where you be?

I've been in touch with Nanao.

Some state grant ($15,000) and Grateful Dead grant ($5,000) were

---

173. Margaret Randall was the editor of *El Corno Emplumado,* a bilingual (Spanish-English) literary journal.

okayed for Kerouac-Naropa Festival, so it looks as if it's off the ground. I go on retreat March 5–23 (Seminary in Altoona, PA) then drive to Naropa for March 30 classes.

Love to Masa and kids,
Allen

251. GARY SNYDER [NEVADA CITY, CA] TO ALLEN GINSBERG [NEW YORK]

[*ca.* March 1982]

Dear Allen,
Can we retain Bedrock this summer as work-crew reading room?—That is, up til mid-July. Twas great to see you!
Gary

EDITOR'S NOTE: *The above note was written on the following undated letter from Lorraine Sloane.*

Friends,
Eleven years ago a small Zen Buddhist meditation group was started by Gary and Masa Snyder when they were building their house on San Juan Ridge in the Northern Sierra Nevada. The first summer people sat in a grove of pines. Later the house became the *zendo*, with local residents, many within walking distance, joining in. In May 1974 the *zendo* was declared formally, and named "Ring of Bone *Zendo*" in memory of the vanished poet Lew Welch. Then the group, having grown larger, moved into a small barn nearby.

Four years ago Robert Aitken Roshi graced us with a *sesshin* and has kindly come over from Hawaii every year since to lead a *sesshin* for us. The *sesshin* with Aitken Roshi gives us an opportunity to have interviews with a teacher during this time set aside for meditation. We are now considering ourselves spiritually affiliated with the Diamond Sangha founded by Aitken Roshi; and the Sanbo Kyodan lineage of Harada Sogaku Roshi—a Soto lineage that has incorporated Rinzai teachings. We have become too crowded in the small barn, so it's time to build a proper "California-barn" style *zendo*. We are raising money for this. We are planning to build it with our own and volunteer outside labor. We want to have the *zendo* built by the 4th of July, 1982. It will seat about 36 people. A mountain temple/*zendo*, locally based, open to wayfarers, hand-made on its own share of land held and managed by the local group of sitters.

We have a start on the cash needed for materials. We still need about $8,000. Any contribution will help. If anyone wants to join in the building (12 June–July 4, 1982) or has building materials to donate, write us about it.

Lorraine Sloane
For the Ring of Bone *Zendo*

252. ALLEN GINSBERG [BOULDER, CO]
    TO GARY SNYDER [NEVADA CITY, CA]

April 3, 1982, 2 A.M.

Dear Gary:

In haste, as ever, goddammit! Just got back from seminary eight-day retreat (with kidney stone in the middle)—to begin classes. Enclosed catalog. Notice Bill Doub teaching with us at last!

I forgot but I think you mentioned I had some rent credit in the bank on my cabin? If so why not apply the bulk of the money to the *zendo* fund? If this is not convenient or useful let me know and I'll find other means. Anyhow if it's ok turn all but $100 (for small repairs) over to Lorraine Sloane for Ring of Bone Zendo.

Yes, use Bedrock any way it'll be useful for building project—till mid-July or later if need be. The folk at Naropa wrote you with more definite proposal re travel housing $. If the conditions aren't ok enough, let me know and I'll make sure they meet your needs one way or another, for however short or long a visit.

It all (the Kerouac celebration) looks great, getting together solid and organized and varied. As per Creeley's suggestion conferees are encouraged to address themselves to any texts they want to of Jack's (or anything else topically). We may try to organize at the end some *dharmic* manifestation relating to nuclear. The question is what *dharmic* non-aggressive form. Any ideas?

Love
Allen

[PS] Please do come. Off to St. Louis this weekend, Cleveland next, then back steady all spring.

253. GARY SNYDER [NEVADA CITY, CA] TO ALLEN GINSBERG [NEW YORK]

April 8, 1982

Dear Allen,

As per enclosed [a letter from Jane Faigao asking Snyder to visit Naropa], if I make it I certainly will. Thank you for your generous gift to the *zendo*! You had $674.74 credit. I transferred $600 to the *zendo* account. $75 should be enough to cover your repairs and if someone rents it for a month or two next winter that will build it back up again.

Incidentally, your land taxes for this year I paid directly out of your credit. Here is a receipt for you too. It is tax deductible.

We've had an amazing three weeks. Scatters of snow and cold weather and then March 31 the big snow storm, and on April 1 we had two feet of snow on the ground. Temperatures are still going below freezing at night, pinched and frozen little buds—and patches of snow everywhere. The flowering Japanese cherry is at least two weeks behind schedule; we are having our Buddha's birthday celebration this afternoon ("flower festival") without much in the way of flowers—snowflakes instead.

Gary

254. ALLEN GINSBERG [BOULDER, CO]
     TO GARY SNYDER [NEVADA CITY, CA]

Sunday May 8, 1982

Dear Gary:

There are a few solecisms in the enclosed Kerouac Conference flyer, but not too many.

Nanao is visiting (he came to see the Dutch poets)[174] and is staying on to perform Snow Woman this week, we have an extra bedroom for him.

If you have any idea in advance at what point you'd like to come for the conference let us know, tickets may be cheaper. The conference schedule

---

174. A group of Dutch poets were touring the U.S. in conjunction with the publication of their City Lights anthology, *Nine Dutch Poets*.

is tentative and can be rearranged. See anything you like particularly? Or make suggestions. We didn't assign you to anything yet except (tentative) poetry reading.

OK

Allen

255. ALLEN GINSBERG [BOULDER, CO]
TO GARY SNYDER [NEVADA CITY, CA]

July 14, 1982

Dear Gary and Masa:

Here's latest big poster—we've left your slots more or less open and tentative. Hope you can make it—looks fine—maybe too huge!! Let us know when you're coming? How's *zendo* building?

Any of the workshops or symposia that interest you you can join. Kerouac Catholicism and Buddhism July 29 Thursday is weak in faculty so far, wish you'd get here in time for that. Amazing job trying to organize housing rides itineraries books roadies, etc. Robert Frank now has money to do film document artwork.

I've been working more with local New Wave bands. Friend of Steve Sanfield Diana Henoring studying here with me.

OK

Allen

256. ALLEN GINSBERG [BOULDER, CO]
TO GARY SNYDER [NEVADA CITY, CA]

July 19, 1982

Dear Gary and Masa:

Our notes (my poster and your last letter to Naropa) crossed in the mail. Alas you can't come! Everybody announced including Ken Kesey, Creeley, Kerouac's early wives and daughters, Diane di Prima, McClure, etc. will be coming—Voznesensky alone couldn't get visa so won't arrive, and yourself.

If you can possibly get away for a day's visit do come! As I said the panel on Kerouac and Buddhism and Catholicism will be weak without you and Philip.

As I wrote I think, we've been emphasizing open-heartedness and tender *bodhichitta* [175] as tone of the celebration, and Kerouac's off chance remark "Lost Generation Beat Generation next be Found Generation" to encourage people to think sanely on future agenda, so it wasn't intended to be nostalgia or rehash, more survey of culture past 25 years and pondering on future, not technical but humane and poetic. That's why I trusted the whole circus to arise, and I think it will be beneficial—give serious students and next generation poets a chance at some small transmission of spirit in a basically *dharmic* atmosphere.

So if you can break away with Masa for a couple days please do, and phone us. If not, please send brief message of encouragement and whatever tiny gigantic *prajna* image you can flash on! I'll read it before I read (July 31 Saturday) or at the Kerouac/Buddhism Seminar (July 29 Thurs).

But come! if you can, even briefly (tho I know flesh gets weary)—yet it (*Road's* birthday) could be used for bodhisattva wheel turning in U.S. context, and there will be considerable national attention—as well as creative moment in itself as Robert Frank is funded to wander at will and make a film as he pleases, documentary or private fancy, and that should turn the mere historic charming moment into conscious art work.

Fine news *zendo's* up preliminary? I guess lots of work ahead and I don't really wanna disturb that—just remember U.S.A. is also a big echoey *zendo*!

Love

Allen

PS We (Trungpa, his secretary and doctrine chief student and I) just finished first dharma poetry course, a tentative inquiry, which we made with students twice a week for a month—including spontaneous oral improvisations. To be continued next year.

---

175. *Bodhichitta.* Awakened mind.

257. GARY SNYDER [NEVADA CITY, CA]
     TO ALLEN GINSBERG [BOULDER, CO]

14 VIII [August 14, 1982]

Dear Allen,

Have been hearing good reports from Kerouac Conference. We're still working several days a week on the *zendo*.

[. . .] Cool breezy summer. When see you?

Love,

GS

258. ALLEN GINSBERG [MEXICO] TO GARY SNYDER [NEVADA CITY, CA]

August 21, 1982

Dear Gary and Masa:

"I wonder what it's going to be like 500 years from now?" Gregory just said in hotel room near Pacific, Las Moches, Sinaloa. From Santa Fe anti nuke benefit for Nanao's friends, plane bus and train over Tarahumara Sierras to town across from Baja California La Paz. Cheapo shrimp, we're talking about meat and spirit. Kerouac Fiesta was exquisite, vacation is exquisite. How's your serious work exquisitives?

Love

Allen

259. ALLEN GINSBERG [NEW YORK] TO GARY SNYDER [NEVADA CITY, CA]

August 25, 1982, Noon

Dear Gary and Masa:

[. . .] Just returned from flying caper with Peter and Gregory to Mexican Pacific Coast over Sierras, bought a wooden Tarahumara doll and some beads and looked into a lot of canyons from train—continuous lightning glows all over sky, flashes, veins, bolts, glimmers—for four hours as we reached Pacific.

Just back 6 A.M.

Allen

[PS] I'm due for Chinese UCLA Conference Sept 21–23, thence back to Naropa for registration. I'll probably go to L.A. September 17–18 and read somewhere or visit relatives.

I'll be in N.Y. till September 15. Aren't you due to attend this Mainland Chinese Lit. Conference also?

I'll write from N.Y.

Saw Nanao's son Issa in Santa Fe—remarkable healthy round eyed boy and got report on Nanao on Mt. Taishan from Carol Merrill. Much bureaucracy she says.

260. ALLEN GINSBERG [NEW YORK]
      TO GARY SNYDER [NEVADA CITY, CA]

August 26, 1982

Dear Gary:

Sorry to miss the opening ceremony. I thought of flying in but lack the meat-jump, having just come from Boulder—Mexico Pacific—N.Y. Going this weekend to teach poetry at Eido Roshi Dai Bosatsu Center. Please give my best wishes to Aitken Roshi—and thanks for his manuscript.

Antler going into hospital for small hernia operation, would like to recuperate at Bedrock Mortar if his dates don't conflict with crowds visiting for dedication day. He'll write you to check it out, or Jeff [Poniewaz] will. Great days!

Love
Allen

261. GARY SNYDER [NEVADA CITY, CA]
      TO ALLEN GINSBERG [BOULDER, CO]

8 IX [September 8, 1982]

Dear Allen,

We had a splendid dedication—would have been complete if you'd been there. McClure, Whalen, Bob Jackson, Dan Welch—many old friends. Don Allen was going to come but didn't at the last moment.

Haven't heard from Antler. But Bedrock is already rented for about six weeks—to one of Aitken's Hawaiian students, Vicki Shook. Then she'll move to Nevada City and the house will be available. See you in Los Angeles directly.

Love,

Gary

262. ALLEN GINSBERG [NEW YORK]
   TO GARY SNYDER [NEVADA CITY, CA]

September 10, 1982

Dear Gary:

Probably see you next week in L.A. at mainland Chinese writers' meeting. Robert Rees the UCLA organizer said you were invited, I forget whether you'd got word last time we met.

Enclosed prospectus for a poetry teaching project for Naropa next summer, we'd like to renew invitation for you to visit—this time with adequate pay.

We haven't set a date, as that will be dependent on our guest poet, yourself if possible. Pay will be $3,000, plus travel with Masa (and family?) and accommodations, for a six-day or week period of intensive work with students.

As it's tentatively planned, it's work with maximum of 40 students who'll be staying with us a three-week period, me, Peter, Anne Waldman, Larry Fagin, and Michael Brownstein carrying the three-week course with a guest poet in for one special week, poet who will see each student one-to-one for half hour each, plus nine hours of teaching as general discourse or workshop or lecture; and one reading. That would amount to 29 hour babbling work-week plus a poetry reading.

I've worked out above general idea with Larry Fagin so we could specify how much work it would be for the week's guest teacher, to have some direct and also mass class contact with students, but haven't worked out structure more specifically as it depends on teaching style of whoever fills the Flying Chair.

Time also depends on when guest poet has open week. When you're not in *sesshin*. Best time for us is late July or early August tho that's not crucial it could be shifted around any time June late or early July or later August. And we're trying to pay enough to make the week useful to the teacher. (I may visit Brazil, June.)

We all thought of you as ever for myriad reasons social aesthetic meditative historic and hiccup. Think it over and we can talk in L.A. or other where. Also if you can't come who do you think would be good?

I wonder what kind of ground plan, method, or also what kind of special curricula we could invent between you, me, and Anne Waldman? Vocalization straight spine and proclamation—air horse—is an aspect I've been encouraging along with Trungpa's general encouragement.

Spent weekend at Daibosatsu Zendo four days with Eido Roshi and sat in on discussion of several Rinzai cases—"I was just washing my feet." Eido said I should sit more and sing more.

OK—this just to give you time to think about real Naropa visit before we meet.

I phoned Don Allen, there are facilities for observers at the Chinese meeting.

I know so little about Chinese culture I feel hesitant about the meet, tho eager to be there and talk to real Chinamen.

Love

Allen

PS: More adventure with rock-n-roll New Wave, I sang with Clash at Red Rocks, Colorado, and one night here in N.Y. on their visit—intelligent and soulful-humor'd thin hairy English kid lads, 8,000 in audience.

PS: Re Masa—has she done short term dance workshops? I wonder if that could be arranged? Is it appropriate?

PS: Enclosed *Washington Post* article on Kerouac Conference—not insensitive except he garbled Trungpa's speech (re knife fight): "The two big enemies have huge sharp knives at each others throats very sharp pressed against jugular vein looking eyeball to eyeball in each others eyes asking 'shall we do it? . . . Better not . . . So because of you (pointing to audience) and Kerouac's dome-passion there will be no nuclear disaster."

Gregory read great new poem re *Bomb* also—long Shelleyan ["The Day After Humankind"].

263. GARY SNYDER [KNIVSTA, SWEDEN] TO ALLEN GINSBERG [NEW YORK]

13 X 1982 [October 13, 1982]

Dear Allen,

I'm at the country home of Reidar Ekner fiery acerbic marathon-running Swedish shamanist poet (who translated *Turtle Island* here). We're about to go look at Norse farm-site-diggings; me catching up on mail while traveling. Back home November 8.

We do want to do the one-week poetry special at Naropa. Best dates would be the final week of the second summer session ending, you said, August 12.

Tentatively (depending especially on when Balasaraswati comes to teach next summer) Masa would be interested in doing a concurrent run of "basic introduction to the world of Bharat Natyam—music, myth, and poetry gathered into dance" workshops. Or, at least, a formal performance one time, with me as explainer.

How was Chinese Disneyland?[176]

Will be in New York City December 1 November 30—December 1–2, do a little reading the 1st at New School thanks to Dr. Diamond. I see you'll still be in Boulder. Then Diamond and I will go to Washington D.C. for the American Anthropologists' conference, I'm to be reading poems! A panel on poetry and author. Harold Bloom part of same panel.

China writers conference: I'm very glad I went, will be corresponding with Lin Bin-yan. Do hope there's a chance to visit there next year. Los Angeles wealth is something again.

The telephone will be installed in your house very soon. The gravelling of the road has also started. It's very tasteful and not imposing on the landscape. The new route for the road above my orchard. Antler will be staying a few weeks from early or mid-October. After he leaves I'd like to seriously rent it for a while at @ $175 a month to help pay back grand, phone costs, and your land taxes, and build up a reserve for you again. Everything's in quite good shape down there.

Swedes are sharp on environment and lots of interest in Buddhism. A sort of stable steady-state little U.S.A. here. Lots of bureaucracy too.

Yours faithfully and truly

GS

---

176. Ginsberg had gone to Disneyland with a group of visiting Chinese writers.

264. ALLEN GINSBERG [BOULDER, CO]
     TO GARY SNYDER [NEVADA CITY, CA]

November 8, 1982, 2 A.M.

Dear Gary:

I got your letter from Sweden, thanks—waited for word from Larry Fagin (now executive poetics manager) to answer you. He'll write all details. Robert Creeley will also come, likely for a week, tho before you arrive he'll be gone. Dance department here delighted Masa will teach, and will contact her too. Both short workshop and duo with you both, I think.

Send me any suggestions re Scandinavia—I'll be in Paris, Amsterdam, and then Denmark January 9–22, Sweden January 22–February 1, Norway a few days. Then Berlin and back to N.Y. February 17. What kind of clothes in winter I wonder?

Your Naropa dates will coincide with Eido Roshi, various lamas, etc., arriving for Christian-Buddhist contemplative conference (third annual). Maybe you can drop in on that. Enclosed last year's announcement. Same personnel this year, except for Situ Rinpoche.

Chinese spent all day at Disneyland—me too—Wu Qiang got lost, we found him 4:30 P.M. at exit gate where he waited.

Peter went to N.Y. to take care of his father, may be there when you're there. I go to L.A. November 19 for *Los Angeles Times'* year's poetry book prize (free trip and $1,000)—Shhh it's a secret till November 19. Tell Harold Bloom I'll be in Yale February 28–March 1 resident at Pierson College via McClure's friend Chas. Mairowitz.

Fine about $175 rent. Wow. But should we check first if Phil wants to use it awhile, now that his *zendo*'s closed?

Dear Masa:

The Dance Therapy Program was planning a folk–anthro–world dance survey as part of summer's program and will be happy to include your work, so that's OK—they'll get in touch soon.

OK, Love to all,

Allen

265. ALLEN GINSBERG [BOULDER, CO]
    TO GARY SNYDER [NEVADA CITY, CA]

November 13, 1982, 2:30 A.M.

Dear Gary:

Did Antler make it up to Bedrock Mortar? If so, let him stay there free, he's living on margin and just recovering from hernia operation. I'll send money if necessary for maintenance, let me know.

Peter Orlovsky's father died tonite, 84 years old—Peter was with him all the last week in N.Y.—went back in time to tend him in hospital.

I'll be in L.A. this weekend again, November 19, to get *L.A. Times* '82 Poetry Book Award. I think I mentioned that in last letter? (I was s'posed to keep it secret till then.)

Been teaching your excellent poetry circa 57–60, Whalen, Lamantia, Wieners, Welch (with letters), and others in Beat Generation Literary History 1957–1960 period—really interesting to re-correlate all the texts.

Possibility this spring you be invited to NYU to read with Burroughs and me and Corso. Will you be out traveling then at all?

I hope to do month retreat next June '83 and after fall term plan on disentangling and some kind of retirement, to cultivate my garden(s).

Love

Allen

266. GARY SNYDER [NEVADA CITY, CA]
    TO ALLEN GINSBERG [BOULDER, CO]

[*ca.* December 1982]

Dear Allen,

Antler's fine and here—ok, if you say, no charge.

Larry Fagin called, I'll be writing him back. I'll be in New York City briefly April 11–12 . . .

Your Bedesman

Gary

PS I'll rent it for money after December to pay back for phone etc. installation.

267. ALLEN GINSBERG [CHARLEVILLE, FRANCE]
     TO GARY SNYDER [NEVADA CITY, CA]

December 21, 1982

Dear Gary and Masa:

Was at Paris for UNESCO, then with Kayuko Shiraishi to Milan and Amsterdam, I invited her to read with me at Kosmos Café–Zen Center. Now staying in Arthur Rimbaud's old apartment in Charleville, where he wrote *Le Bateau Ivre* and *Lettres du Voyant*. Tour of farm in Roche where he writ [*A*] *Season in Hell*. Grey city, big as Lowell Massachusetts, very similar. Dutch Poets International request your presence next fall. On to Denmark, Sweden, Norway for a month, then Berlin, etc. Back February 17 to New York.

Love

Allen Ginsberg

268. ALLEN GINSBERG [STOCKHOLM, SWEDEN]
     TO GARY SNYDER [NEVADA CITY, CA]

[January 23, 1983]

Dear Gary:

Me, Peter, and Steven Taylor are here for a few days on to Helsinki, Oslo, Bergen, Stavanger, Berlin, etc.

Love

Allen

[PS] Reidar [Ekner] helped us with translation. Uppsala (January 26). Lovely reading Reidar translated "Birdbrain." Peter climbed Viking mounds barefoot in snow. Tomorrow slow nite boat to Helsinki. Staying with Ann and Sam Charters, also Izzy Young of folklore center where we gave small reading for his circle of musicians and longhairs. AH!

269. ALLEN GINSBERG [BOULDER, CO]
    TO GARY SNYDER [NEVADA CITY, CA]

[*ca*. Feb. 24, 1983]

Dear Gary:

I called and talked to Masa—Creeley may have called you to consult about scheme for educational month at Naropa Poetics, i.e. is there any integrated curriculum? He'll deal with "personal environment"—"local" speech and (he sez) as per Olson "you (one) and It = you: what leans out; It, what leans in." and he'll cover Pound, Williams, E. A. Robinson. Anne Waldman probably cover [Gertrude] Stein. Pat Donegan [will cover] Korean Chinese Jap poetry haiku U.S. Imagists a little, as background study. Larry Fagin, minimalism and oddity; Peter wild mind ape; me, some dharma poetics, some "close to the nose," some music/poetry, some politics, and whatever others leave out. I guess your own plan's already sent.

Thanks for taking care of house, phone. How much have you put out to pay for phone etc., and when are taxes due? I expect to have money coming in from one source or another this coming two months so can send reimbursement and advance $ for taxes and expenses.

Yes rent place out thru winter. If possible leave it open for Antler in spring, late March or April. But I don't know if this is practical. Let me know. I'll be reading with Antler at St. Mark's in New York in March.

I hope to retire somewhat from Naropa after another year.

When China? I'm committed now to fall '83 but will maybe maybe have five weeks free August 15–September 23, 1983. Tho that may be too short a time. Orville Schell says he'd like to come along on the poets' trip to China. Have you written Peking yet? Any plans formulated? Maybe could do it after December '83 anytime—spring '84? I'll be free from then on.

OK, Love

Allen

PS Religion Department at University of Colorado might pay for your services while in Boulder (they'll contact you to inquire).

Also the New Wave / Organic Food / Social Center Mercury Café in Denver (where I sing occasionally with local rock bands) would like to hold a reading for you while in area. Could pick up $500–$1,000 for that probably—with Masa dance also. Could be done some evening during your visit or right after.

Also religion contemplative/Christian Buddhist will overlap your stay at Naropa. So, lots of action, teaching, and blabbing in the Buddha-fields.

Anyway I am aiming to retire a bit from world. Will probably do a month solitary retreat at Rocky Mt. Dharma Center just before our poetics meet.

OK, Love

Allen

PS Did you get xeroxes of Lisa Law's startling clear pictures of Lew Welch at Human Be-In 1967? She had four of Suzuki Roshi onstage which I gave to Trungpa.

I sent you a Naropa newspaper with a talk of mine on poetics and dharma.

270. GARY SNYDER [NEVADA CITY, CA]
TO ALLEN GINSBERG [NEW YORK] AND OTHERS

29 IV 83 [April 29, 1983]

Friends,

A long cloudy winter—90" rain—has gone by. The Cor-ten steel roofing on the *zendo* has taken on the stable rust-color that it will now hold indefinitely. The cut ground edges begin to heal over, and the building begins to settle in, be part of surrounding nature. The Yamabushi (mountaineer Buddhist of Medieval Japan) used to say "the whole universe is our meditation hall." But it's nice to have a roof over your head when you sit on a rainy night.

So here are two pictures of the Ring of Bone Zendo taken last July, just at the end of the intensive three-week work-*sesshin* that built it. We thank you for your help on this, and hope you can join us in it someday.

A *sesshin* in the old barn *zendo* led by Robert Aitken Roshi was the push that got us into building a proper one. Robert Aitken's book *Taking the Path of Zen* came out last fall from North Point Press in Berkeley—it's a most useful book on the nuts, bolts, and non-nuts-bolts of Zen practice. I recommend it to old timers and newcomers alike.

The Ring of Bone *sangha* remains basically the local people, "peasant Buddhists" who have been sitting together for almost 10 years. But we welcome the participation and shared concerns of neighbors, especially in Northern California, our natural nation. So keep in touch.

Yours in the dharma

Gary

271. ALLEN GINSBERG [BOULDER, CO]
     TO GARY SNYDER [NEVADA CITY, CA]

October 22, 1983, 2 A.M.

Dear Gary:

Enclosed article on agrigenetics enterprise. [. . .]

I cooked lobster supper for Robert Bly at home here and saw him read—he has really good lines and I do like his fairy tale structure of poetry reading and stage manner tho—he put down Esalen but seemed Esalen.

Barbara Meier here organizing Buddhist peace fellowship.

I told Bly I thought we ought to revive the Vietnam anti-war readings for Central American war, he thought it was time also. Maybe we'll do it.

I'll be up in Portland Reed College November 10–13 weekend, and down in Eugene for a benefit for Nyingma Lama Center in Cottage Grove—Chakdud Rinpoche Trungpa's beginning to teach Ati (Dzog. Chen) which is Nyingma specialty (something like Shehen Taya?). "Rime" Movement 18th Century Tibetan brought together Kagu Mahamudra and Nyingma Ati styles and practices.

I hired an agent to peddle my collected works.

If by chance I'm free August '84 would there be possibility of me crashing in barn or loft and doing sitting with you? I don't want to displace Aitken Roshi at Bedrock Mortar. I don't know if I will be free—may have deadline on *Collected Poems* before China trip.

Received *Axe Handles* [North Point Press, 1983]. At first glance (tho already familiar with most of the texts) I liked best the poems where you have a definite narrative structure—or understand them best—Title poem "Axe Handles"—Incidentally I finally read Lu Ji's *Wen Fu* last year—I compared "Trust the face of his mood" to "Mind is shapely, Art is shapely," and—"Nothing can be measured along one line of measurement" to W.C.W.'s [William Carlos Williams'] measure as variable foot. Also "Bows to Drouth," one single image—"Changing Diapers"— "Painting [the North] San Juan School," "Fence Posts" has narrative plot—"Look Back" and "Soy Sauce"—Naha ["Fishing Catching Nothing off the Breakwater near the Airport, Naha Harbor, Okinawa"] as lyric not narrative, fine—["Working on the '58] Willys Pickup" has beginning middle and end story—"White Sticky" in between lyric—Narrative— a small anecdote anyway—"Coaldale Nevada [24:IV:40075, 3:30 PM"]— Whyncha really describe the before and after and middle—do you know Wordsworth's similar passage—The Prelude Book Fourteenth Conclusion (l. 15–48 in Norton English Literature anthology)—climbing a mountain at night "The mist soon girt us round . . . when at my feet the ground appeared to brighten, and with a step or two seemed brighter still / . . . " etc.

Also, Sign at Toki's ["Under the Sign of Toki's"], like a little story— Talking with Governor ["Talking Late with the Governor about the Budget"] has China like ending shift—"The Governor" made is classic in that one—"Dillingham, [Alaska, the Willow Tree Bar"] not narrative but has sharp clear point or editorial last three lines amassed from details. "Uluru [Wild Fig] Song" tho notes has continuity—"Money [Goes] Upstream" OK—but "Breasts" tho didactic is clearly witty thought out—tho I didn't think you needed the Yeats paraphrase at end—"Tough enuf / for a few more good days" was a better end by itself. Decay's ["Old Rotting Tree Trunk Down"] alright, especially the sudden woodpecker's cry. Stockholm Woman ["For a Fifty-Year-Old Woman in Stockholm"] and "Old Woman Nature" and "The Canyon Wren" have less structure than the complete anecdote poems but have specific flashes, and "For All" is both clear lyric and didactic charming yak. I liked the bulk of the rest but the above are my favorites, a few I didn't know or notice before. Thanks for sending the book. Cover is bright and clean!

"Bubbs Creek Haircut" still sticks in my mind for exemplary structure to use in teaching as model for students by the way. Tho there are random or obscurer passages in it, the floating mind between beginning conversation and end wake-up admits any material, which is fine that way.

OK—I started a brief note and got carried away.

Love to Masa and Gen and Kai—I'm beginning to pack books to

retire to New York. Saw my mother in a dream and wrote longish poem ["White Shroud"]—also narrative—sort of minor epilogue to *Kaddish* 20 years later.

Allen

272. GARY SNYDER [NEVADA CITY, CA] TO ALLEN GINSBERG [NEW YORK]

22:XI:83 [November 22, 1983]

Dear Allen,

What are you doing up at two in the morning still writing letters? Thank you for the article on David's Company, and your literary comments on the poems in *Axe Handles*. You've been up to Portland, Oregon, and back by now I guess. Charles Leong wrote me and said you were coming but his emphysema would keep him from attending the meeting. He is old and frail now, but still writes a beautiful calligraphy, and very witty sharp letters on the evolution of Chinese communist culture and politics.

Maybe Barbara Meier should run for the board of directors for Buddhist Peace Fellowship. We need to hold another election. We'll write her. I'm enclosing our little local Ring of Bone *Zendo* sitting announcement—we're out of fall schedules already, but we'll be sure and get you the spring schedule, and have no fear; you can be sure to sit in the August five-day *sesshin* with Aitken Roshi if you want. There will be good lodgings for everyone.

A few notes on my schedule ahead—December 9, talking on animals, poetry, and magic in Reno; doing an introduction to Zen practice class on the Ridge December 17; Buddhist Peace Fellowship study group on December 15; Lee Swenson talk on anarchism and the peace movement; January, I'll teach four Friday night classes on Mahayana Buddhist lore as reflected in the daily Zen sutra book; and a weekend *sesshin* toward the end of that month. In February do a day-long workshop for University of California extension on Zen and poetry, and a workshop at Intersection with Lee Swenson on Buddhism, anarchism, and political economy. In early March, to Yale (Pierson College three days) and one or two little colleges down Maryland and North Carolina way. Then in all of April, Alaska, community and consultancy work. Through the later part of May, work weekends every weekend on the "*hojo*" (little tea-house, *sanzen* interview house for Aitken Roshi to be just by the *zendo*), a big work weekend in June—three day—to finish it off. Then from early August sometime roshi will be coming and leading at least one five-day *sesshin*, but staying for three weeks or a month, and giving Zen interviews almost nightly, along with whatever classes he proposes to do, and lots of sitting. So, if you can be here for two or three weeks in August, you can have a good taste of Zen, meet Aitken Roshi, and run around with Masa, Kai, Gen, and me. And if you are on the West Coast in latter May or early June, you could have fun joining in a work-weekend up here which is always a big party.

My most exciting reading this past year has been Ivan Illich's *Shadow Work*, Lewis Hyde *The Gift* (see his chapter on Ezra Pound!), and Murray Bookchin *The Ecology of Freedom* (first new contribution to anarchist thought since Kropotkin).

We much appreciated your energy and hospitality last summer in the midst of all that busyness, the chances to spend some time with Burroughs, the great dinner at your house with Peter broiling ribs in the backyard, and hope we can reciprocate with some good hospitality here. If you could come in August, it might be that roshi would be living in the little *hojo* building itself; it might be that if he was with Anne (his wife) that he might want to use Bedrock Mortar, in which case we would provide you with full room and lodging in the barn-studio, which has unfolding double sofa-bed, stove, rug on the floor, and other amenities. Or, some use could be made of Shobo-an—we'll see.

We all took a six-pack of beer and a coffee cake and went down to a neighbor's last night to watch "The Day After." As Kai and Gen commented, it was nowhere near as realistic or gruesome as the comic book that everyone in Japan reads, *Barefoot Gen*, which they read in English translation when they were 9 or 10. It was good enough, but the panel afterwards—all male, right or left, was disgusting. Only Robert McNamara seemed sincere, moved and to the point. From [Carl] Sagan to [William F.] Buckley, the others were self-serving.

In another direction, wild turkeys have begun to appear in our local landscape and a flock of nine or so is regularly seen strolling by. I saw them again this morning, by the pond, and walking on down through the meadow toward your house. They are huge! And a big four-point buck this afternoon resting in a sunny patch on some dry pine-needles, after many days of rain and a very cold night last night. Are we going to let these super-powers blow up turkeys and deer?

Gary

273. ALLEN GINSBERG [DURANGO, CO]
     TO GARY SNYDER [NEVADA CITY, CA]

November 28, 1983 1 A.M.

Dear Gary and Masa:

Snowed out of Denver Airport after Albuquerque Kinio Theatre reading—stayed with Carol Merrill and Issa in Corralles. So took 6 A.M. bus to Durango—drove out on lightly icy roads to Mesa Verde and visited cliff condominiums of 15th century. Will read at Ft. Lewis College tomorrow—L.A. New Wave kids with hiking boots, and lots of student poets here. I'll return to Boulder for end of term, thence New York December 8 for the winter and spring. See you in China or before probably. They'll invite you here, if you want to visit Four Corners area again.

Love
Allen Ginsberg

274. GARY SNYDER [NEVADA CITY, CA] TO ALLEN GINSBERG [NEW YORK]

9:IX [September 9, 1984]

Dear Allen,

Thank you so much for your hospitality to Jerry Tecklin under trying conditions. It meant a huge amount to him to be able to do this and he couldn't have afforded rent. Jerry has put in years of volunteer work on the Ridge for community affairs—researching and fighting the mining—he's much loved—so we all felt moved that he could get away and do his own studies.

I'm using Bedrock as an office now, it improves my life and work a lot. Much thanks again to you. I'd be happy to pay rent if that would be a help. See you in New York City November 7 Japanese poets . . . ?

Love,
Gary

275. ALLEN GINSBERG [CHINA] TO GARY SNYDER [NEVADA CITY, CA]

November 13, 1984
Airplane Wuhan to Beijing

Dear Gary and Masa:

Successful trip Canton to Chungking. Poets there took me to eat at last in market shops, all different dishes, sweet and pork dumplings. Boat three days two nites comfortable two person cabin (charming basic lounge-windows at boat bow to see) (OK food too) and fourth and fifth class passengers sleeping on stairway landings, passageways, steerage and eight- and sixteen-person dorms. Yangtze Gorges vaster than Li River trip, and one magnificent hairpin bend of river around mountain—village hill-cliff—sharp mountain, a complete U-turn walled by immense peaks with grotesque mythic rock formations atop. River brown—then widened out on plains the last day. Inexpensive hotels, but was met and accompanied everywhere except for three days on river. Wuhan—fantastic hall of 500 life-size arhats[177] intact. Your camera a blessing, thanks.[178]

Allen Ginsberg

276. ALLEN GINSBERG [BAODING, CHINA] TO GARY SNYDER [NEVADA CITY, CA]

December 2, 1984

Dear Gary and Masa:

I'm packing to leave Baoding and take trains to Shanghai (overnite sleeper). Enclosed "Dagoba Brand" emblem for toilet paper—maybe that indicates industrial Marxist view of stupa.[179] Baoding is "real" China—non tourist town, no active temples open in all the 50,000,000 population of Hebei Province. Talked to some intelligent Christians and Allah followers who said they were all decimated during anti-rightist campaign beginning 1958. The later Cultural Revolution was deeper

---

177. Arhat. A person who has attained the highest level of Hinayana.
178. Snyder had lent his camera to Ginsberg.
179. Stupa. A Buddhist memorial monument that often contains the ashes or remains of important leaders.

extension of that, like Ai Quing the poet was sent off in 1957–8 with a million others.

Official figure for persecutions now, I heard, is 27,000,000 people plus their children's disgrace—other elder says twice that.

Enclose some random papers—the 35 years gives account of present views. Apparently the Great Leap Forward was also a fiasco that ruined industry by decentralizing it into the hands of loudmouth hippie party hacks. Production of iron went up but quality down so unusable. During Cultural Revolution 80% of machine tool industry was crippled—and other industry and professions—so said Chinese man I met on Yangtze River Gorge boat, who'd written history of machine tool industry in Modern China—"O" [opium] production, all imports, in 1880–1890.

Students are terrifically affectionate and eager and shy. The cadre at "Foreign Relations" branch of this university whom I paranoically thought a sour spy cop turned out tipsy at last nite's farewell banquet and revealed he was an old vaudeville trooper from Chinese opera, read a scene of old sage with beard, Li Po (Li Bai) poems about Yangtze Gorges and monkeys chattering, and ended with song of Mao, "Snow Covers all North China."

I'm still sick with bronchitis. Hope it goes away in the south.

Love

Allen

[PS] Thank God for your Olympus Camera! once more!

I spent another afternoon leisurely at the temple—here's more info on it—Sixth Patriarch's place you photo'd.

Tho Buddhism seems stamped out, in talking with students and old Chinamen, the breath activity practice which seems officially OK is *Ch'i Kung* (*Qigong*) involving something parallel to *Tso Chan* or belly-sitting—also involving the chakras.[180] Do you know anything about the relationship between the *Chan* and *Ch'i Kung* styles of practice? Maybe they got some kind of Zen here without anyone knowing it.

Students do practice wushu[181] and varieties of exquisite tai chi chuan[182] so there is some awareness practice, very sophisticated, without the

---

180. Chakras. Used here as the term for the centers of subtle or refined energy in the human body.

181. Wushu. A modern Chinese martial art.

182. Tai chi chuan. A Chinese martial art form.

dharma except as theoretic Marxism provides bodhisattva turnabout of energy.

OK

Allen

[PS] Approaching Yangtze Gorges

Two hours down river from Yichang* / The rooster in the galley / Crows dawn.

*Yangtze stopover at 7 P.M., boat waits till 3 A.M. and starts down the gorges to pass them in daylight. We ate the chicken that day I guess.

277. ALLEN GINSBERG [SHANGHAI, CHINA]
TO GARY SNYDER [NEVADA CITY, CA]

Monday, December 10, 1984

Dear Gary and Masa:

Our Writer's Association tour translator, Xu Ben, who met us in Süchow, came to listen to my lectures and brought me two copies of newspaper with your "[At] Maple Bridge" poem he'd translated, and a verse of mine I'd written for him but not kept copy.

Enclosed the *Süchow News*. I'm slowly recovering from bronchitis by now, and getting active—visit Nanking this weekend, next weekend, Kunming I hope.

Lecturing on Whitman is fun.

Love

Allen

PS Letter from San Francisco says a Trungpa *dharmadhatu* shrine hall building repair benefit is being organized by Diane Di Prima, who asked me to read when I'm out March 15 for College of Marin and teach McClure's class. I said yes. Janet Carter who wrote me for Diane asked if I'd invite you. If you're free and inclined and don't have any benefits of your own cooking it'd be fine if you got the time. Diane or Janet Carter will write you, let them know.

278. GARY SNYDER [NEVADA CITY, CA] TO ALLEN GINSBERG [NEW YORK]

January 1, 1985

Dear Allen,

Welcome re-entry to the non-socialist world. I hope you are well. And don't have any more colds. It was good to hear from you as you were traveling.

Snow fell here and has been slow melting. A black bear ate chicken food and then later made off with the whole corpse of a buck that had died near the house.

I have a favor to ask—I'd like to use Bedrock Mortar as an office and study for a year or so—ditch hut is too small for a spread-out project as I have in mind; several prose jobs. You could of course have it any time you were around; I'd just have a desk, some books, papers, etc. there. But nothing I couldn't move around.

You might want to consider it a grant? The value of a year's rent—and deduct it. I could formally apply if you'd like (rent value annually could be said to be about $2000). It would be splendid for my purposes for a spell.

(When Aitken Roshi comes to lead *sesshin* again in June I'll be able to turn it right over to him again too.) So let me know if this is OK.

And how you are. Nice piece on you *New York Times*; saw Lewis Hyde review also. And when are you on the West Coast next?

Love

Gary

279. GARY SNYDER [SANTA BARBARA, CA]
      TO ALLEN GINSBERG [NEW YORK]

February 19, [1985]

Dear Allen,

I'm down at UC Santa Barbara for two weeks Regents' lecturer work—sponsored by Germanic and Slavic department—cool and foggy today. Am writing to remind you to contact Thea Lowry at some point if you want to take up her offer of a party after your reading the 15th in Marin.

Also: Jerry Tecklin, whom you once met on the Ridge (supplied us with freshly killed rattlesnake just before we went hiking in the Five-Lakes Basin). He was from St. Louis originally—parents fled Poland. In recent years he taught himself to read Yiddish, and sits in his log cabin nights reading the New York Yiddish paper. He got a grant—only $700—to go to New York City this summer for an intensive six-week course at some famous Jewish Yiddish culture institute in Yiddish. He's an amazing man—trained as a biologist—now researching Polish shtetl life too. Anyhow: he's real poor and needs a place to stay in New York City June 24–August 1. Any chance there'd be empty space at your place? Got any ideas?

Also: I never tried to do anything with your camera—and I don't have the proper papers for it. I'll leave it with my sister Thea for you to pick up, and you could leave mine there too. Maybe Shig can help you get yours fixed in the Bay Area.

Wendell Berry will be in the Bay Area that weekend. Jack Shoemaker was musing on how nice it would be if you and he could meet. When are you going back east? I'll not get down there. Leave dawn the 18th for Penn State. Talk all day 16th in the *zendo* to local *sangha* on "this path to intimacy with demons: Zen and Poetry" (a quote from Ikkyu . . .)

Am talking publicly on the China trip, here, tomorrow night.

Edibly,

Gary

280. ALLEN GINSBERG [NEW YORK] TO GARY SNYDER [NEVADA CITY, CA]

March 13, 1985

Dear Gary:

Yes, I'll be partying at Thea's 15 March, if you get in early enough, be nice to meet. I'll send ahead or bring an Olympus—lost yours in shuffle with Peter, he's in Bellevue, will go on Antabuse to Karme Chöling[183] a month when he gets out, good psychiatrists. I'm seeing a psychiatrist too, as is his lady Juanita.[184] What fun!

---

183. Karme Chöling. A Buddhist retreat near Barnet, Vermont.
184. Juanita Lieberman. Peter Orlovsky's girlfriend at the time.

I think it's possible, if by time Harry Smith (who designed *Collected Poems* book cover and three fish) now recovering from a car bump bruised knee has found himself a place to live. Not sure, but expect he'll be gone. I'll be in New York off to Naropa April 8–15, home and then *Collected Poems* comes out in England so will be there a week end of April. Then Naropa Ethnopoetics July 15–August 15. Turned in mass of *Selected Prose Essays* to Harper I got to edit with Bob Rosenthal. China poems went out on UPI wire—three of them.

Love
Allen

281. GARY SNYDER [NEVADA CITY, CA] TO ALLEN GINSBERG [NEW YORK]

18.IV [April 18, 1985]

Dear Allen,
Thanks for camera! I trust you got yours back.

Mark Silverman, a neighbor who does expert painting, has started a complete maintenance painting job on your house. He'll paint the whole exterior (with linseed oil stain) and varnish doors and windows, and seal the deck, and fix window glazing, etc. He estimates the job will cost $1,000–1,500 depending on whether one coat seems enough, or two coats are called for. I've advanced him $500 for purchasing paints. It will be really good for your house!? Hope it still is what you want . . .

About New York City in May—I'll be arriving around 11 P.M. on May 7—doing reading the 8th with Nanao. 12th with you, fly home 13th. Can stay the whole time at YMCA free, it seems—so I'll use the room there—but hope to come visit you, too.

Saw Ed Sanders in Woodstock end of last month. I was around Albany several days—had a funny good visit, saw his maple-sugar-making process. He's become a passionate environmentalist.

Roshi Aitken will be here 4 June til the end of the month. Two *sesshin*.
See you soon,
In the dharma and all,
Gary

24.VII [July 24, 1985]

Dear Allen,

Finally getting Bald Mountain and Ring of Bone *Zendo* business settled—I hope. Please read this new agreement, keep it, sign the last page of original herein included, and return to me. Official B.M.A. meeting scheduled for 9:30 A.M. August 24 at Kriyananda's house. Come if you can. (I'll be back from Alaska August 22.)

Thanks again for your hospitality to Jerry T. [Tecklin]. And I'm in your nifty house right now writing, typing, and reading. Am arranging fire insurance too. It will be most useful for me this coming winter to get prose projects done.

100,000 bows,

Gary

September 18, 1985

Dear Gary:

Just returned from one month Naropa and three weeks practice retreat at Rocky Mt. Dharma Center. Found your Bald Mt. Association papers here, so enclosed, it's signed—what changes were made? [. . .]

I'll be going to Russia with Harrison Salisbury delegation Soviet Writers' Union November 18—I suggested he invite you (and Masa!).

I'll go to Managua January end for Reuben Dario International Festival, and Vargas speaking for Cardinal would like you (McClure, too) and others to "Invade"—i.e. an invasion of poets.

I'm not sure who's right or wrong but U.S. seems to be the bigger bully right now, and so I'll go and be peaceful and literary—mainly they need our "presence." Might help.

No need rent Bedrock Mortar right now, your care taking over the years. If I need to visit will it be hard to shift over to my occupancy? Guess not.

My brother says I should get regular home insurance as well as fire insurance (and that will cover my N.Y. land, different from COP Inc.). The difficulty was Bedrock was unoccupied; but if you're using the place I think that might change conditions and so it be OK to apply for home insurance (with clause covering other property as my brother suggested). Shall we do that? Can you find out how much I'll need to pay?

OK, love

Allen Ginsberg

[PS] I'll be in L.A. area—San Diego, Santa Barbara, UCLA—November 10–14. Is Masa going to Alaska? I'll try to look up Balasaraswati photos from India.

Jerry Tecklin was a pleasure and I learned a lot.

284. GARY SNYDER [NEVADA CITY, CA]
TO ALLEN GINSBERG [NEW YORK]

2:X:85 [October 2, 1985]

Allen,

Have a good trip to Russia. I hope I can go sometime. Here are a few things—the interview in *Nuclear Strategy and the Code of the Warrior* opens up some new ground to play in. The whole book is good (re: idea on war). I'll mention it to Anne Waldman, and David Padwa.

Your house is always useable by you. Thank you. I had fire insurance started and paid for, then it was withdrawn because of some new company rule—it's hard getting insurance out here. The easiest way (now) would be if I tried to add it on to my existing insurance (AAA) by simply declaring it another of "my" buildings. That is full homeowners' coverage. If you lived here or visited and walked in and started a policy on it directly yourself—there'd be no problem. If I go in as a user (or worse a "renter") they have rules against it—or extra charges.

Later (October 17)—I'm still trying to figure this insurance stuff out. Meantime—please sign and return sheet for Bald Mountain Association.

Onward,

Gary

285. GARY SNYDER [NEVADA CITY, CA]
    TO ALLEN GINSBERG [NEW YORK]

13.V.86 [May 13, 1986]

Dear Allen,

Warm May New York City evening—night rain sprinkles "Annapurna" for food—Old India Hands—old poetry comrades, lovely evening. Here's a check, I don't know quite why, for you from the insurance company.

Onward

Gary

286. ALLEN GINSBERG [BUDAPEST, HUNGARY]
    TO GARY SNYDER [NEVADA CITY, CA]

August 31, 1986, Sunday P.M.

Dear Gary and Masa:

Worked with translator (Gary's too) and Hobo Blues Band on LP pop record with music *Howl, Mescaline, Supermarket, Café in Warsaw* poems, in Hungarian, I sang *Gospel Noble Truths* in English. Thence 10 days ago to Struga on vast blue skied lake Ohrid, Albanian-Macedonian border, to receive deluxe Macedonian bi-lingual prize book and a real 27-carrot [*sic:* karat] golden wreath on marble stand with velvet-lined leatherette box—marvelous sexagenarian rare toy, nice glitter. Vojo Sindolic there in Belgrade has translated a selection of your poems in Serbo Hrvatski. You back from Alaska yet? Saw Dylan after Kansas City concert a month ago, said if I send him 200 untitled photos he'd write captions for book or show. Robert Frank helped me select good ones, the day I left New York on to Krakow and Warsaw tomorrow, home September 13.

Love,

Allen G.

287. GARY SNYDER [NEVADA CITY, CA] TO ALLEN GINSBERG [NEW YORK]

[*ca.* November 4, 1986]

Dear Allen,

Thanks again for the high quality well presented B&W prints![185] Come
see us soon. "Poetics of Emptiness" gathering at Green Gulch will be April
10–11–12. Am inviting Phil [Whalen]. Anne Waldman might come—I'm
offering her a reading at [UC] Davis, which would pay transportation.
Any chance you could come? We're not paying honoraria—but might
figure out ways to pay transportation.

Having fun here. Lots of good talks with Masa (now that the boys are
at school).

Gary

288. ALLEN GINSBERG [NEW YORK] TO GARY SNYDER [NEVADA CITY, CA]

November 26, 1986

Dear Gary:

Here is a *Samizdat* ecological Eastern European action paper summarized on p. 16 in English, that I picked up in Hungary.

Will you be passing near New York this spring at all? If so come to
my class at Brooklyn College, they'll be a few hundred dollars—Monday
afternoons mostly.

White Shroud'll be sent you, this month, and *Howl Annotated* next, a
week or three later.

Love to all. Hi Ho to Masa.

Allen

288. GARY SNYDER [NEVADA CITY, CA] TO ALLEN GINSBERG [NEW YORK]

December 1, [1986], beginning Rohatsu

Allen,

Thanks for *Samizdat* . . . (we're still working on forest issues here . . .)
Nelson Foster's here, leading Zen interviews for Rohatsu Sesshin, starts

---

185. Ginsberg had given Snyder some of his captioned photographs.

tonight—eight days—I'm Head of the Hall (*tanto*)—and that will keep us sitting til Bodhi Day dawn . . .

[. . .] I'm clearly not going to be east this spring. (But let me counter-offer $200 any time you might be in our area—especially April and May.)

Later, I want to invite you quite properly and with full pay etc. for a big reading at Davis—in conjunction perhaps with several other poets of our ilk and a class on literary West Coast / renaissance / Beat / history, that I'll put together. In a year or two.

Might even shape up a new poetry conference to be held at Davis. If I don't have to actually organize it.

All's well here—persimmon tree finally fruiting, after eight years growing.

Gary

290. GARY SNYDER [NEVADA CITY, CA] TO ALLEN GINSBERG [NEW YORK]

[*ca.* 1986]

Dear Allen,

Here at last are the two tapes you left here. Teaching has been a lot of work, but good work—did Cabeza de Vaca text (via Haniel Long) with the class—caught them by surprise!—do you know it? Spanish soldiers lost in Texas for eight years early 16th century.

Gary

[PS] Nanao returned to Japan. North Point [Press] will publish his *Collected*—he'll come back next spring to work on it with the press. I'm delighted!

Come visit your house again soon.

291. ALLEN GINSBERG [NEW YORK] TO GARY SNYDER [NEVADA CITY, CA]

February 7, 1987

Dear Gary:

If you're passing thru New York any Monday this spring please come to my class 2–4:30 P.M. This reading series is mostly by local N.Y. State and

City "assets"—except Philip [Whalen]. Trying to arrange other dates here for him.

"Distinguished Professor of English" turns out to be a lot of work and fully half my salary goes to Federal State City taxes, Social Security, insurance, union, and who knows. Maybe it's not $ so hot or I should get married and have six children fast.

Getting my apartment here painted all white and shining and floors sanded and polyurethane'd—Steven Taylor and work crew do the job nicely.

My first photo show at Dallas Museum of Art two weeks ago went OK. I gave poetry reading to go with pix—an old Kyoto snapshot of you on the wall there among 33 other "images" as they say in photo biz buzzwordese.

I sent your copies of *White Shroud* and *Howl* this last week, hope they arrive. Best to Masa.

As ever
Allen

292. GARY SNYDER [NEVADA CITY, CA] TO ALLEN GINSBERG [NEW YORK]

11:III:87 [March 11, 1987]

Dear Allen,

White Shroud and *Howl*'s new edition—variorum—both came, thank you. Many poems in *Shroud* new to me—and its variety.

Masa and I will both come to New York City for ceremonies of induction at the Academy.[186] Thanks again for your fraternal support! over the many years.

Please write a sentence to quote on the back of Nanao's book! Send it to Jack Shoemaker, North Point Press. It's a fine-looking manuscript. Title will be *Break the Mirror!* for the whole collection. I just wrote an intro for it.

Plans ahead: We'd like to invite you to UC Davis spring quarter '88. Read, and speak in a colloquium—the series "Places on Earth" April or

---

186. With the help of Allen Ginsberg and others, Snyder had been elected to the American Academy and Institute of Arts and Letters.

May. Can pay transportation + $1,500—not much—but something—you could do "The mind as a place"—or what you'd like.

University: Make them pay you more. And supply some secretarial aid and support. (If I were to work at UCD the full nine months September–June my salary would come to $70,000. And I have tenure and title of full professor. You deserve that and more, dear comrade!)

Gary

293. GARY SNYDER [NEVADA CITY, CA] TO ALLEN GINSBERG [NEW YORK]

6:IV:87 [April 6, 1987]

Dear Allen,

Just heard of Trungpa Rinpoche's *paranirvana!*[187] The *zendo* will do a little service for him.

Here is information on Dick Nelson—who I have recommended for a Strauss Living. His most notable recent books are *Make Prayers to the Raven* and *Shadow of the Hunter* (University of Chicago—both) and his in-progress creative work can be seen in recent *Antaeus* #56 (Autumn 1986)—"The Gifts."

Dharma Greetings.

Yrz

Gary

294. GARY SNYDER [NEVADA CITY, CA] TO ALLEN GINSBERG [NEW YORK]

3:VIII:87 [August 3, 1987]

Dear Allen,

My great thanks to you for help with entering the Academy-Institute. It is something useful and appreciated. You have always helped and supported me, I know, and I'm very grateful. Should we talk about nominations for new people next year? I'll be home steady after 19 August.

Yrs,

Gary

---

187. Chögyam Trungpa, Ginsberg's meditation teacher, had died in Halifax on April 4, 1987.

295. GARY SNYDER [NEVADA CITY, CA] TO ALLEN GINSBERG [NEW YORK]

30:VIII:40087 [August 30, 1987]

Dear Allen,

[. . .] Wild turkey flock (19 birds) walking stately through the meadow.
Warm days—last night it was 80° at midnight.

I've decided not to get into nominating anyone for Academy this my
first year. Also too much work backlog piled up right now.

May I, at my own expense, put in a skylight in the main room of your
house? It is rather dark in here, I use a light at the desk all day. It's a simple
roof to work with, the pitch is to the north so the skylight wouldn't be
hot, and I think it would really enhance the place. Please let me know.

I'm running the Mac [computer] every day now, getting pretty good
at it. A marvelous tool. Soon I'll launch into a lot of prose-writing
on it.

I might indeed come to the Academy dinner November 4 . . .

Yours ever

Gary

296. GARY SNYDER [NEVADA CITY, CA] TO ALLEN GINSBERG [NEW YORK]

23:X:87 [October 23, 1987]

Dear Allen,

Some sort of rains have arrived, two nights of sprinkles and far flashes of
lightning. This is the first rain since late February, one of the longest dry
spells on record. I sit at Bedrock with the stove going, taking pleasure in
the new feel of the air and the smells. Masa is in Japan visiting her parents
until mid-November, and Gen's at the house today, a day off from his
landscaping job on account of rain. Kai's back in UC Santa Cruz as a
junior and taking a legal studies / environmental studies major finally,
and very excited about it.

Quick bit of business. Nanao will return to the West Coast from Japan
on October 31. His book will be in bookstores that week. He reads and
signs at Black Oak Books[188] on November 11. Elliott Bay Books in Seattle
has asked him to read there on December 7, and after that he may wish to

---

188. Black Oak Books. A bookstore in Berkeley, CA.

go to the East Coast, I know it was part of his plan to go east in December. So (I guess this is a question to Bob Rosenthal) is there a chance of Nanao doing a reading in New York City, a bookstore or a college—right after December 8 or 9? A good season for it, just before Christmas. Please have Bob look into that directly because time is creeping. Nanao would need that they'd pay at least transportation.

And a reminder that you are scheduled to speak at UC Davis in our "Places on Earth" series, for May 24–25, Tuesday and Wednesday. Other writers next spring will be Will Baker and Peter Matthiessen. And my memory is that you were planning to come to stay at Bedrock Mortar for a few days around that. It would be great if you could come the weekend before and sit in the *zendo* on Monday night with us, maybe give a little talk for the *zendo*. Also I was wondering if you might be up for doing something for the larger community, at the old school house cultural center, an "Evening with Allen Ginsberg" because I know how many of the old time reinhabitants here know your work and love you and etc. and have long felt a desire to hang out a bit with your ideas and poems. Whether you are planning to visit the ridge before or after the Davis talk and reading, I wonder if you'd be interested in doing the cultural center appearance? The previous week, May 18 I guess, would be the annual ceremony at the Academy-Institute and I will probably try to attend that, too. So we might just fly back to the West Coast together and I could drive you up to the ridge with me. Either way we'll have plenty of rides for you.

I have a 4' by 4' laminated tempered glass aluminum frame skylight on order for the Bedrock house, and a carpenter lined up to install it. It will help this main room enormously, putting light on the desk and saving on using the batteries from the solar system days. The whole job is going to cost a bit over $500, because the skylight alone is 375. I think you'll like it.

So that's the daily life dharma details. I'm writing a few poems on the side of my prose project these days, here's some samples. [Snyder's poem "The Sweat" was enclosed.] Climbed and hiked a lot this summer, Baranof Island, Alaska, the head of Lynn Canal and into the Yukon ranges, and then several hikes in the Sierra Nevada. Masa and I—and a number of *sangha* friends—did Mt. Conness in August, a white blade of granite in the central high Sierra—she is stronger and healthier than ever thanks partly to the demands of her dance. I hope your own work flourishes and the health. Had a long letter from Phil, wants to move back to San Francisco. Dick Baker's restaurant went bankrupt. Arrgh, American Buddhist character politics and problems. Enough.

Yrz,

Gary

297. ALLEN GINSBERG [NEW YORK] TO GARY SNYDER [NEVADA CITY, CA]

November 8, 1987

Dear Gary:

Just recovering from invasion of body lice and an ambulatory knee operation—football player's microscopic surgery to clean up torn ligament.

My itinerary next May's as follows:

Wednesday, May 18, 1988—Academy of Arts and Letters Ceremonial
Friday, May 20–21—San Jose Poetry Center w/ Alan Soldofsky
Sunday, May 22—S.F. Jewish Community Center w/ Jason Gaber
Tuesday, May 24–25—UC Davis w/ you

May 25–June 1—Bedrock Mortar / Kitkitdizze so we can fly back to West Coast together but I have these dates May 18–22 and will come up to Davis I guess by bus May 23 or May 24. Then go back (with you?) to Kitkitdizze and I have the week—or more—free. My next date would be probably (thus far) Naropa beginning June 20 or so and I hope to keep this time clear and rest.

Any kind of Ridge Cultural Center activities you want to plan is just fine because I'll have time and leisure till early June. Skylight sounds great, send me the bill.

I'm limping around on crutches for the next week so your springy activity on Baranof Island, Lynn Canal, Yukon Ranges, and Sierra Nevada Mts. makes me abashed for my sloth and physical glop. Once my leg heals I'll get back to swimming and walking Brooklyn Bridge with Russians and Chinese.

Our Chinese poets project has been set for fall 1988 and I've been in touch with Wang Meng and the Writer's Union in Beijing, they've ok'd it—now for the final selection of poets. Any last months' suggestions?

I'm having a reading series with my course Living Poetry spring 1988 aside from late May (at which time course'll be over—last meeting May 9 is Kenneth Koch) will you be on East Coast at all during spring with an afternoon to spare? Not much money—$300—but I'd trade you equal cut-rates off your Davis budget. My compeers at Brooklyn are eager for you to visit and it would strengthen my hold on their brains if you could ever show up. Spring or the future any time during terms you're in East Coast megalopolitan area. Might be able to get bigger budget later, tho.

I heard from Nanao—aside from a few low-paid readings at Gas Station (Ave B and Third St.) I don't know how we can arrange anything yet for him. His book looks fine. I should've used just his first name Nanao in last verse of my blurb.

OK—going back to bed to recuperate. Love to Masa Kai Gen.

As ever

Allen

298. GARY SNYDER [NEVADA CITY, CA] TO ALLEN GINSBERG [NEW YORK]

24:XI:87 [November 24, 1987]

Dear Allen,

OK for your suggested activities and itinerary in late May '88. It will be good to have you around the ridge for a few days. Get your body into working condition, we'll go for some walks!

Wrote Bridget Goldschmidt I can't read at Brooklyn this spring. Until April I have to keep writing; after April will be teaching and that allows no slack. I'm sorry, but my effort to finish prose project must come first this year.

Am going from Lhasa to Kashgar across Tibet next fall, as co-leader on a trip. David Padwa coming too.

Have a good thanksgiving.

Gary

PS Nanao's book doing very well!

299. ALLEN GINSBERG [NEW YORK] TO GARY SNYDER [NEVADA CITY, CA]

December 21, 1987

Dear Gary:

Lhasa–Kashgar trip! I don't know if I've physical stamina! My left knee healing tho weak, lost some thigh muscle, taking physiotherapy.

Well any time you're in New York area give me some notice and please spend a few hours reading at Brooklyn for students and small crowd, it would likely also do me good toward fast tenure track I'm already on. Faculty and students all consensus ask for you. As is this spring Ashbery Koch Baraka Waldman Cope DiPrima Wieners and locals Bob Rosenthal, Eileen Myles, New Jerseyian James Ruggia, and Sanders, Tuli Kupferberg, and Steven Taylor and Eliot Katz (N.J.)—have all OK'd series for "Living Poets." Course, undergrad excitement Mondays. Also Simon Pettit downstairs and Alice Notley a few blocks away will read—good full program one semester.

I finished mixing on 24-track computerized studio in Woodstock—a spoken poetry record [*The Lion for Real*] with lively haunting jazz melodies, somewhat an innovation since the musicians chose the poems and extended their art with deliberate compositions allowing for improvised solos—which they don't often get with their pop songs—and they went all out. My "producer" may next try Burroughs with symphony and old time Glenn Milleresque background.

Burroughs in town new *Western Lands* novel his late period best. "The old writer has run out of words . . ." + 300 pages and then had gala art gallery vernissage 60 or more of his shotgun art painting collages. He'd been doing calligraphic mazes and collage books since 1958 but last two years in burst of energy employing shotguns chance and paint filled balloons he got activated. *Tout* New York was there—the European star painters [Francesco] Clemente and Sandro Chia—and many younger artists who've been returning to narrative and dreams and chance after long minimalist arhat dryness, so it was a prize cultural party.

Peter's more or less stable these weeks, Julius [Orlovsky] stayed with me a month, talkative—we'll try to get him moved down to an adult home nearer the city so he can socialize again after years rusticating in distant halfway houses. I think I mentioned?, I spent a week intensive in Minneapolis Hazelden Institute the mother hospital for AA, Family Services Co-Dependent Program run by one Terence Williams ex-drunk former special collection librarian of University of Kansas, Lawrence, at whose house I stayed February 1966 writing "Wichita Vortex" series. Old home week for us broken-down reprobates, Beverly Isis[189] came with me but Peter wouldn't. Interesting—most all of us suffering from low

---

189. Beverly Isis. Peter Orlovsky's girlfriend at the time.

self esteem and worthlessness illusions—the crux of codependency with alcoholics and junkies and nuts. Love to Masa and kids if you see them.

As ever

Allen

300. ALLEN GINSBERG [NEW YORK]
TO GARY SNYDER AND NANAO SAKAKI [NEVADA CITY, CA]

January 2, 1987 [*sic:* 1988]

Dear Gary and mainly Nanao:

Enclosed find a copy of letter from Mrs. Watari. I had a photo show, not very big, at her gallery in May. I won't be able to go to Japan this spring as I am already dated up to my nose. Fall is possible, but next spring 1989 I'll be really free. What do you think? I could probably manage three weeks there or a month, unless I go in summer, when I'd have more time. I'll be in Israel with Robert Frank from January 5–January 28 return.

Happy New Year,

Allen

PS I'm preparing a book of 108 photos for Twelvetrees Press, a fine-grade publisher of photo books—large size—and will include literary material in the back, short one-paragraph character biographies of the people photo'd plus brief samples of their poetry and prose—more or less the same as what Mrs. Watari requests—so that material would be on hand in any case. Book due this spring but it won't be done in time, i.e. the above-mentioned annotations won't be done till later in spring.

PPS Gary—New Years Eve party I met one Laurence Allen, executive vice president of *Financial Times* (London N.Y. Frankfurt), who's a fan and close reader of yours, even had "left out in the rain." Perhaps you could write an op-ed piece on real "value" for them, he said that would be great. I gave him your address. He seemed quite good and intelligent—met him at George Soros' house—Hungarian multimillionaire acquaintance of my Hungarian translator Istvan Eörsi—manager of two billion $ Soros Investment Fund, and patron of literary culture exchange China Poland Hungary Soviets. Soros will help fund our Chinese poets' visit this fall 1988.

301. GARY SNYDER [NEVADA CITY, CA] TO ALLEN GINSBERG [NEW YORK]

January 18, 1988

Dear Allen,

When you get this you'll be back from Israel. The news has been uniformly bad the whole period you've been there. My friend Ari Sherman who was in Israel three years, when I mentioned to him that you said you'd try to control your temper, said "Why should he control his temper? Let him get mad!" Another radical Jewish voice heard from. I hope you can meet Ari this spring, he's one of my best poets: full of both intellect and soul. He and Gen get along extremely well.

Working in Bedrock Mortar calm, Monday January 18, patchy snow on the ground and the sun just rising. Just at freezing outside. Masa and I have spent the whole weekend here, working and talking together, and also escaping from the big house where Kai is entertaining four guests from UC Santa Cruz—three huge girls (including a sansei lass from Seattle) and one boy, an artist. They have taken over the big house with tapes of music, sleeping bags on the floor, bottles of beer, and great laughs. So, Kai is back to the spirit of friendship and laughter, even though he still wears his halo and brace. He has great youthful spirit of rejuvenation and energy of growth—I'm sure he'll be able to take up his scholarship of Okinawa in April.

Did I tell you about that? He was awarded a scholarship from the Ryukyu government on a special program to study Japanese and Okinawan history and culture for a full year, all expenses paid. This scholarship is offered to overseas kids who are part Okinawan, he'll be with 20 or so others from Indonesia, Thailand, but mostly Brazil, Argentina, U.S., and Canada.

Your house is cozy and working well, the skylight has totally changed the main room with an even clear northern aspect light that makes it feel like an architect's or artist's studio, and gives me plenty of light all day for working at the Macintosh and other office tools. Between now and April I expect to be pretty much working here hoping to round up and finish this prose essay book I've been engaged in which I am now calling *The Practice of the Wild*. At the same time the *zendo* involvement goes on, this weekend is the great cold *sesshin*, which I will be leader of, some guys coming down from Washington even for it. In February our semi-annual meeting, and the annual Valentine's Dance with live music in the *zendo*.

Gen continues living at home and working, when the weather's right, for Jim Pyle, doing landscape labor. He has an interesting affinity with it, saying as he does that it's good for his body, and he needs to balance his body out against his mind. Much of the time he's a pleasure to be around—especially with Kai here.

So that's the current report, we are all looking forward to your visit here in May, and your night at the North Columbia Cultural Center on May 27. I'm still hoping to arrange somebody to cover my classes so I can come to New York around May 16 or 17 and go to the Academy ceremonies on the 18th, and then maybe fly back to the West Coast with you on your way to San Jose. I guess we should say I'm going to do it, then maybe have to cancel later. And finally, here's the account of our *zendo* art exhibit last September—at least my contribution to it. It was a charming Ridge spirito-aesthetic event, with a lot of esoteric art mani-fest. Oh yes, David Padwa and I are going across Tibet in September, with Jack Turner, a climber and philosopher from Jackson Hole, and a few others who can afford the trip. You would be most welcome if you wanted to come!

Yrz

Gary

302. GARY SNYDER [NEVADA CITY, CA]
    TO ALLEN GINSBERG AND BOB ROSENTHAL [NEW YORK]

February 1, 1988

Dear Allen/Bob,

Gents—a response to the next step in our poetry reading etc. arrange-ments for May for Allen. I was down in the office last week, and saw the xerox sheet of Allen's reading needs, it's a pretty good one! Some of the people in the office were quite frightened by it, and I said all of this makes excellent sense. My poetry workshop students will take care of those details as part of their apprenticeship. Especially, tea-making and flower-arranging. Anyhow, rest assured that one way or another will be adequately handled, and those that aren't you won't notice. I do have to tell you, Allen, that the only place we could line up for you that is of adequate size is the Main Theatre. Which is fine, but there is one small thing to be noted, mainly that a play is on set there—and we were told that in the nature of the set (of which I have not yet been able to find out) the curtain cannot be closed. Therefore, you will have the opportunity to do your talk and reading in front of some kind of a dramatic setting. I thought—since I've done readings on sets before—that this would pose no problem to you. If there is some difficulty with this, give me a call right away and I'll see if there's any way we can find a smaller room. Trouble is, it might be drastically smaller.

Also, I would appreciate it—for our poetry budget—if your ticket purchases could be done early enough in the game to get lower fares. The way we do it at Davis, you keep your receipts and also receipts for motel, and turn those in later for reimbursement; the basic honorarium check should be ready for payment when you're there, since you already have given out your Social Security number! You might think when do you want to arrive? I guess you'll be coming up from San Jose—the 24th has a 2 P.M. colloquium scheduled, if you can get to Davis by say noon or one, that would be fine. I have a motel reservation made for you for Tuesday, Wednesday, and we'll be coming home together to the Ridge Thursday afternoon after my poetry workshop is over at 3 P.M. I hope all this is OK. I could get a secretary at the campus to be in touch with you guys, but it's actually easier and surer and more fun if I do it myself.

Enough administration. Last week the Great Cold *sesshin* started with snow on the ground and chilly temperatures, then shifted towards spring by the end of the *sesshin*. It's not exactly spring yet, but the little cheeps and peeps of birds beginning to mate, and the mating activity of squirrels around on the ground, is a sign of the change of the year. Kai is feeling great and obviously healing, Gen is back working at landscaping, and I am plugging away at the work of the literary country gentleman which means cutting some firewood, typing on the computer. Sitting in the old jeep in the sun in Nevada City, waiting for Masa to come out from giving a dance lesson, writing this letter on my tongue to you.

Best,

Gary

PS This was dictated and my new secretary typed it. One way to keep things moving. Was in Hawaii last weekend looking at Polynesian artifacts visiting Aitken Roshi.

G.

303. ALLEN GINSBERG [NEW YORK] TO GARY SNYDER [NEVADA CITY, CA]

February 13, 1988

Dear Gary:

All your letters at hand, and I'm woefully behind with letters. Main theater and backdrop is OK. We'll get ticket purchase done in time for reduced fare. I'll be up May 24 in time for colloquium schedule, and probably be staying as usual with Shig Murao. Tell Ari Sherman every time I get mad lose my temper I put my foot in mouth and say something inaccurate and wind up losing "credibility" and anyway gotta apologize later in order to communicate whatever little I do really know about.

Skylight news bright! Best to Gen [*sic:* Kai] with his brace halo.

I'm supposed to teach in Brooklyn September, so alas Tibet, but I wonder if I'd be up to it physically. I may be in Japan October 19–November 5 if plans with Nanao go thru—despite my lethargy it seems like an educational trip.

Noam Chomsky on Orwellian attitudes in media—whenever I read him I'm overwhelmed by feeling I missed the horror of what's going on unreported by *N. Y. Times* or whatever I read. Ever see his summary round-ups of Central American politics, or his books? Hard going but such detail, amazing.

Nanao sleeping all day, upset stomach after our reading last nite—had to read twice, too many people came in snow to small cabaret "Gas Station" around the corner in the bombed out neighborhood 2nd St. and Avenue B where I lived 1960 wrote *Kaddish*.

I looked at a brick townhouse there—lowest neighborhood—but still too expensive $300,000! for a messy place take years to fix up—ever receding horizon tho I keep having dreams of a long lost permanent place house apartment room in New York or some archetype lost city.

Love to Masa and Kai

Allen

304. GARY SNYDER [NEVADA CITY, CA] TO ALLEN GINSBERG [NEW YORK]

25.III.88 [March 25, 1988]

Dear Allen,

I heard big wild turkey squawks and gobbles in the woods the other day and thought it was coyotes attacking, went out to see. There was the flock, running not away but in big sweeping circles. And then I saw the toms (two of them) leaping up in the air periodically, with tail-fans open, and realized it was just a spring dance. What a privilege.

Kai got his brace and halo off his head and neck two days ago. He says his neck feels weak and slow and painful still. April 1 he'll leave for his year of scholarship studies in Naha Okinawa—we'll have a potluck in Berkeley to see him off.

And news to tell you, lest you hear it as unclear gossip will write it now, though Masa and I would rather we could talk face-to-face with you.

Masa and I are realigning our lives, staying close to each other and together on the Kitkitdizze land, but about to begin to live with other partners. For over a year now, we have both been seeing other people part of the time, even while living together. There have been no secrets or betrayals from the beginning. This experience together with our new friends has evolved to a clear point of wanting to realign, even while keeping affection, friendship, and our many shared projects. Kai and Gen have known about this almost from the beginning, and are quite supportive.

Nelson Foster, who has been a Zen student of Aitken Roshi's for many years, is Masa's new partner. Nelson lives in Honolulu and has begun to do some Zen teaching work, both here at Ring of Bone and at Koko-an in Hawaii. Nelson and I have been close friends for 10 years, and I welcome his coming to Kitkitdizze, and to Ring of Bone. He will gradually be moving his domicile here over the next half year. My new friend (who was Masa's friend before I got to know her) is Carole Koda. Carole lives in the San Joaquin valley, north of Merced. Carole and her two daughters, Mika (nine) and Kyung-jin (four) will be moving up here over the summer and fall. Carole came to sit at the *zendo* two years ago, and that began our acquaintance. There has been a certain amount of difficulty and pain in these changes, as you can imagine, but for the most part this has been a flowering and discovery of new depths for both Masa and me. We have become deeper and franker with each other as well, and look forward to the richness of this new extended family. Nelson and Masa (it looks to me) share a subtlety of spirit, and a gentleness of style. Carole and I share, among other things, our love of mountains and wilderness, and of poetry.

It seems as though our friends are gradually adjusting to this, though it does shake some people. We try to tell them it is not exactly that Masa and I have broken up. It is more interesting and far more intimate than that. A lot of it is new territory, and we are going step by step, finding out what works. The openness, frankness, and continual communication that the four of us manage amongst us in all directions makes it work. So please don't worry about us, and please welcome Nelson and Carole into our lives.

Living arrangements aren't clear yet. Looks like Nelson and Masa are going to remodel the barn into their own quarters . . . the main house will be Gen's room plus commons library, reading room, guest room, big kitchen. I hope I can continue to use this house as my studio, and Carole and I may build something additional, or buy a nearby house. All of us being involved with the *zendo* will make it that much livelier in the future.

Masa's in Boston right now, until the 31st, with Nelson, doing some fund-raising for the American Friends Service Committee. Carole's coming up next week to walk some trails and study the place and its needs together with me. If I go to the Institute-Academy ceremonies in May I'll bring her with me.

Spring quarter at Davis about to start up. I teach two classes: the one called "Literature of Wilderness" gets about 90 students and will run every Wednesday from 7 to 10 P.M. Poetics workshop for graduate students runs every Thursday from 12 to 3 P.M. I trust you will enjoy the time around Davis meeting these youngsters and also a further few of my new-found friends on the faculty. I brought James Laughlin to the campus for two days in early March and he was much appreciated. Incidentally: Is not J. a worthy candidate for membership, or some sort of recognition, from the Institute-Academy?? Let's talk about that.

I was glad to see Liu Binyan[190] recognized. I had put his name down myself, little knowing there was a push in that direction anyway.

OK, see you soon,

Love

Gary

---

190. Liu Binyan. A dissident Chinese writer.

305. GARY SNYDER [NEVADA CITY, CA] TO ALLEN GINSBERG [NEW YORK]

12.VI.88 [June 12, 1988]

Dear Allen,

It was good having you at Kitkitdizze and the Ridge. Seriously, call up, come visit your house, we'll send someone to meet you at the airport anytime.

Finishing up UC Davis and getting ready for *sesshin*.

Peter Matthiessen is good company. His work on Indian politics and the FBI is outstanding.

Love
Gary

306. ALLEN GINSBERG [HAMBURG, WEST GERMANY]
     TO GARY AND MASA SNYDER [NEVADA CITY, CA]

June 13, 1988

Dear Gary: Dear Masa:

Greens Party here divided between "Realos" (i.e. "realistic" political compromisers) and "Fundies" (i.e. fundamentalist purists who refuse to compromise) and so while North Sea's dying (hundreds of dead seals and some sort of algae red tide) the Greens have been losing votes. Maybe we need green Democrats and green Republicans? Our opera seems successful. Heading back to New York City today.

Love, tell Nanao
Allen

307. ALLEN GINSBERG [NEW YORK] TO GARY SNYDER [NEVADA CITY, CA]

June 16, 1988

Dear Gary:

[. . .] I hope things work out for Masa and Nelson in the ex-gay-guy's-house. If not let me know. Hope to be back within a year.

Returned from Hamburg opera opening. I don't know if you've heard about North Sea dying—"Eco-Catastrophe" multiplies. I'm glad we did the Blue Coral show.

Off to Lowell June 2 read with Ferlinghetti and McClure. Thence to Naropa.

XX to Gen and Masa
Allen

308. ALLEN GINSBERG [KYOTO, JAPAN]
      TO GARY SNYDER [NEVADA CITY, CA]

October 29, 1988, Fukumura,
North of Kyoto—Kutsuki 11 P.M.

Dear Gary:

It's hailing outside, Nanao and Sogyu and young Soto priest just ate noodles over fire pit in Fukumura's farm barn after driving down from Obama. Started 10 days ago in Tokyo big reading 1,000 people, theater with Kazuko Shiraishi and blues saxophone, then with American Literary Society, Kanasaki and Kenji Inoue, and assembled professors and your friends all very sympathetic and hospitable, great reading for them, big reception with Nanao present singing and reciting; poor Yu Suwa a little soused as always apparently took us long way home roundabout on subway. I spent hours at Akihabaru electronics stores wandering bewildered, visited foreigner's bar with poet Simon Schuchat working U.S. Embassy old acquaintance. Then Watari Gallery photo show party/interviews/poetry reading with old Noh flutist; party with 82-year-old butoh master Ohne dancing my mother's Kaddish ghost. Then to Noh with Nanao, thence to Northern Mountains outside Matsumoto; thence to Jirka Wein's Southern Mountain longhair farmer's community just like San Juan Ridge only old Jap farmhouses on steep footpaths crowded nearby, with little veggie plots, overlooking Oshikamu Village and Akaishi Mountain (I think). Supper with his friends who're helping prepare Kyoto Shirako for reading. Then train and drove with Sogyu to Obama, visited Myotsu-Ji anti-nuke priest, then Mihama Nuke Power Station tour, then Buddhist/Shinto shrine Jin Gu-ji for green tea with young anti-nuke priest in pretty teahouse—two Tendai ex-monks, one Soto, Nanao and me, Kagyu sitter, rainy day tomorrow, anti-nuke demo in Osaka, then Kyoto.

Love
Allen

309. GARY SNYDER [NEVADA CITY, CA] TO ALLEN GINSBERG [NEW YORK]

3.I.89 [January 3, 1989]

Dear Allen,

Snow still sticking here and another storm predicted for the 5th. The 4-wheel drive is amazingly useful back on these roads this year. I'm sending you this tax letter for your information, but not for you to pay, I have paid it and there's no reason you should repay me seeing how much use we are getting out of Shobo-an. I'd be happy to pay the annual fire insurance on it too. And did I tell you about this bear that has been leaving scats and tracks and signs everywhere in the neighborhood?

Sun on the snow—drips off the eaves—deer eating the compost tossed out on the snow.

Gary

310. ALLEN GINSBERG [NEW YORK] TO GARY SNYDER [NEVADA CITY, CA]

June 14, 1989

Dear Gary:

Just a note in haste—tried calling phone no answer. I'll nominate Carl Rakosi for [American] Institute. Robert Creeley suggested Ferlinghetti. I said I'd second it. That was a bold thought of Creeley's. Do you have anyone I should second? I'll write Rakosi's citation. Creeley will write Ferlinghetti's. Should you also second these?

As ever,

Allen

PS John Hollander also discovered Rakosi and recommended him for an award—which he didn't get.

Regards to Carole, Gen, and Kai.

311. GARY SNYDER [NEVADA CITY, CA] TO ALLEN GINSBERG [NEW YORK]

June 23, 1989

Dear Allen,

I don't plan to nominate anyone this year for Academy Institute. Sure, I'll second anyone you wish, if called on.

Is PEN or anyone keeping track of possibly killed or arrested Chinese writers? I'm totally pissed with Chinese government.

Gen and Kai both living in Bedrock and working around the ridge for people.

Cheers,

Gary

312. ALLEN GINSBERG [NEW YORK] TO GARY SNYDER [NEVADA CITY, CA]

August 26, 1989

Dear Gary:

Here is an interesting Antler poem (with few minor flaws). How you doing? Hope you'll get to Naropa for Ecologic–Latin America Conference next summer.

My Great Jones/Island record comes out next month, *Lion for Real* title. I'll send a tape. Occasional letters back and forth from Nanao. Enclosed also a note from PEN on recent censorship moves—please respond to them.

Allen

PS I've been in touch with Masa, pleasantly. My Brooklyn College "tenure" date is September 1—next week. Also enclosed a letter from Swiss gent, young communard host of trip with Peter O. and Steven Taylor to Berne about five years ago. He's OK. Dispose as you will. He seems to be working hard.

313. ALLEN GINSBERG [NEW YORK] TO GARY SNYDER [NEVADA CITY, CA]

September 27, 1989

Dear Gary:

Enclosed some photos most from last year's visit—you and Nanao working, two large photos of your mother, one of you and Gen (for both of you, however). I'm sending Masa a large portrait of Gen. And sending Gen a photo of Masa and you. I meant to send all these out before.

Hope you're feeling better and asthma passes on to the fish in the pond or the pines in the breeze. Is it a karmic inheritance from Gen? Odd thought!!

As ever

Allen

PS Irving Rosenthal's visiting here, so talking over old times.

314. GARY SNYDER [NEVADA CITY, CA] TO ALLEN GINSBERG [NEW YORK]

10.XI.89 [November 10, 1989]

Dear Allen,

All's well with Gen and Kai following an earthquake. I'm going for a week to Okinawa—reading and talks—late this month—won't see Nanao though. Your place is renting now, Sean O'Grady, nice Irish (American) lad writing Ph.D. I'm charging him $225 a month (for you) and something extra for using my inverter, etc. I miss your company! Sorry we'll miss in March.

Love,

Gary

315. GARY SNYDER [NEVADA CITY, CA] TO ALLEN GINSBERG [NEW YORK]

17.XI.89 [November 17, 1989]

Dear Allen,

I get various reports of the San Francisco poetry festival reading. Kai said he sat right up front. McClure thought it all was great.

Thanks for having the large and handsome photos sent. I gave Gen his portfolio along with birthday presents on November 1. He is in Santa Cruz. Masa is in Hawaii and I'll give her the pictures when she gets back. The two photos of Lois [Gary's mother] you sent me are the deepest and truest pictures of her I've seen. Thank you for everything.

I'm off to Okinawa in a couple more days. Carole said she enjoyed talking with you.

Gary

EDITOR'S NOTE: *Near the end of 1989, Gary Snyder had surgery to remove a growth on the right lung lobe. The doctors hadn't been able to perform a needle biopsy on it, but the growth turned out to be benign. His recovery from the surgery was slow and painful.*

316. CAROLE KODA [NEVADA CITY, CA] TO ALLEN GINSBERG [NEW YORK]

Solstice [December 22] 1989

Dear Allen,

Gary received a check from the Academy early this week. It will help a lot—thanks for making calls for us. He's having a good day today—after a few days of heightened pain and fatigue. Doc sez he oughtta feel better next week. Good. Boys coming home this weekend, we're heading down to Greensfelders now for solstice bonfire.

Warm greeting to you,

Carole

317. GARY SNYDER [NEVADA CITY, CA] TO ALLEN GINSBERG [NEW YORK]

6.II.90 [February 6, 1990]

Dear Allen,

Just finished the manuscript [of the] book in progress [*The Practice of the Wild*] this last weekend and handed it over to Jack Shoemaker of North Point Press on Sunday—in a little snowstorm—he was visiting here to get it and to hang out.

Snow still on the ground, but no more falling. Now that I have finished that push I can feel how my body is doing and it is still pretty stiff and weird, with numb areas all around my right side chest, and pins-and-needles sensations in the flesh and referred sensations, such as if I stroke the underside of my right arm I feel it weirdly on the surface of the stomach. All of this we hope will gradually correct itself.

Academy-Institute did come through with help money, $3,500, the maximum they can give. I am really grateful for that and for your assistance in getting it through. Blue Cross pays only 80% of the bills, and this thing came to around $20,000.

Next day:

Snowed last night again—it's a good day to stay home and work instead of rassling the truck around. Three more days and Carole and I will drop the girls off with their father in Fresno and drive on down to Tucson to visit with Dave Foreman (Earth First!) and then further to Drum's place [Drummond Hadley] up Guadalupe Canyon on the Mexican border. Haven't seen Drum in several years. We'll be back at Kitkitdizze on February 19.

As for the end of the month. Carole and I will be with McClure on the 1st, give a reading. Morning of 2nd I have a meeting with North Point Press people, and Carole will enter a weekend *sesshin* with Joko Beck in Oakland. I'm free afternoon / eve of March 2 so if there's a chance let's get together. I could meet you in San Francisco, if I can remember how to drive in North Beach and find a parking place.

Your interview with that forgettable character [John Lofton] that was reprinted in *Harper's* was a model of intelligence, etiquette, forbearance, and teaching. Bob Greensfelder brought it by and showed it to me.

Carole has started serious negotiations with Dick and Ginny Baker to buy their share of Bald Mountain Association, and Shobo-an with it. We agreed on a price of $100,000 for the whole thing, house and land. I think this is just about right.

Allen, I hope your health's OK. I appreciate better what health means. See you in March,

Gary

318. ALLEN GINSBERG [PRAGUE, CZECHOSLOVAKIA]
TO GARY SNYDER [NEVADA CITY, CA]

April 30, 1990

Dear Gary:
Nanao, Anne Waldman, Japs Rolling Dragon Bum Academy Band, and Czech "Midnite" (formerly "Plastic People") band performed together in Cesta Budejovice, Southern Bohemia. Then we went walking in ancient Boubin medieval forest. Mayor of Prague will present me on main square May Day.

319. GARY SNYDER [NEVADA CITY, CA] TO ALLEN GINSBERG [NEW YORK]

28.VI.90 [June 28, 1990]

Dear Allen,
A cool early summer here, most refreshing. Nanao is with us, staying on the other side of the hill at Ditch Hut, which is perfect little place for him. He loves it. He and I have been working together on a new translation of *Turtle Island* in Japanese for a new edition. All the buildings here are in use at the moment: Jerry Tecklin's son David is in Shobo-an, from

whence he is venturing out daily to work with the Beckwitt's "Forest Issues Task Force" on timber appeals, some of which have succeeded. The graduate student from Davis has left Bedrock (here is another rent check—final until I get a new renter—maybe—in the fall) and at the moment it is occupied by both Kai and Gen, here for a few weeks from college, planning their next moves. Kai will go back to Berkeley for his final year, Gen will either transfer to College of the Redwoods (a community college up near Arcata, from which he would go into Humboldt State) or take off for a year to do some good intern-type work. And the *zendo* at the moment is running a full-out *sesshin*.

Carole and I will be leaving in a few days, with Nanao, to drive to Boulder. Nanao's plan is to go on from there to New Mexico, to visit with his son Issa and Carol Merrill. We plan to return in a leisurely way across the basins and ranges, exploring some desert peaks and visiting some giant gold-mines. The girls will be with their father for the month of July. We'll be staying at David's [Padwa] apartment on 20th Street while in Boulder. See you there.

[. . .]

The [Philip] Glass/Ginsberg collaboration is delightful [*Hydrogen Jukebox*]!

Gary

320. ALLEN GINSBERG [ROME, ITALY] TO GARY SNYDER [NEVADA CITY, CA]

[*ca*. July 2, 1990]

Dear Gary:

Here's the Great Mother original 8,000 years old a small statue in Ankara Hittite Museum [reference to picture postcard image]. Visiting Pythian Oracle's site at Didyma at end of II'd millennium: "At sunset, Apollo's columns echo with the bawl of the one god." More Greek antiquity on Aegean Asia Minor shores than I realized: Homer, Herodotus, Cybele, Astarte, Diana all from Turkey! On to Spoleto for Phil Glass opera my text very melodious *Hydrogen Jukebox*, now with Pivano in Rome one day, see you at Boulder Naropa next week.

Love,

Allen

321. ALLEN GINSBERG [NEW YORK]
      TO GARY SNYDER AND CAROLE KODA [NEVADA CITY, CA]

August 6, 1990

Dear Gary and Carole:

Back from Naropa. If there's any rent money due next from Bedrock Mortar please apply it to battle mountain gold battle initiative. Your round-robin notice is dated 6 May 1990 and I'm only now opening mail that came whilst I was traveling London–Turkey–Rome–N.Y. one day–Naropa Boulder.

I have new office right on Union Square, one big room on 14th floor overlooking vegetable market by Union Square's 17th St. bandshell—an old classic building with ornate 1898 cornices (or 1915)—more room than before.

Peter is in worse shape than before, his apartment a wreck, but Robert Frank just shot French-subsidized one-hour "real time" video with Peter manic on Broadway in subway, streets, and van—hilarious and tragic both at once.

Just answering mail.

As ever

Allen

PS Rest of Naropa trip fine. Harry Smith produced xerox anthology— two 52-week sets of creation myths, one set male and one set female for his lectures.

322. ALLEN GINSBERG [SOUTH KOREA]
      TO GARY SNYDER [NEVADA CITY, CA]

September 1, 1990

Dear Gary:

Been in Korea two weeks, met "mad monk" poet painter Jong Kwang, lots of versifiers and professors, now up in mountain temple near East Sea, Soroksan National Park, a few days out of Seoul—Koreans noisier than Chinese. Raw fish last nite at oceanside restaurant, the flat fish was sliced alive and head still gasping on the plate full of snail meat and cuttlefish "outside palace walls cicadas sing in bright sunshine to empty rooms." Lectured on your work and William Carlos Williams yesterday, they need books tho! Love to Carole, Gen, and Kai—returning tomorrow.

Allen

323. ALLEN GINSBERG [NEW YORK] TO GARY SNYDER [NEVADA CITY, CA]

December 5, 1990

Dear Gary:

I see your book is listed among best seller paperbacks at St. Mark's Bookshop—here's souvenir.

Next year I'm retiring! (to Vajra Purgatory perhaps), or try to cut down activity, all except for workaholic neurotic flamboyant urban messianic excitation!

Love

Allen

324. ALLEN GINSBERG [NEW YORK] TO GARY SNYDER [NEVADA CITY, CA]

January 1, 1991

Dear Gary:

I called, spoke to Carole, heard your mother was ill, give her my regards. Phil [Whalen] seems very weak on phone, I've been in touch with Hartford Street,[191] Diane di Prima, and Leslie Scalapino—any news?

Spent a day with old love black lady Alene Lee[192] hospital bed, dying of cancer, near expiration, the room space seemed calm, grounded— extremely peaceful—perhaps her mind in that state so open and gentle I sense it—felt very good—carried me for days—been talking with Gehlek Rinpoche[193] about that passage, the final mind so to speak, or procedure. He recommended concentration, focus, on whatever level of practice

---

191. Philip Whalen was living at the Buddhist center on Hartford Street in San Francisco.

192. Alene Lee. As Mardou Fox, Alene Lee appeared as the main character in Jack Kerouac's book *The Subterraneans*. She had once been Ginsberg's girlfriend.

193. After the death of Chögyam Trungpa in 1987, Gehlek Rinpoche became Ginsberg's meditation teacher.

most familiar, cultivation of sympathy and openness or emptiness attitude sounds alright. He thought my "Laughing Gas" notions might be relevant.

Happy New Year to Carole and you and Gen and Kai if you see them around. Say hello to Bedrock Mortar.

Love
Allen

---

325. GARY SNYDER [NEVADA CITY, CA] TO ALLEN GINSBERG [NEW YORK]

January 2, 1991

Dear Allen,

A vigorous and mindful new year to you and your labor brigade. What a beautiful full moon the night of the 31st it was! I'm going to teach "The Rise of West Coast Poetry and the Beat Generation" spring quarter. Teach Rexroth, you, McClure, Phil, Diane di Prima, Lew [Welch], Duncan, Spicer, myself. A good exercise to review.

I miss seeing you—travel this way. (I don't know when I'll be east . . .)
Faithfully,
Gary

---

326. GARY SNYDER [NEVADA CITY, CA] TO ALLEN GINSBERG [NEW YORK]

29:I:91 [January 29, 1991]

Dear Allen,

Here's the Ring of Bone book. The Heart Sutra translation in there.

So dry here. So far driest year on entire historical record.

Will see you, into town Sunday March 10 Eve—Hang out Monday 11—Book-signing. Tuesday 12th, probably fly back the 13th.

Just finished the foreword to Shambhala's anthology of poets who meditate.

Gary

327. GARY SNYDER [NEVADA CITY, CA] TO ALLEN GINSBERG [NEW YORK]

[*ca*. February 1991]

Dear Allen,

Peter Howard[194] loaned me an extremely useful unpublished manuscript on the history of San Francisco–area poetry scene 1918–1960 by a woman who used to be a librarian at the Bancroft [Library]. Am enjoying filling out the picture of that little bit of literary history . . .

We're on for March 10 (I arrive—March 12 book-signing in the evening). You interested in going to dinner with Burt Watson and Phil Yampolsky and me and talk old Japanese hand stuff on the night of the 11th? (Not set up yet.)

Yrz in all sorts of enterprises . . .

Gary

328. ALLEN GINSBERG [NEW YORK] TO GARY SNYDER [NEVADA CITY, CA]

February 10, 1991

Dear Gary,

Enclosed letter will do I hope for Bald Mt. Assn.

Enclosed my latest caper for Poetry Reading Rainbow Shoestring Series at Brooklyn College, and a notice of an elegant nudie show at Aperture's Burden Gallery near the Flatiron Building.

I'm glad you feel ready to go ahead with transferring Bedrock Mortar. I'm hoping to find some way to finance the sale in a way that I can get a lump sum in a lawyer's hands in a trust to pay Peter O's rent as he gets out in half a year. Rather than using up the principal (principle?). Not having done much real estate I've just begun ruminating. Do mortgages cost too much in interest? That's a classical way. Think on the problem. See you March 10.

As ever

Allen

PS I teach Mondays till late but could show up at Yampolsky's by 9 P.M. maybe, cabbing into Manhattan as usual.

---

194. Peter Howard. Berkeley rare book dealer.

329. GARY SNYDER [NEVADA CITY, CA] TO ALLEN GINSBERG [NEW YORK]

12.IV.91 [April 12, 1991]

Dear Allen,

A charming interlude with you down on that rocky *bajada* of Clare-
mont—the Japanese flowering cherry is in full bloom! And a clear, but
cool and breezy, springtime.

The book of photographs has a definite and astringent / *shibui* / power.
You have caught well. Thank you for your unfailing generosity.

Aff'c'ly

Gary

[PS]And here is the syllabus for the spring course.

330. GARY SNYDER [NEVADA CITY, CA] TO ALLEN GINSBERG [NEW YORK]

[April 28, 1991]

Gary Snyder and Carole Koda are happy to announce that they were
married in a ceremony with family and a few friends in the Kitkitdizze
Meadow 18 April 1991. Yellow-rumped warbler, flicker, nuthatch, acorn
woodpecker, orange-crowned warbler, Anna's hummingbird, purple
finches—rufous-sided towhee, varied thrush, many juncos, also there.

Sarvamangalam: Good luck to all.

331. GARY SNYDER [NEVADA CITY, CA] TO ALLEN GINSBERG [NEW YORK]

6.VIII.91 [August 6, 1991]

Dear Allen,

Back from a fine 20 days in Alaska under the north Pacific cloud-cover,
enjoying Sitka spruce raindrips and spongy wet moss.

I was invited by Poets' House to come join in the discussion on Buddhism and poetry this fall, but have decided to decline so that I can stay
on top of a steady fall writing project plan. I notice that you are expected
to participate in that (in conjunction with the Shambhala meditation
and poetry anthology). [. . .]

Yr comrade,

Gary

December 18, 1991

Dear Gary:

I've nominated (for third time) Barney Rosset for American Academy's "Distinguished Service to the Arts" for his long and successful 1958–65 + battle against censorship in books—and later film. Nowadays unrewarded, and as he's lost Grove Press, he seems deserving of recognition, moral support, and acknowledgement of his historic campaign. Reading Ed de Grazia's new vast tome on censorship history [*Girls Lean Back Everywhere*], I realized again how crucial and heroic Barney's role was, other publishers lost, went to jail, went broke—he won though.

As ever

Allen Ginsberg

PS Perhaps you could also second this nomination—before January 10?

EDITOR'S NOTE: *Early in 1992, Gary Snyder bought Bedrock Mortar from Allen Ginsberg. Allen put the money from the sale into a trust for his lifelong partner, Peter Orlovsky.*

15.III.92 [March 15, 1992]

Dear Allen,

Just sent off payments for Bedrock Mortar to Bob Rosenthal. It's good to have this finished, I guess, but sad to lose you as a partner. I'm sorry it didn't work out—over the years—that you could make better use of your place, maybe too far away, it was sure fun to have you here when you were here. Now the whole of Bald Mountain Association (except Ananda, which will soon get its own deed) is Carole, myself, and the Ring of Bone *Zendo*. The three of us will probably draw up a new agreement amongst us patterned to our smaller numbers and reflecting our current understanding. Carole now owns Shobo-an, and although she shared in the purchase of your land, I am the sole owner of the house. I expect the house will serve as a working base for our young people as they do more lively ridge work, and that is splendid. I will be in touch with you later about the matter of rent owed you for the last 5½ months. Kai and Gen have been living there.

Got your message from Reno a bit late—you were gone. I've been to Seattle, San Francisco, doing programs for forestry expert types on clear-cutting and management, and now heading back down to Berkeley for a reading in Wheeler Hall, and a conference on environmental history and thought sponsored by the whole UC system. My travels have been focused on the West Coast lately, fairly political, bio-regional, and I would say very effective.

Back to Bedrock Mortar: Gen and I will go through your books down there and put them in the mail to you. I will either hold the didgeridoo for you, or package it up and send it UPS—as you prefer. I will go through the clothing, and select gear that still looks useful and mail it on to you if that's what you want. Any further thoughts, please call me. [. . .]

Gen is plotting his next move. [. . .] I finally got some papers from him that he wrote last year on environmental ethics that wowed me with their perspicacity. He needs to find a tutor, in the Oxford System, that would take him on as a personal student in philosophy or history, and let him work at his own pace. The regular university environment is not quite right for him. At the moment he is depressed and feeling that he cannot go back to college, and that he has no future. Yet in a certain way he is a genius, and we all are casting about for a means to enable him to develop his real potentiality. Do you know any universities or colleges that do Oxford style tutorials? I don't think I do at the moment, but need to research it.

Three inches of rain, and now warm clear days. Skiing two days ago, plum blossoms and almond blossoms today.

Yours in the Big D.

Gary

334. ALLEN GINSBERG [NEW YORK] TO GARY SNYDER [NEVADA CITY, CA]

May 7, 1992

Dear Gary and Carole:

Thanks for letter and check for Bedrock, it's in the bank and the Anheuser Busch stock is also cooking—so Peter has his nest egg via COP. Enclosed an old memento from Beijing. I don't think it got published before, transcribed from Writer's Conference tape and notes, and lightly edited—from *London Observer Magazine*.

I got your letter and will write—enclosed also a much edited conversation with W. S. Burroughs.

As ever
Allen

335. ALLEN GINSBERG [NEW YORK] TO GARY SNYDER [NEVADA CITY, CA]

January 25, 1993

Dear Gary:

Here's an impractical wish list ["New Democracy Wish List"]—not much on World Bank, indigenous folk, bioregionalism, ecology. Do you have some handy condensed aphorisms or praxis to add in?

As ever
Allen

336. GARY SNYDER [NEVADA CITY, CA] TO ALLEN GINSBERG [NEW YORK]

18 III [March 18, 1993]

Dear Allen,

Came home to more rain and snowfall.

Am now writing up advance plans for big all-UC conference spring of '94 on the natural world and the humanities.

New York's grit and speed is fun. Thanks for your time and place. See you in April, and here are the keys.

Gary

337. GARY SNYDER [NEVADA CITY, CA]
      TO HELEN TWORKOV (Tricycle MAGAZINE)

18.VI.93 [June 18, 1993]

Dear Helen,

We had a wonderfully turbulent spring out here in California with storms of rain and dipping temperatures surprising us several times over—just when we thought California spring had come. Now suddenly the 80-degree heat has come on us, and thick grass growing from all those rains.

It has been over a year now since those exchanges in regard to Asians, Buddhism, and Ryo Imamura's letters and distress have gone by. I recently went back and looked over the whole correspondence. I also had a chance to read Charles Prebish's paper, the one he wrote for *Tricycle* but which was rejected. I am frankly very disappointed that so much time has elapsed and nothing has yet been done to address the question of the role of Asian-Americans in the evolution of American Buddhism, and how they are feeling about Caucasian Buddhist assumptions. Norman Fischer's recent article is useful and charming, but he continues the same oversight we were trying to draw to your attention: when he says "American Buddhist" he automatically assumes it means white faces. The brown faces are not, it is true, in his *zendo*, but they are across the street at the Jodo-Shin (or other) temple which is full of fellow Americans who happen to be non-Caucasian. All you have to do is say "Euro-American Buddhists" if you must make some such point.

For that reason, I will regretfully resign from the advisory board as of now. The only power an advisor has is to resign, and since the advice I offered you—to deal with the question and deal with it right away—was never taken, I feel my presence on the board is unnecessary.

I make this move not only for the sake of large (and very real) issues, but also from some very personal loyalties to my Asian-American Buddhist teachers and comrades. I have not always understood and supported their concerns as well as I should have, but I will continue to make an effort. I support *Tricycle* and will continue to do so, with the hope that some day it may engage with this perspective. And my personal best wishes to you.

Gary

338. GARY SNYDER [NEVADA CITY, CA] TO ALLEN GINSBERG [NEW YORK]

1.VIII.93 [August 1, 1993]

Dear Allen,

Over a year ago Ryo Imamura had a problem with assumptions* about "white" and Asian-American Buddhists—as published in *Tricycle* in a column by Helen Tworkov. He wrote her a letter. She wouldn't publish

it. I wrote and said, go ahead and publish it. She didn't. Charles Prebish
wrote an article on Asian-American Buddhism which he thought she
wanted. After receiving it she turned it down. So I resigned from the
Tricycle advisory board. She accepted my resignation. All this for your
information.

Yours,

Gary

* That "American Buddhism" will be the well-informed, cosmopolitan,
real Buddhism, and it is being created at this time by white / Euro-American people. That "Asian" (and "Asian-American") Buddhism is "ethnic"
and somehow limited, and has not made any contribution so far to whatever "American" Buddhism should be. Ryo's argument, and mine, is that
Japanese-Americans etc. are full American, and whatever the contribution their Buddhism makes is as American as the next (white) guy's. And
that Euro-American (with its "cosmopolitanism") is just another ethnic
strain on the Turtle Island landscape.

339. ALLEN GINSBERG [NEW YORK] TO GARY SNYDER [NEVADA CITY, CA]

August 2, 1993

Dear Gary:

Returned tonight from Naropa—saw Tom Hayden who was addressing
our Ecological Studies section. We mentioned Peter Warshall's work in
unbuilding a dam in Malibu. Hayden said he'd got the money out of
state legislature for some project (but hadn't met Warshall except maybe
briefly). Interesting, he seemed to've moved (as ex-Catholic) to spiritual
ground for ecology, focusing on local politics. Knew your work and had
read Rick Fields (who was present at lecture)—strange circles.

Back in New York, leaving for 10-day retreat with Gehlek Rinpoche
August 10. Then leave September 7 for Europe, ending in Barcelona and
several weeks free in Mediterranean December.

Enclose a note I just received re Suwa Yu—his *paranirvana*!

Love to Carole and Gen

Allen

PS Mr. Randy Roark from Boulder/Naropa will be with Philip Whalen
this month—Pound student, etc.

September 30, 1993

Dear Gary and Carole:

"Join the Magyar American Club for Antifascist Dishwashing!"

Stayed 10 days in giant studio 15-foot ceiling French windows overlooking Buda Hill castles and Danube. Before, with Andrew Schelling
and Anne Waldman, at Naropa offshoot ex-students founded in Vienna.
Wanna teach a week or two in Vienna some season? Good pay and travel
and hotel.

There's alas a cultural blockade of Serbia which serves the war government. So Istvan my host drove to Belgrade via Novi Sad (Yugoslavia)
auspices Soros Fund, to join dissidents, peaceniks, and pacifists isolated
from outside news, info, and supportive culture—gave poetry readings
and saw translators and old friends and learned a lot about the old and
new politics of the Bosnia War.

I'll go to Krakow overnite train next.

Love

Allen

October 21, 1993

Dear Gary:

Well now I've been in Serbia and Belfast! Not seen much action except
stone crashed thru train window and loutish lads exploding firecrackers
on train up from Dublin. Visited Drumcliffe Churchyard and Ben Bul-
bin in Sligo, and Yeats' tower (huge! five stories and solid!) near Galway.
Folks here anticipating your trip to Galway next year. Bob [Rosenthal]
sent me copy of article featuring your mother—tho embarrassing and
maybe off center, it's not as bad as you might think—humanizes the
situation somewhat and oddly does you and your mother credit for per-
sistence and funny harmony. Don't worry.

Love

Allen Ginsberg

342. GARY SNYDER [NEVADA CITY, CA] TO ALLEN GINSBERG [NEW YORK]

31.I.94 [January 31, 1994]

Dear Allen,

Thanks for the postcards from Europe, Nacho of Madrid told me about you, I hope your health held up and presumably now you're back home catching up on certain projects and getting well. I just wrote Anne [Waldman] and Andrew [Schelling] saying that I figured out a way I could come to Naropa this summer, so I will be joining you guys for the third, fourth, and fifth of July. I was feeling bad thinking that I would miss it this summer. Work on *Mountains and Rivers* is going quite well, and I'm thinking it will be done within the year.

Just talked to Kai on the phone, he's doing mapping in Botswana, and was just on a visit to South Africa. He got mugged in Johannesburg, and lost his journal. He sounds pretty cheerful though, and Gen and I are going over to visit him for all of April. We'll travel around Botswana, Tanzania, and Kenya most likely. (Any angle on how to contact writers there? Useful contacts? Is USIS ever of help?)

Over the last few dry weeks Gen and I managed to burn more brush piles and thin more of the forest. A slow and steady exercise toward protecting the land from fire. I'm off to Indiana now to do some readings, see you one of these days.

Love,
Gary

343. GARY SNYDER [NEVADA CITY, CA] TO ALLEN GINSBERG [NEW YORK]

14.II.94 [February 14, 1994]

Dear Allen,

While it's fresh on my mind: I've just been organizing your things at Bedrock, Gen's helping, and most of what we've found goes to the Goodwill but I wonder about several items: your big net hammock, a pair of work boots, a pair of semi-dressy black shoes, your metronome, and a transistor portable radio. Which of these, if any, would you like to have sent to you? And one other thing, a black and red wool buffalo check jacket. Next I'm going to look over the books. Sorry this has taken so long—Lois has been sick, lots of work here, etc.

Trust you had a good trip around Europe. Nacho mentioned seeing you.

And see you in Boulder if not before . . .

G.

PS Am getting a fax! will send you the #.

344. ALLEN GINSBERG [NEW YORK] TO GARY SNYDER [NEVADA CITY, CA]

March 10, 1994

Dear Gary and Carole:

Settling back teaching at Brooklyn and N.Y.U. after Europe trip and diabetic ups and downs (caused leg doctor's heart congestion pill)—everything normal again. Finished proofs of poem book 1986–92 [*Cosmopolitan Greetings*] out May 18 from HarperCollins, and working on four CD set from Rhino—are there any compilations of your work (Gary) on records or CD's? You're not on the excellent Fantasy collection. Rhino may do another collection of poets.

OK

Allen

345. ALLEN GINSBERG [NEW YORK] TO GARY SNYDER [NEVADA CITY, CA]

March 14, 1994, Midnight

Dear Gary:

Just exhumed your note 1/31/94 from pile of uninspected mail—alas my secretaries are all overwhelmed. Karen Kennerly of PEN could probably connect you with writers in East Africa—I haven't been there since 1961.

I meanwhile sent you a card the other day, not having seen your letter. Finished proofs of poems 86–92, and today finished 30 pages close work liner notes to four CD record—third time round for this essay. Glad you'll be in Boulder. Saw Peter Matthiessen in Santa Monica writing conference with Anne W. and just returned from weekend with John Daido Laorie [*sic*] Zen Mt. Woodstock.

Love

Allen

346. GARY SNYDER [NEVADA CITY, CA] TO ALLEN GINSBERG [NEW YORK]

[March 26, 1994]

Dear Allen,

The radio will come a bit later—with some books—after I return from Africa.

Would the British Museum want to buy my deerskin jacket made by hippies? It's too small now.

Yrz

Gary

347. ALLEN GINSBERG [NEW YORK]
      TO GARY SNYDER [NEVADA CITY, CA]

March 26, 1994

Dear Gary:

I'm months behind answering mail—finished new poetry books proofs, liner notes to four CD Rhino Collection (*Holy Soul Jelly Roll: Poems and Songs 1949–1993*) for December issue, Philip Glass opera CD notes, etc. etc.

Your earlier note 14 II 94—I'll have to pick up the didgeridoo somehow. Is that around safe?

If you folks use the hammock in summer you're welcome to keep it—otherwise I'll take it to Cherry Valley or a loft if I ever get one.

Work boots—can they be kept in barn for a next visit? Buffalo jacket—anybody want it? Metronome—I have one here, any local musician want it?

Transistor portable I can always use here—leave it for me at City Lights with didgeridoo—those two items.

I received your excellent Le Ecologic discourse and notes on *Tricycle*. I think the magazine's too useful to savage, especially with Kerouac serialization "Wake Up!" I'll review all the correspondence—it'd seem merely dead end no win to leave it (the tangled knot) still tangled and walk away. There seems some element also of now—substantive personal pain rather than, ultimately, a substantial disagreement once everybody's terms are understood. I'll review it all. The honky chauvinist complaint seems real enough, but sinking the magazine isn't going to help that, or firing the editor. This seems a situation to enrich not destroy or boycott permanently. Some element of acrimony that's not workable seems present in the conflict. I'll read all the letter exchanges again.

I took on too much teaching this year and it's exhausting me—Beat History and two classes in "Historical Poetics"—i.e. Pre-literate indigenous oral thru Sappho to Corso to post literate oral rap. Gigantic book by Strehlow with Australian aborigine poetry and explanations and music notes I got in Australia's on my shelf—rescued from Harry Smith after his death (he'd purloined it for two decades).

Had sent card to Masa from Europe and got a nice note from her, from Sacramento, seems happy with a vocation there.

Living alone in my apartment for a change, blessed solitude for a while.

Love to Carole, Gen, and Kai and folks on the Ridge and off. 2 A.M. answering mail.

As ever

Allen

PS I'll be in San Francisco for Harper new book signing May 31–June 1 then for my birthday June 3 with my brother Gene whose birthday's June 2!

Enclosed some postcards sent me by photographers. I did Gap ad, after two years' refusing, asking for a lot! of money to be donated to Naropa Poetics Department, and it worked—same as postcard shrine photo.

348. GARY SNYDER [NEVADA CITY, CA]
    TO ALLEN GINSBERG [NEW YORK]

30.III.94 [March 30, 1994]

Dear Allen,

Hasty note, thanks for your letter about *Tricycle* and the Japanese-American Buddhists. I have not tried to make an issue of this, nor do I want to embarrass Helen publicly. I did not notify the board of advisors about my resignation from it, with the exception of you and Peter Matthiessen, and that in a low-key way. I don't expect you to do anything about it, except be aware of it, and if small opportunities for correction come along, take them.

I've had somewhat contradictory instructions as to what to send back to you—but a package is already on its way, so you'll get the hammock and the metronome and the red buffalo plaid jacket and some other items. The radio, which is a Grundtvig, will be coming later together with some books. After I get back from Africa I'll get your books in the mail, and also UPS the didgeridoo to you; it is in fine shape.

I'm on sabbatical this spring, that's how I get to travel for once, and have been steadily finishing sections of *Mountains and Rivers*, seven or eight more and it will be done, after almost 40 years of keeping it in mind. There may be some projects associated with it that will carry on later, I have been educated into new fields like Landscape Ecology, and will have to let some of those insights mature.

Zowie, Botswana and Zimbabwe! Gen and I leave in two more days. See you in July in Bowlder [*sic:* Boulder].

Gary

349. ALLEN GINSBERG [NEW YORK]
TO GARY SNYDER [NEVADA CITY, CA]

Tuesday, June 21, 1994

Dear Gary:

I'm leaving this Saturday to spend almost a week with Burroughs in Lawrence, Kansas, then on to Naropa. As we'll be together with Creeley, maybe we can join minds to nominate poets and foreigners to the American Academy of Arts and Letters. I just got the papers from them and I'll bring copies to Naropa. So ponder it. Corso says he'll accept (he said "no" before but he's aging a little more gracefully)—Anne Waldman? [Kenneth] Koch? McClure? any ideas? I've been traveling. I'll ask Harpers about hemp paper. I'm going to East November—December free, maybe Bali—December 15, Madras music fest with Philip Glass.

OK

Allen G.

January 12, 1994 [*sic:* 1995]

Dear Gary:

Above see my blurb for Pendell's book. Enclosed also xerox of a letter from Spiros Meimaris, Athens bookseller and teacher—who last year published translation, entire book of *Journals Early '50s Early '60s. Journals Mid-1950s ('54–'58)* are now in final proof state, completed, for spring (April).

Old letter from Nanao says he'll be in California this month—you heard from him?

Dreamt I saw Jack Kerouac last nite, told him he'd done enough work, he should take it easy and maybe write one book every 10 years and live to be 80 or 90 years old. I guess that's advice to me.

Spent December in London and Paris, new books out bilingual from Bourgois ed. (*White Shroud,* 1 volume, *Mind Breaths* and *Plutonian Ode,* 2nd volume) and *Cosmopolitan Greetings* in Penguin edition—so I did a lot of interviews and went to museums. Assistant Peter Hale came along to carry bags and laptop with modem, so could fax from Ritz Hotel to office in New York. *La Nouvel Observateur* put us up in Ritz for three nites @ $690 per room per nite—so saw Paris hi life a few days. I'll start teaching February 1. Enclosed last week's poem. Best to Carole and your family. Did anyone send you my four-CD set *Holy Soul Jelly Roll?* Volume 3 with Blake is easy listening. Living alone in my apartment. Peter Orlovsky now six months clean, at present at Spring Lake Ranch in Vermont, I'll visit him this weekend, after three months in rehab in New Jersey. So there's some hope after 10 years, maybe he hit bottom after all.

My heart's still pumping but especially in travel I get out of breath easily, feel older and less energetic—so I guess the Kerouac dream applies. Hope to finish *Collected Essays and Blurbs, Selected Interviews,* and *Selected Correspondence* in next years and *Selected Poems*—different editors working on all books except myself last—all done in-house (i.e. people I assigned and pay to edit)—Bill Morgan bibliographer, Miles, etc.

I'll be at Stanford and in San Francisco February 9–13. Stanford with Rakosi, and to look over my archive site.

Love XX as ever

Allen

351. ALLEN GINSBERG [NEW YORK]
      TO GARY SNYDER [NEVADA CITY, CA]

April 10, 1995

Dear Gary:

I talked with Nanao, and invited him to stay with me in New York end of May, and said I'd give him $1,000. If I can rustle up a reading I will—it'll be too late for my Brooklyn series, maybe find a place at Nuyorican Café.

Hey, and Uma Thurman is Bob and Nina Thurman's daughter! (of Columbia U. and Tibet House).

Re: Burton Watson: We could nominate him for membership in Academy itself. Or Gold Medal for lesser, Vursell Memorial Prize. Or dignified address. I'll ask Bob [Rosenthal] to see if there are other prizes elsewhere—I think we have a directory of some sort.

Just returned from Wales and Galway. U2 rock band chief Bono drove down from Dublin and introduced me at great length; I gave him booklets by Geoffrey Manaugh 19-year-old extraordinary poet and Bono sent him a fan letter. I'll send you the pamphlets.

Don't forget to send me printout of *Mountains and Rivers*, if it's convenient. Eager to see the long hauled text. Bei Dao will be at Davis teaching this fall. I've seen him several times in New York and Ann Arbor. Also saw Shu Ting via PEN Club two years ago. Yes, I've been in touch with Colin Still[195] and will sit for him. Love to Gen and hello Carole and Kai. Tell Gen to come to Naropa! Or I'll tell him. Gen! Come to Naropa! You'll have fun!

Love

Allen

PS I'm not yet computer literate so don't email you. Peter Hale in my office can.

---

195. Colin Still. London filmmaker who later produced a movie about Ginsberg entitled *No More to Say & Nothing to Weep For*.

352. ALLEN GINSBERG [NEW YORK]
     TO GARY SNYDER [NEVADA CITY, CA]

April 10, 1995

Dear Gary:

Here's pamphlets by 19-year-old poet—I really enjoyed. If you scan *Mystic's Fists* (first book age 18) p. 3 "Threshold" poem and then "Position," it's got bodhisattva impulse and a lot of self empowerment. I think I mentioned him in Shannon Airport?

All went well in Galway, met a marvelous drunk thin dying poet reminded me of gentler [Basil] Bunting—Michael Hartnett—in Galway. I gave extra reading, three nites in row, to accommodate students who couldn't get tix to first two scheduled, and repeated same in Swansea. Went to bardic contest and met fine Welsh language big-rough-handed gentle farmer poet Dic Jones, present champ bard!

Love
Allen

353. ALLEN GINSBERG [NEW YORK]
     TO GARY SNYDER [NEVADA CITY, CA]

April 16, 1995

Dear Gary:

Enclosed *Irish Times* F.Y.I. I have arranged Nanao dates at Nuyorican (June 1) Café, Kerouac Poetry Festival NYU June 5–6, and *Tricycle* Central Park open air dharma fest for Nanao. I'll give him $1,000 COP and whatever other hundreds in fees will add more. Kerouac Fest is primarily literary (not "Beat") and will end with reading at Town Hall as last year with Anne Waldman and others. I think you were invited, don't know your answer.

OK—I sent you Geoff Manaugh pamphlets last week.

As ever
Allen

354. ALLEN GINSBERG [NEW YORK] TO GARY SNYDER [NEVADA CITY, CA]

May 22, 1995

Dear Gary:

I'm still mining old negatives, and found this—never before printed. I'm not sure I have the technical begging monk's gear (robes and hat) right—send me proper terms—before I publish or show the photo—it's amazing time-travel! I leave June 7 for Venice Biennale where I have a show of 108 new and old photos—be there a few days, see Fernanda Pivano, stay a week and travel with Francesco Clemente family in Amalfi where I've never been. Back end of June after preparing *Selected Poems* big big book in Milan. Working on that now for England, U.S., Italy and Germany, etc. Were you sent my new *Journals Mid-1950s* book? Yet?

Nanao was here a week, good humored desert ninja said I was city ninja—at least he didn't put me down as city dweller twerp. I gave him $1,000 COP Inc. money, he read with me last night of five successive nights at Knitting Factory, *avant-garde* music place near City Hall, below Chinatown.

Then he went to Massachusetts and Nova Scotia, so we rendezvous'd in Halifax for Sawang (Trungpa's son) celebration/confirmation as Shambhala King, performed by Penor Rinpoche present head of Nyingma sect, with whom he'll study in Southern India monastery. Saw Kobun Chino and others there, huge assemblage of Trungpa students from all over, with Shambhala arts week, so he and I read there together for the *sangha*, 800 audience or more, big hit (Nanao) and he may go on to Gampo Abbey on north point of Cape Breton. I xeroxed three copies of his new manuscript and made him a copy of his old "Four Poems" from early '60s which he'd lost sight of. So his visit worked out well, some profit and much exposure—he found New York and Halifax audiences wide awake and lively in response "exciting."

After 23 or more years, Dave Haselwood finally unearthed my cache of original 1962–63 Indian photo negatives a few of which he used in *Indian Journals.* I'd been inquiring for a decade from City Lights, Berkeley archives, David, etc. He couldn't remember, tho he'd sold "dirty matter" (working designs, proofs and some copy negatives to Columbia Special Collections years ago)—finally found my photos intact and preserved at bottom of a trunk. What a boon, gift, relief.

Photography hobby is turning to larger business—Venice Biennale show, Tibor de Nagy Gallery New York in fall, later big show at Raymond Foye's giant Gagosian Gallery, a number of photos at Whitney Museum in fall also, and big Japan show at Fuji Museum of Veno near Tokyo, 1996, and Venice show goes next year to San Diego probably. Plus new book for Aperture, more recent photos.

How's your health? Nanao said the lung operation was not necessary—nothing found bad?

Peter O. returns from Detox Hospital in Atlanta, will be in Hazelden Fellowship House here in New York. I'm signing to buy sizeable loft around corner—405 E. 13 Street right of First Avenue, my neighborhood—tomorrow! Peter will inherit inexpensive E. 12 Street pad—if he can stay straight.

Love to Carole—all well with my weak heart!

Allen

355. ALLEN GINSBERG [AMBOISE, FRANCE]
    TO GARY SNYDER [NEVADA CITY, CA]

                        June 22, 1995, yesterday longest day of the year
Dear Gary and Carole:
Enclosed a "story" from *USA Today* which you may've seen—from June 19—in which Gary's name's mentioned in passing.

I'd a painful week in bed late May with a pulmonary embolism, knife-like hurt in right chest with blood clot detached from thickened and slightly corrugated right hand heart valve—fortunately not left side of heart which would've been dangerous. As it was, fatigue and lassitude and codeine and I recovered in time for two brief obligations at NYU Kerouac/Poetry (J.K. as *litterateur* and poet) Conference. Then June 7 flew to Venice for show of 108 photos during Biennale week—great deal of interest since there's another crest of admiration in "Beat" literary character in Italy and Milan publishers are preparing a big *Collected Poems* translated by Fernanda Pivano—first book with new poems since 1974 when Maoist and multinational egotists took over Mondadori. Mondadori's gay nephew now in charge.

There were a couple photos of you in the Venice show—but alas the bulk of my negatives from *Indian Journals* disappeared in early 1970s when book was published. I'd asked David Haselwood, City Lites, and

Berkeley UC Special Collections—nobody knew where they vanished. Suddenly I got a call from Haselwood, he'd found them after 25 years at the bottom of his trunk when cleaning house. So the original negatives now are safe in my office in New York—enough for a small show this fall. Photo activity more remunerative and expansive, I have secretary-curator lady who's efficient and big museum shows in Japan and Europe are in preparation.

So, after Venice I went down below Naples to Amalfi where Francesco Clemente's wife Alba was born, grew up, and had 10 days of convalescence in Mediterranean sun on a veranda overlooking town and ocean and sky, eating fresh pasta and local veggies and fruit—hundreds of thousands of lemons in terraces up and down town hillsides. Then strength recovered have been traveling with Clementes and their four kids by overnite wagon-lit train to Loire Valley where he has opening in a few days of 108 pastels he did over last year in New York, India, Amalfi, New Mexico—huge display of poetic images, he's an excellent poet mind and Pound devotee—intelligent sensitive couple who honeymooned age 21 in India for two years. We've worked on projects together the last decade. He did collaborations with McClure, Creeley, Wieners, and Gregory Corso. Grew up in '60s and treats Beat Culture with serious European insight and charm. So now vacationing with his family and 82-year-old father in Loire Valley visiting Chateaux which'll get a million visitors this year, most during summer.

Before I left I talked with Rick Fields whose voice was whispery, he's got cancer, lung or esophagus. And a call from Timothy Leary inquiring means to sell his archives to Stanford, which offered a deal. He said, "I don't know if you've heard of my condition, I have terminal cancer." He seemed ready and cheerful or as Jack Kerouac said, "coach-like," Irish football coach, said he had 75 years, was satisfied and ready. Prostate, with metastasis awhile back aggravated by fatigue from foolish 15-city lecture tour to support his extended family. Gregory fine in New York financially secure with monthly stipend from Japanese painter, Hiro Yamagata, who sponsored my photo show in Venice and donated a quarter million $ to Naropa last year and sez he'll continue yearly—with extra stipend for Anne Waldman to ease her penury directing Poetics Department.

I keep writing—journals and poems, much about physical aging or obvious deterioration of body—with ⅔ of my heart working I have less physical energy approaching age 70—tho I feel like 16 emotionally—but sightseeing I've got energy for one castle a day and lots of naps. Peter Orlovsky now OK in Hazelden Fellowship Halfway House East 17th Street six blocks from our apartment, for a few months.

With ⅓ left of my Stanford archive sale million, after Federal State Local Taxes, 1/10 to Bibliographer/Archivist Bill Morgan for 14 years work, every item retrievable cataloged, and 5% to Agent [Andrew Wylie]—I purchased a nice big loft around the corner from my apartment from painter Larry Rivers. So I'll move in the fall and Peter gets our old apartment.

PS New loft 2,100 square feet, lots of open space, windows on three sides five flights up with new stainless steel elevator with keys. Nanao visit New York and Halifax was fun.

PPS I'll be back in New York June 28, thence to Naropa two weeks and third week June with Burroughs in Lawrence, Kansas, before settling back in New York for all fall and prepare U.S. English–German *Selected Poems* and teach in Brooklyn.

Index